000022

Economics in Our Time:
Macro Issues

Economics in Our Time:
Macro Issues

Robert F. McNown
Dwight R. Lee

University of Colorado

SCIENCE RESEARCH ASSOCIATES, INC.
Chicago, Palo Alto, Toronto, Henley-on-Thames, Sydney, Paris, Stuttgart

A Subsidiary of IBM

To Lauri and Brenda

Library of Congress Cataloging in Publication Data

McNown, Robert F
  Economics in our time.

  Includes index.
  1. Macroeconomics.   2. United States—
Economic conditions—1961–   I. Lee, Dwight R.,
joint author.   II. Title.
HB171.5.M173   330   76–374
ISBN 0–574–19260–3

Preface

In recent years the United States economy has been jolted by a complex array of macroeconomic events. The simultaneous occurrence of inflation and unemployment, dollar depreciation and the abandonment of fixed exchange rates, the threat of resource scarcity limiting economic growth, and an episode of general wage and price controls have all contributed to a reawakening of interest in the analysis of macroeconomic problems. However, many students remain unconvinced that traditional economic theory has much to say about the problems we face. Too often the introductory economics course is devoted to the extensive development of graphical analysis and theoretical fine points, which can obscure rather than illuminate the essentials of macroeconomics. When a devotion to analytics displaces a discussion of applications, the student may lose the connection between economic theory and the real economy.

This book applies the fundamentals of macroeconomic theory to the analysis of contemporary issues and a number of historical episodes. The essential tools of economic analysis are developed in a rigorous—yet readable—verbal style, and these tools are applied directly to the problems of unemployment, inflation, income distribution, international trade, and economic growth. It is our belief that, by limiting the theoretical discussions to a relatively small number of essentials and avoiding the distractions of graphical analysis, this book provides the student with a clearer grasp of economic theory and its application to contemporary problems facing the macroeconomy.

The usefulness of a theoretical framework in analyzing economic issues is well accepted by most economists. However, a complementary framework for the analysis of political decision making remains a serious omission from the discussion of economic policy in most approaches to introductory economics. This book attempts to remedy this omission by the explicit analysis of political decision making and the examination of how these principles have affected the development of economic policy over time. The theory of social choice employed in this book clearly points out the limitations of economic policies likely to be forthcoming under a system of representative government. Because of these constraints on public policy, it must be recognized that the alternative to the imperfect market mechanism is often an equally imperfect government policy. The limitations of government policy are clearly and repeatedly stated in numerous examples of policy failure: the Great Depression, recent ups and downs of the business cycle, inadequacies in income redistribution policies, and policy errors in the field of international economics. It is also the position of this book that economists have the obligation to be honest about the limitations of economic policy and to describe what cannot, as well as what can, be accomplished through policy actions.

In addition to political constraints on the formation of policy, there are also limitations imposed by purely economic forces. The solutions to some problems come at an extremely high cost to society, and these situations should be clearly stated. However, despite the limitations imposed by both political and economic forces, there are policy proposals that offer the possibility for an improvement in the functioning of our macroeconomy. Here we may learn from the past in discovering what elements characterize effective policy as contrasted with ineffective or even harmful government actions.

We feel, and we hope others will agree, that these elements of political economy combine to form a realistic approach to the analysis of contemporary issues and will appeal to today's introductory economics student. We have written the book to appeal to students in introductory courses in economics at the principles or preprinciples level offered at most colleges or junior colleges. Because the theory is rigorously developed, the book can stand on its own as the primary text in a class oriented toward the analysis of macroeconomic problems. It is equally well suited as a supplement to a main text on introductory economics. The book is also offered as a companion to our earlier *Economics In Our Time: Concepts and Issues*, which focuses primarily on microeconomic issues.

A number of people have contributed substantially to the writing of this book, and we take this opportunity to express our thanks: to Bruce Caldwell and Carol Harris, our editors, for many helpful suggestions and technical assistance with the manuscript; to James Gwartney (Florida State University) for his numerous recommendations on the theory of social choice, as well as other general comments; to Fred Glahe (University of Colorado), our colleague, for his consistently useful comments; to Thomas Duchesneau (University of Maine), Courtenay C. Stone (California State University, Northridge), Craig MacPhee (University of Nebraska, Lincoln), and Daniel Orr (University of California, San Diego), whose comments helped shape the book into its present form; to Lauri McNown for assistance with discussion questions, the index, and some materials on political information; and to Brenda Lee for her continued interest and encouragement.

Although the book bears the markings of all those mentioned, the final product remains the responsibility of the authors.

University of Colorado, Boulder   Robert F. McNown

Dwight R. Lee

Contents

chapter I

The Aggregate View of Things

No one is insulated against economic events. No matter who you are or what you do, economic conditions will strongly influence your activities and well-being. For this reason, economic events make news. We want to know whether the total output of the economy is increasing or decreasing because our standard of living will increase or decrease accordingly. And since it takes people on the job to produce the economy's output, we are concerned about the rate of unemployment regardless of our own employment status. The inflation rate is no less a concern; it affects everyone's cost of living, as well as the overall performance of the economy. With these and other economic conditions attracting wide interest, it follows that policies designed to improve economic performance are also newsworthy. People are interested in what policies are recommended and implemented for bringing the economy back to full employment, for reducing the rate of inflation, for stimulating economic growth, and so on.

With all this exposure to economic news, one might suppose sound economic knowledge to be widespread. Unfortunately, this is not the case. Few people have any real understanding of how the economy works. As a result there are any number of misconceptions about important economic phenomena which influence economic policy making. Consequently, it is not difficult to find economic policies which do more harm than good. Some of this is unavoidable because economics is a long way from being an exact science, and honest differences of opinion will always exist on many economic issues. But a little economic theory will go a long way toward dispelling many misconceptions. Straightforward economic theory provides an indispensable framework for analyzing and discussing important economic problems in a meaningful and useful way.

In the chapters to follow we will be making use of basic economic theory to give the reader useful insights into some specific economic issues. The issues with which we will be primarily concerned are grouped under the heading of *macroeconomic* issues. By macroeconomics we mean that branch of economics that is concerned with broad economic aggregates. For example, macroeconomics is concerned with the determination of the aggregate economic output, or the total value of what is produced in the economy in any given year. Obviously this attention to the value of aggregate output, or *Gross National Product* (GNP), ignores important questions like what determines the composition of this output. But questions which are concerned with the details behind economic aggregates fall outside the realm of macroeconomics. The problem of *inflation* (increase in the general level of prices) is another aggregate that macroeconomics deals with. The causes and consequences of inflation are areas of major interest in macroeconomics. Again, questions of detail, like why do some prices increase more rapidly than others, are not investigated. Yet another example of a macroeconomic aggregate is the *unemployment rate* (the percentage of the work force which is out of work). Macroeconomics is interested in understanding and explaining the relationship between the unemployment rate and other economic aggregates such as inflation and *aggregate demand* (the total demand for goods and services) of which *aggregate consumption* (the total consumption expenditure in the economy) and *aggregate investment* (the total investment expenditure in the economy) are major components. Once more, such questions as why some employment opportunities are expanding while others are contracting or what influences the composition of consumption and investment decisions are not of primary interest.

The particulars underlying economic aggregates are the result of decisions made by individual economic decision makers in their roles as consumers, workers, and investors. Questions of how these decisions are made and what economic factors influence them are the concern of *microeconomics*, the other major branch of economic analysis. Microeconomic analysis is interested in how economic decision makers respond to the problem of economic scarcity (resources inadequate to satisfy all human wants). People are constantly faced with choices of how to allocate their limited resources (time, effort, and financial means). Individuals have to decide how to divide their time between work and leisure, what type of employment opportunities to pursue, which goods and services to buy or do without, which investments to make, and so on. Microeconomics is not only concerned with how individuals make these decisions, but also with how these countless individual decisions come together. Clearly some mechanism coordinates the desires of consumers with those of producers if the economy is to operate efficiently at using scarce resources to satisfy consumer desires. Here microeconomics is concerned with the role of markets and relative prices in coordinating economic activities.

Although the topics we will be considering in this book are, for the most part, macroeconomic topics, the basic principles of microeconomic analysis will often be useful in our discussion. Though we will be interested primarily in economic aggregates, it will help us to understand something of the decision-making processes behind these aggregates.

With this background discussion we are ready to look ahead for a brief glimpse of the topics to be considered. In the second chapter we will look at the problem of unemployment, defining what is meant by this concept and looking at some of the positive as well as undesirable aspects of unemployment. In chapter three the concept of aggregate demand is developed with the discussion centering on the pivotal role played by aggregate demand in the performance of the economy. The fourth chapter deals with the role played by government spending and taxing policies (fiscal policy) as a means of influencing aggregate demand and smoothing out undesirable fluctuations in economic activity. Some historical episodes in the use of fiscal policy are discussed to add some useful perspectives to the discussion. Chapter five turns to the role of money in the economy and the use of monetary policy to stabilize economic activity through its effect on aggregate demand. Once more some historical episodes are discussed, and the issue of the relative effectiveness of monetary and fiscal policy is considered. The role of the political decision-making process in formulating economic policy is the topic for chapter six. This discussion comes to grips with some of the practical problems in applying monetary and fiscal policy, as well as understanding important aspects of economic problems discussed later in the book. Because of this, the discussion in this chapter will be referred to often throughout the remaining chapters. Chapters seven and eight deal with the problem of inflation. Chapter seven concentrates on the primary cause of inflation, again with some historical examples, and the relationship between inflation and unemployment. Chapter eight is concerned with the economic consequences of inflation and policy measures designed to fight inflation. In chapters nine and ten the problems associated with income inequality and poverty become our main concern. Chapter nine focuses attention on the economic explanation of income inequalities, and considers evidence on the amount of social and economic mobility that exists in our economy. Chapter ten discusses some of the institutional arrangements for reallocating income and wealth among different economic groups and the effectiveness of these arrangements. The topic of international trade comes up in chapters eleven and twelve. Chapter eleven discusses the economic basis for trade between countries and considers the arguments for restricting this trade. Chapter twelve is concerned with the mechanisms for financing international trade, dealing with such topics as the balance of payments, the gold standard, and floating exchange rates. In chapter thirteen we examine the pros and cons of a value judgment that is implicit throughout the book: that economic growth is desirable. Some of the problems associated with economic growth, such as depleting natural resources and polluting the environment, are examined. The important question here is whether or not these problems make it imperative to bring economic growth to a halt. Finally, in chapter fourteen we take a brief look backward, summarizing the main topics of the book.

chapter 2

Unemployment:
Frictional or Fictional

Contrary to popular opinion, much of what is called unemployment is quite desirable. Unfortunately, capitalistic economies (and many not so capitalistic economies for that matter) are periodically plagued with unemployment rates far exceeding what could possible be justified as desirable. The most notable example of this in the United States occurred during the Great Depression of the 1930s, when as much as 25 percent of the work force was unemployed. Although this was the most serious episode of unemployment in our country, there have been many other periods when high levels of unemployment were of national concern. At the time of this writing, unemployment has grown to more than 9 percent (the highest rate since the beginning of World War II). It has become the source of much economic hardship. Now as before, the causes and cures of this problem are topics of growing interest.

To the individual who wants a job but can't find it, the problem seems painfully obvious: there just isn't enough work to go around. However, this explanation of unemployment doesn't take into account the enormous number of things that we would like to have people producing. We live in a world of scarcity, where the possibility of producing enough to provide everyone with as much of everything as each desires is not even a remote possibility. Our impressive increases in productive ability, cannot equal our ability to want more goods and services. There are always jobs that we are anxious to have done, jobs that require human effort. Unemployment can't be explained by a lack of work to be done.

But before turning to some of the important factors explaining the phenomenon of unemployment, let us address the question: What is unemployment?

4

1. To Work or Not to Work

Many people who could be employed in traditional jobs choose not to be. While there are advantages to working, there are also costs. These costs are measured by the value of opportunities forgone when people take jobs rather than engaging in other activities. For example, most college students could find full-time employment instead of going to school. These students don't quit college and enter the labor force because they feel that the value of their college experience is greater than the value they would receive by taking full-time jobs. The same can be said for women who choose to stay home, raise the kids, and pursue other activities in the home. When a woman makes this decision she feels that her value is greater in the home than in the job market.

Therefore it seems reasonable to include in the category of the unemployed only those who are looking for work and can't find it. But what happens if more people want to work? It is possible for both the percentage of those of working age who are employed and the unemployment rate to increase at the same time. This is exactly what has been happening in recent years. Specifically, there has been an increase in the percentage of women seeking employment outside the home. As a result, even during recent periods of high unemployment the percentage of employed working-age population has increased. For example, in 1955 the unemployment rate was 4.4 percent, and employment as a percentage of working-age population was 61.4 percent. In 1965 the unemployment rate was 4.5 percent, but 62.4 percent was employed. In May 1975 unemployment was at 9.2 percent, the highest it has been since the beginning of World War II; yet employment of the working-age population was 62.9 percent. While unemployment figures can provide us with information, they don't give the whole story.

In order to look at the concept of unemployment more systematically, it is helpful to consider the importance of the wage rate in the relationship between the willingness to take jobs and the availability of jobs. While money is not the only consideration for taking a job, it is obviously an important factor. The more wages go up relative to other prices in the economy, the more attractive employment will appear relative to other opportunities. Consequently, increased wages mean more people who want to work.

It is important to emphasize that we are talking about a situation in which the wage increases relative to prices. We refer to this as an increase in the *real wage*, an increase in the quantity of goods and services the wage can purchase. A *money wage* increase is not always associated with an increase in the real wage. If the money wage goes up by 10 percent and all other prices go up by the same percentage, there is no increase in what that wage can buy. The real wage has remained the same. To determine the real wage, we must have some measure of the price level, a number that reflects the money prices of all goods and services in the economy. This number is referred to as a *price index* and represents our best effort at measuring the current cost of a representative bundle of goods against its cost in an earlier period.

So it seems reasonable to expect that an increase in the real wage will entice a larger number of individuals into the labor force.* Correspondingly, a decrease in the real wage will result in fewer people attempting to participate in the labor force.

The real wage also influences employers, who hire workers because labor is an important factor of production. Labor, when used in conjunction with other productive factors such as machinery, tools, and land, results in the output of salable goods and services. When deciding how many workers to hire, employers are primarily interested in the revenue from the workers' output. When only a few workers are being used with a given amount of other productive factors, an additional worker will produce a healthy increase in output and therefore in the revenue received. This, in part, is explained by the fact that workers will be used first in those jobs where their productivity will be highest. But after a large number of workers are employed, the productive opportunities awaiting the next worker will have diminished. As a result, the additional revenue that employers can expect from hiring one more worker will decrease as the number of workers employed increases.

It follows that when the real wage is high, employers will not find it profitable to hire large numbers of workers. We will not find employers anxious to employ additional workers when the cost of hiring them is greater than the resulting revenue. With a low real wage, employers will find it to their advantage to increase the number of workers. Thus, the number of workers demanded is inversely related to the real wage.

It is now easy to describe a situation that will result in unemployment. If the real wage is very high, the number of people looking for jobs will be greater than the number that employers are interested in hiring. Many people who are looking for work will not find it. These people can legitimately be considered unemployed.

Also possible is a very low real wage that results in the number of jobs exceeding the number of people willing to take them. This can be described as a full-employment situation, since there is an available job for everyone who chooses to work. However, there is a higher real wage at which employers will continue to hire everyone who wants a job, and at the same time more people will seek jobs.

The real wage at which employers will be willing to hire exactly the number of workers that desire employment lies somewhere between the two wages just discussed. This is the real wage that will result in the largest number of people actually hired; at a higher real wage more people want to work, but fewer can find jobs; at a lower one more people could find jobs, but fewer want to work. It can be referred to as the *full-employment real wage*. This is the only wage at

*This doesn't mean that these individuals want to work longer hours. In fact, the opposite seems to be true. Over the years the work week has diminished because individuals are consuming more leisure as real wages and incomes have increased.

which the number of people wanting employment will equal the number that employers are willing to hire.

If the real wage deviates from the full-employment real wage, there will be pressures to bring it back. But this tendency does not mean we will always have full employment. Before we discuss the reasons for this, let's first turn our attention to some of the adjustments that are constantly occurring in the labor market.

2. Changing Demands and Changing Jobs

So far we have been talking as if there were only one real wage for all workers. While this is convenient for purposes of discussion, we all recognize that workers have many different skills, and in general each will command a different wage. The demand for workers reflects such things as their skills and the value of the output they produce. On the other side of the market is a supply curve determined by such things as the pleasantness of the work, the duration and difficulty of the training required, and the alternatives available.

This means that there is a full-employment real wage for every type of job. Full employment requires that the full-employment real wage exist for each category of employment. Then, given enough time, everyone willing and able to participate in a given job should be successful in finding it.

But the full-employment real wages are constantly changing with shifts in consumer preferences and technology. If, for example, consumers decide to keep their old cars for longer periods of time rather than purchasing new ones so often, the demand for automobile assembly-line workers will decrease. This means that at every real wage, fewer auto workers will be demanded than before. This *change in demand* refers to a shift in the demand curve and is to be distinguished from a *change in the number demanded*, which means a movement along a given demand curve in response to a change in the real wage.* After this decrease in demand we will find more potential auto workers at the prevailing real wage than employers want to hire at that wage. There will be unemployment among auto workers.

On the other hand, with people keeping their old cars longer, the demand for automobile mechanics will increase. At every real wage, more auto mechanics will be demanded than before. This means that at the prevailing real wage, the number of auto mechanics that employers want to hire exceeds the number of people willing to do the work.

---

*The decrease in demand for automobiles may have the effect of lowering the price of cars. Since this has the effect of increasing the money wage of auto workers relative to another price in the economy, we could argue that the real wage has increased, causing a movement along the demand curve for auto workers. This effect is being ignored here, however, since we will assume that one price (in this case the price of automobiles) will have an insignificant effect on any meaningful measure of the price level or the price index that is being used.

Unemployment in the labor market for auto workers will exert a downward pressure on the real wage these workers receive. The money wage may not decline, but it will increase less than other prices, which includes other wages, in the economy. This downward pressure on real wages results from workers, either individually or through their union representatives, electing to accept a lower real wage in return for a higher employment level. As the real wage declines some people who wanted to be auto workers at the higher real wage will decide that it is to their advantage to do something else. Of course, a decrease in the real wage will find employers willing to increase the number of auto workers they hire.

The downward pressure on the real wage paid to auto workers will continue as long as unemployment exists among these workers. One should not get the idea, however, that there will be a rapid adjustment in the real wage. It may take time and, as we will see, this has important implications for national economic policy.

While unemployment and a falling real wage afflict the auto workers, things will be looking better for auto mechanics. The real wage received by people capable of repairing cars will tend to increase as employers find they can't hire as many auto mechanics as they want at the original real wage. More people will find that, of the different alternatives open to them, becoming an auto mechanic is the most attractive. As long as there is excess demand for this skill, there will be an upward pressure on the real wage and an increase in the number willing to prepare for and practice it.

These adjustments are desirable, despite the fact that they require some workers to be laid off. When consumers decide they want fewer cars and more auto repair, it is desirable that scarce productive resources, which include labor, be shifted out of auto production and into auto repair.

The resulting unemployment and reallocation of workers are an unavoidable cost of shifting resources in response to consumer desires. Because of changes in consumer demand, as well as in productive technology, the value of labor employed in different jobs is constantly changing. If the labor force is to respond to these changes, we will find a certain number of people who are unemployed because they are between jobs.

Neither should we overlook the fact that many people leave a job, not because of a change in demand or technology, but because they reassess their alternatives and choose to look for another job. Also, individuals who are just entering the labor force may look for some time before accepting their first job. Most people mistakenly believe that anyone who is unemployed has lost his or her job. The truth is that, normally, less than half the unemployed have involuntarily left their jobs. The majority includes those who are entering the labor force for the first time, are reentering it after a long period of voluntary unemployment, or have quit their jobs.

For example, in December 1974 the unemployment rate in the United States reached 6.5 percent, or about 6 million people. While this is certainly an undesirable rate, it doesn't mean that 6 million people lost their jobs. Approximately 772,000 were looking for their first job, mostly young people. Almost 1,660,000 hadn't been working or seeking work for some time and had decided to enter the labor force again if they could find what they wanted. And 770,000 had voluntarily quit their jobs. In other words, fewer than half those listed as unemployed had left their jobs involuntarily.[1]

Unemployment of the type discussed in this section is often referred to as *frictional unemployment*. Regardless of the name economists give it, unemployment will often be unpleasant for those experiencing it. But given these economic facts of life, a certain amount of frictional unemployment is desirable in a dynamic economy.

3. Full-Employment Unemployment

When a worker is laid off because of a change in demand or technology, there are several options open to him or her. One possibility is that the worker will find it best to drop out of the labor market and pursue some other activity, such as going back to college. If this is the case he or she will not be seeking a job and therefore will not be considered unemployed. However, if the worker does intend to remain in the labor market, there are still a couple of possibilities. By not being very particular about the type of job or the acceptable real wage, an unemployed worker should be reemployed very quickly.*

Of course, most people will not accept the first job that comes along. By taking time and exerting some effort, they hope to find a better job. If we lived in a world of perfect information, searching for the best job would never be a problem. People would immediately know where their best opportunity was.

But information about job opportunities, like almost everything else, isn't free. It takes time and money to acquire. Unemployed workers will look for jobs in which they can be most productive and therefore earn the most. Up to a point, time spent in search of the right job will have a payoff that exceeds the value of the income that would be earned by taking the first job that comes along. Because of the costs, we will not find people acquiring complete information about employment prospects. Once the point as been reached where the cost of additional search is not offset by the expected benefit, the unemployed individual will find it to his advantage to terminate the search and take the best employment offer he has received.

Many examples of this type of job search come to mind. Students about to

---

*There are certain laws and institutional arrangements that restrict the worker who is willing to accept a low real wage in order to get a certain job. For example, minimum-wage legislation makes it illegal for an anyone to work for less than a federally established wage in many jobs. Also most union agreements are specifically designed to prevent workers from competing for jobs by offering to work for a lower real wage.

graduate from college spend time and effort writing letters to and interviewing with prospective employers. Each job possibility differs in pay, type of work, chances for promotion, and location. Each student will evaluate these considerations differently, and the more information he or she can obtain on the different possibilities, the better the employment decision.

Because of the benefits associated with employment information, people are willing to pay for help to get it. Employment agencies, by providing a place where job seekers can find out about prospective employers (and vice versa), facilitate the exchange of information between these two groups. The fact that these agencies are able to charge enough to warrant their continued operation indicates that the value of their services exceeds the cost of providing them.

Government statistics list individuals who are in the process of looking for a job as unemployed. But if we are to consider all those people unemployed, we must alter our previous definition (those who are looking for work and not able to find it). We would now have to include in the ranks of the unemployed those who are looking for work, but are unable to find a job they are willing to accept. From this viewpoint, much of what is commonly called unemployment is socially desirable. Given the advantages of having people employed where they are most productive, we would not want to reduce unemployment by requiring everyone to take the first job that came along or keeping workers in their present jobs when they felt it was possible to find a better one. In an important sense, job seekers are not unemployed. They are employed in the production of a very valuable commodity, knowledge. As long as they choose to continue in this employment rather than accept a conventional job, there is reason to believe that the knowledge their job searches are producing is more valuable than what they could produce in the alternative activities open to them.

Many things affect the amount of frictional or job-search unemployment. In a dynamic economy with consumer tastes and productive technologies changing rapidly, there will be more people shifting jobs and therefore more frictional unemployment than in a more static economy. Another important consideration is unemployment compensation. In many cases there is little cost to the worker for extending a period of unemployment. For example, in Massachusetts a person earning $6000 per year would, with unemployment compensation, lose only a little over $60 in income after taxes for every month unemployed. When such employment-related expenses as transportation and union dues are considered, the financial cost of being unemployed can be quite small. An unemployed worker would actually lose money in most cases by taking another job that paid much less than the previous one.

There can be little doubt that when it is less costly to be unemployed, workers will be less reluctant to quit their jobs and unemployed workers will be less anxious to become reemployed. For example, "inverse seniority" clauses are part of the labor agreements in several industries. These clauses give workers with the most seniority the privilege of being laid off first and rehired last. Evidence from Britain supports the view that the unemployment rate is sensitive to unemployment benefits. In September 1966 unemployment benefits in Britain were increased significantly. Immediately there was an increase in unemployment. Registered unemployment rose from 340,000 in September to 543,000 in November, with the unemployment rate for males more than doubling between August 1966 and January 1967.[2] The increase in benefits was obviously a major factor in the increase in unemployment.

A large amount of unemployment is voluntary. Many people choose to be unemployed rather than take available jobs because they feel their time is better used searching for more information on job opportunities, or simply taking a little more time off. So in many respects unemployment will be an attractive alternative, particulary when there is little financial cost associated with it.

At this point you may wonder if we are telling the whole story. So far we have talked about unemployment as if there were little reason to get upset about it. In fact, we have alluded several times to its desirability.

Actually there is much more to the unemployment story than we have discussed so far. Frictional unemployment can be expected to be around 3 to 5 percent of the labor force. This figure is often referred to as the natural rate of unemployment. Many economists define *full employment* as a situation in which unemployment rate doesn't exceed this natural rate. It could be referred to as full employment unemployment. Unfortunately, the unemployment rate has not always cooperated by remaining in this natural range. Periodically it climbs into the 5 to 10 percent range, occasionally going even higher. (Recall the 25 percent unemployment rate of the Great Depression?)* Attempting to explain unemployment rates of this magnitude with changes in demand, technology, and job preference strains credibility somewhat.

4. Unemployment and Aggregate Demand

Implicit in our discussion of frictional unemployment was the assumption that when the demand for labor decreased in one part of the economy it increased somewhere else. This will not always be the case. Occasionally the decline in the demand for labor will be very general. Demand will not be going down everywhere, but increases in the expanding sectors of the economy will not be large enough to offset the decreases elsewhere. When this occurs we say that the level of *aggregate demand* is declining. The quantity of goods and services that people are buying is going down, and as a result the demand for workers, as well as other productive resources, will be reduced. Although somewhat simplified, at this point it is convenient to say that a decrease in aggregate

*Data on unemployment is obtained from surveys. Those who respond that they are both without work and actively seeking employment are listed as unemployed.

demand is the result of people having less money to spend. Just as it is possible for aggregate demand to experience a decline, so it is possible for it to increase. We will take up increasing aggregate demand in later discussions, but for now we are interested in the effects of a decline.

5. The Problem of Expecting Too Much

If a worker is laid off during a decline in aggregate demand, getting a new job will be difficult because the demand for workers is decreasing throughout the economy. Unemployment resulting from a decline in aggregate demand can persist because neither firms nor workers will immediately recognize that the problem they face is part of a larger phenomenon.

The individual worker who has been laid off will see the problem as a decline in the demand for labor in his area of employment, not a general decrease in labor demand. Therefore, he will expect to find another job at a wage similar to what he was previously receiving. The individual will equate the real wage with the money wage he is offered. This isn't to say that workers don't know the importance of the price level in determining the real wage. It simply means that unemployed workers do not see the decrease in demand that caused their unemployment as part of a wide-spread reduction that will tend to reduce most prices in the economy. Therefore, in their search for new jobs, workers will hesitate to accept money wages much lower than what they were previously receiving. Unemployed workers will have in mind an *acceptance wage*, a wage below which they will not accept employment.

The reluctance of workers to accept lower money wages for their services in the face of falling demand is matched by a similar reluctance on the part of others in the economy. Sellers of products that are in decreasing demand will not necessarily be aware of a general decline in demand, which will exert downward pressure on the prices of many of their productive inputs. In other words, they will not expect their costs to decline. As a result they will be hesitant to lower the price of their product even though they are selling less than they expected at the existing price. They will elect instead to maintain the price and sell less.

With producers cutting output rather than price, the quantity of productive inputs needed (labor included) will be reduced. The reluctance of producers and workers to reduce their prices in response to a decline in demand causes a decrease in the number of workers hired as well as a decrease in the output of goods and services.

This implies that if all money prices and wages adjusted downward by the right amount in response to a general decrease in demand, then output and employment would not be affected. If employees were quick to lower their acceptance wages, sellers of products would see their production costs, in money terms, going down and would be willing to lower the price of their products. With prices lowered throughout the economy, the real wages would remain the same even though money wages declined. With the lower prices of goods and services, the same amount would be sold even though consumers had less money to spend. Nothing would change except money prices.

But another implication of our analysis is that prices (including money wages) will not respond appropriately, at least not without a long lag. Unemployment will persist because job seekers' expectations of finding high-paying employment exceed their ability to locate it. Eventually, of course, expectations will begin to fall, and unemployed workers will adjust their acceptance wage downward. But by the time this happens it may not have much effect on the level of unemployment. Because of the unemployment that occurred and persisted in response to the initial drop in aggregate demand, we can expect the level of aggregate demand to fall further.

When people are unemployed they will decrease their expenditures and consume less. This may not be dramatic, because they can draw on past savings or public programs such as unemployment compensation, but some reduction in consumption can be expected. What is reduced consumption for one person is reduced income for another. With people consuming less, businesses will find that they are selling less. This results in less demand for factors of production, including labor, and therefore more unemployment.

So by the time unemployed workers get around to lowering their expectations regarding the money wage they will accept, the further reduction in aggregate demand is such that these expectations are still too high. Higher than normal unemployment rates will persist.

On the other side of the coin we can expect to find businesses finally reducing their prices somewhat in the face of a chronically low demand. But as with labor, by the time this price reduction occurs it is likely to be inadequate. Depressed sales will still be the rule and, of course, demand for labor will remain low.

6. Time Heals All Wounds

What we have just described seems like a vicious circle: a reduction in aggregate demand increases unemployment, which causes a further reduction in aggregate demand, which increases unemployment, and so on and on. Is there any mechanism that will bring the downward spiral to an end? The answer is yes.

The downward spiral includes decreases in prices and wages which tend to moderate the decline (although at first they are too little and too late to do more than moderate). As long as unemployment is greater than normal and the demand for output is less than is being produced, money wages and prices will continue to decline. However, even though consumers will be demanding less, they will not reduce consumption expenditures by as much as the decline in output. With demand falling less rapidly than output, eventually output will decline enough to equal demand. This will finally bring a halt to the decline since everything that is being produced will be demanded. Of course, this bottoming out of employment and output is likely to occur at a high level of unemployment.

Because businesses are now selling everything they produce, the downward pressure on prices will cease. However, with unemployment exceeding the natural rate, the downward pressure on money wages will continue. With money wages falling and output prices remaining the same, real wages will be declining and employers will hire more workers. Employment will start to increase. As employment rises so does the level of output and aggregate income. This increase in income may lead to an increase in aggregate demand sufficient to absorb the additional output. This being the case, real wages will be declining and the demands for goods and services will be increasing. Both of these changes encourage employers to hire more workers and increase output, which once more may be translated into increased aggregate demand. This upward spiral in output and employment continues until the unemployment rate has declined to the natural rate.

When this has occurred there is no longer a tendency for output to be expanded by bringing unemployed resources, including labor, into the productive process. Those people not actively employed in the labor force are either in satisfactory alternatives to traditional employment or between jobs as a result of changes in the relative demands for productive skills. What economists refer to as a *full-employment equilibrium* has been reestablished.

In the last few pages we have given a brief and incomplete description of the *business cycle*.° The phase characterized by declining output and employment is commonly referred to as a *recession*, unless the decline is really dramatic, in which case we change the name to *depression*. That part of the cycle which exhibits increasing output and employment is known as a *recovery*.

Those of you who have followed recent economic events may be a little puzzled by the fact that we emphasized the tendency for money wages and prices to decline during the recession phase of the cycle. In late 1974 and early 1975 the annual rate of *inflation* (an increase in the general price level) was over 10 percent at a time when the unemployment was at the highest rate of the post-World War II period. This certainly doesn't seem consistent with our previous discussion. It is true that the relationship between changes in the general price level and the rate of unemployment do not always hold with the precision implied in this chapter. Lags exist in the real world that, for a time, appear to contradict relationships that are predicted by elementary economic analysis. As a rule, a deeper look will remove many of the apparent conflicts

---

°Our discussion has concentrated on the adjustments in the labor market during the business cycle. Obviously other sectors of the economy are involved. Such important factors as interest rates, investment demand, and demand for monetary holdings are also playing important roles as they adjust to changing economic conditions during the course of a business cycle. Although this analysis is incomplete, it allows us to focus on adjustment in the labor market.

between the analysis and real-world observations. In chapters 7 and 8 we will examine the relationship between inflation and unemployment more carefully in order to shed some light on economic problems.

Finally, you probably noticed that full-employment equilibrium occurred automatically in response to the unemployment that followed the reduction in aggregate demand. No overt government policy was required, just a policy of patience.°

7. The High Cost of Patience

Patience may be a virtue, but it's certainly not its own reward. While patiently waiting for the economy to regain its "natural" full-employment posture, billions of dollars' worth of output can be lost, with high levels of unemployment bringing misery and frustration to millions of households. The amount of time required for natural adjustments to restore the economy to full employment once a recession or depression gets under way may be substantial.

Are there government policies that can be used during periods of unemployment to encourage the return to a full-employment economy? Yes, there are. This is where macroeconomics can be useful. It gives us insights into the types of policies that will smooth economic activity. Macroeconomics provides us with important theoretical understanding of the effects some policies will have in stimulating aggregate demand when it is deficient and moderating it when it is excessive.†

Unfortunately, theoretical understanding doesn't always translate into practical know-how. Many problems exist in formulating and implementing policies that will move the economy in the desired direction. There are cases of attempts to improve the performance of the economy that had the effect of pushing the economy in the wrong direction, making the situation worse than if no active policy had been pursued at all.

Be that as it may, there is plenty of evidence that people are not content to sit back and do nothing during economic hard times, waiting for "natural" economic forces to correct the situation. People in economic distress want something done. And political decision makers will invariably respond to constituent demands by doing something. Therefore, we must develop some understanding of how given policies are likely to affect the economy.

°A fundamental criticism of the previous analysis was provided by John Maynard Keynes, an important Twentieth-century English economist. One interpretation of his position has been that a less than full-employment equilibrium is possible. An alternative interpretation of Keynes's views is that the only true equilibrium is at full employment, but that a less-than-full-employment disequilibrium can be very persistent.

†Excess aggregate demand is the opposite of deficient aggregate demand and means that the total demand for goods and services exceeds the ability of the economy to produce them.

In the next chapter we will take a close look at the components of aggregate demand. These components are not only influenced by economic conditions but they also in turn influence economic conditions through their effect on aggregate demand. By identifying these components and looking at the relationships that exist between them we will take an important step in understanding how we might be able to nudge the economy in desirable directions.

DISCUSSION QUESTIONS

1. What effect would the following have on the amount of frictional unemployment found in the economy:
   a) Improved and more accessible information on job opportunities
   b) More rapid changes in technology and consumer preferences
   c) A reduction in people's attachment to particular locations
   d) A tax that applied only to the unemployed

2. On strictly economic grounds (forgetting considerations of fairness or compassion), why do you think it would be unwise to enact a tax that applied only to the unemployed?

3. Many occupational groups have been legally empowered to restrict the number of people who can enter their occupations. Those supporting the restrictions argue that they provide a public benefit by protecting consumers against incompetents. Can you think of some costs these restrictions impose on society?

4. It is often argued that centrally controlled economies have lower unemployment rates than decentralized market economies, and this is one of the advantages of central control. How would you argue that this low unemployment reflects a disadvantage rather than an advantage of a centrally controlled economy?

5. If the money supply were cut in half and this was accompanied by a 50 percent reduction in all prices and wages, nothing would have changed in real terms. Workers would be receiving the same real wage for their labors and producers the same real price for their products. However, based on your reading of this chapter, what do you think would happen to the unemployment rate if the money supply was suddenly reduced by 50 percent?

6. Many college students find it discouraging to struggle through school in an effort to prepare themselves for a good job when the unemployment rate is high. Are there any advantages to going to college during a period of high unemployment?

chapter 3

The More We Spend, the More We Get: Aggregate Demand and the Multiplier

As we have seen, there is an important connection between the level of aggregate demand and employment. Therefore it is vital that we understand how the total level of demand is determined. The purpose of this chapter is to examine the demand for goods and services by the major sectors of the economy—consumers, producers, government, and foreigners—and their interaction in determining total demand. This will set the stage for our subsequent discussions of policy.

1. King Consumer

By sheer volume, the household goods we consume every day make up the most important component of total demand. Small shifts in consumer psychology or savings habits can shake the best predictions of economic events. Fortunately consumption demand, in the aggregate, is related in a fairly stable way to several variables. With a knowledge of these determinants of consumption behavior, we can predict quite accurately the level of consumption demand for the economy. The key variables are income and wealth, though there remains some debate as to the correct way to measure these two determinants.

We are obviously constrained in our expenditures by our income level and, more explicitly, income after taxes, or *disposable income*. Consumption expenditures can therefore be expected to rise and fall with disposable income. The business contraction that began in 1974 provides some data in support of this view. Between 1973 and 1974 real disposable income declined by 2½ percent—the first year-to-year decline since 1947. This drop in disposable

17

income came about in spite of a 8½ percent rise in money wages, for this wage increase was more than offset by the rise in consumer prices over the year. The resulting decline in real disposable income was accompanied by the first annual decline in real consumption expenditures in over thirty years. With real disposable income and consumption restricted to an unusual degree, it is not surprising that the business slump was so severe.

The earliest attempts to forecast consumption expenditures were based on this kind of simple relation between disposable income and consumption. However, some problems with this formulation soon arose. Forecasts of consumption expenditures in the early years after World War II seriously understated levels of consumption demand that were actually realized. In fact economists' expectations of a sluggish post-war economy were contradicted by the tremendous economic boom led by buoyant consumption demand.

A simple relation between disposable income and consumption is not adequate to explain certain types of consumption behavior. For example, it has been found that low-income families spend a very large percentage of their incomes, sometimes incurring debts to spend even more than they earn, while higher-income families save a substantial fraction of their incomes. However over long periods of time the fraction of total disposable income spent on consumption goods has remained fairly constant for both groups, and hence for the economy as a whole, in spite of the increase in the average level of income over several decades.

These observations led to the development of alternative theories of consumption behavior. One view is that an individual family's consumption is determined by its income position relative to its peer group. Low-income families spend a high percentage of their incomes in order to keep up with the middle class, and higher-income families can consume at a relatively grand level while spending a smaller percentage of their incomes. For the economy as a whole, income grows over time without altering the percentages of high- and low-income families, so that relative income groupings remain unchanged. Consequently the various income groups will still spend the same fractions of their incomes as before, so that total consumption as a fraction of total disposable income will remain unchanged over long periods of time.

Another view is that individuals determine their consumption spending according to long-run expectations about future income. Families commit themselves, both contractually and psychologically, to a particular life-style, and they are unlikely to alter their expenditure patterns radically because of year-to-year fluctuations in income. Consequently, families with incomes below their long-run-expected-income level will spend a very large proportion of their incomes to maintain the life-style to which they have become (or would like to be) accustomed. On the other hand, some high-income families are only temporarily in such a position, and they expect their incomes to fall back to some lower level. These families are likely to spend a smaller fraction of their incomes rather than splurge with the temporary windfall earnings of the year.

For the economy as a whole such ups and downs in individual incomes average out in the long run, so that we observe a fairly stable fraction of total income spent over long periods of time.

Some examples of this kind of behavior are available. You as a student probably anticipate an average lifetime income considerably higher than you presently earn. Consequently you are quite willing to go into debt, take gifts or loans from your parents, and otherwise live beyond your current means. This shows you are letting lifetime expected income, rather than current income, influence your consumption pattern.

In 1975, with the economy severely slumping, tax rebates were enacted on 1974 taxes in the hope that this would stimulate consumer spending. The above theory suggests that a *temporary* change in disposable income would have little effect on consumption. In fact a number of surveys in early 1975 indicated that many consumers planned to save their tax rebates or use them to pay off past debts. Such behavior, which is entirely consistent with the above theory, substantially limits the expansionary effect of this kind of temporary tax-reduction program.

This view of consumer behavior is essentially equivalent to the position that consumption is determined by wealth or expected wealth. All families have income-earning assets—some in the form of stocks, bonds, land, and so on—but mostly in the form of human capital—those human skills and abilities that are productive and hence marketable. It is reasonable to suppose that the form in which wealth is earned has an important influence on consumption habits. A person who earns $20,000 per year on interest from large holdings of government bonds probably consumes at a different rate from one who receives an equivalent income in wages or salary.

Furthermore, the composition of one's financial wealth directly affects the level of consumption expenditure. One way to hold wealth, other than stocks or bonds, cash, bank deposits, or real physical, is in the form of consumer durables, such as cars and houses, which provide a stream of psychic income in the form of services rendered over a period of years. Families that experience an increase in financial wealth, expecially in the form of money or assets closely related and easily converted to money, are likely to channel some of this increase into the acquisition of consumer durables. In fact one explanation of the unanticipated boom in consumption expenditures immediately after World War II is that households had accumulated monetary wealth that was released in the acquisition of durable goods not available during the war.

Although certain aspects of income and wealth are important determinants of consumption behavior in our economy, there does not appear to be a simple relation between consumption and disposable income. A less direct connection, including such considerations as relative income position, long-term expectations, and wealth holdings, is involved. As we will see, these refinements have important implications for the effectiveness of alternative measures for affecting total demand in the economy.

2. The Fickle Firm

The most volatile component of aggregate demand is the demand by firms for machinery and other equipment used in their production processes. These items are called *capital goods*, and an addition to the stock of capital goods is referred to as *investment*. Investment is the purchase of real capital goods, and as such it constitutes a direct demand on the output of goods in the economy. The economist's use of the term *investment* should be distinguished from everyday usage, which refers to the acquistion of stocks, bonds, and other securities. The purchase of stock does not directly involve real capital goods, and hence it is not investment in the economist's dictionary. Your stock purchases may enable the issuing corporation to acquire capital goods, but this is a different transaction altogether. Only the purchase of real capital goods is an investment, and this is the business sector's direct contribution to aggregate demand.

The volatility of investment demand depends on the expectations of people in business, which are extremely difficult to anticipate. Firms are willing to commit themselves to large investment projects only if they expect handsome returns in the fairly near future. Firms are likely to base their expectations about future sales possibilities on current sales activity, the rate at which sales or revenues are growing, or possibly some feeling for overall consumer sentiment toward the state of the economy.

An optimistic or pessimistic business climate is likely to affect the business community as a whole, with investment activity moving up or down across a broad spectrum of industries. When the economy is on the rise and business expectations are buoyant, investment demand will be correspondingly strong. During an economic boom, it is easy for firms to overestimate the strength and persistence of the expansion. When sales level off, many firms will find themselves capable of producing more than they can sell and forced to production below full capacity. At this point, with businesses in a large number of industries throttled with excess productive capacity, investment activity will be reduced drastically and will remain low until increasing sales restore production to full-capacity levels.

Such was the situation in the first half of 1975. Real disposable income, and hence consumption demand, declined sharply causing a sales and production cutback. Because the sales slump was so severe, manufacturing firms in mid-1975 had less than 70 percent of their productive capacity in use—another post-World War II record. The prospects for a swift recovery were particularly dim because very little impetus could be expected from the producing sector of the economy. With considerable unused capital goods sitting around, businesses had little interest in spending money on new investment projects.

Unusually high interest rates also retarded investment activity, particularly in the construction of housing. High interest rates and the difficulty in borrowing money to finance housing purchases in 1974 made the construction industry the weakest sector in the economy. One-half of the reduction in output between 1973 and 1974 was accounted for by the decline in housing demand.

Businesses, as well as home buyers, are affected by borrowing costs and unavailability of funds, and this provides an important channel for governmental control over economic activity. Interest can make up a significant portion of the total cost of an investment project and is therefore an important consideration in the investment decision.

The cost of funds for investment depends upon which of three fund-raising channels is used—internal financing, borrowing, or stock financing. In the first method the firm simply uses funds left over from the profits of previous years. Some observers claim that the extensive use of internal financing by large corporations (about 50 percent of corporate financing is internal) shelters these firms from the pressures of financial markets and enables them to act independently of any policies affecting these markets. However, there is an *opportunity cost*, which is equal to the income that the firm could receive if it were to lend the funds to some other firms or individuals. In deciding whether or not to use these funds for its own investment purposes, the profit-seeking firm takes into account the value that those funds have in alternative uses, such as the prevailing market cost of funds for investments of comparable risk. Thus the cost of internal financing bears a close relation to the cost of obtaining funds in the organized financial markets.

The markets for stocks and bonds are not merely casino parlors or adventuresome wealth-holders. Through these markets, firms can get funds for investment and financial policy makers can influence the investment decision. Stocks are shares of ownership in particular corporations. New stock may be issued by a firm and sold in order to raise funds for investment. The cost to the original owners of the firm is the dilution of ownership and the consequent dissipation of earnings over a larger number of shareholders.

Corporate bonds are IOU's of a firm, and these certificates of indebtedness offer a promise to pay the lender a certain amount of income each year. This yearly income as a percentage of the purchase price of the bond (allowing also for changes in the price of the bond as it reaches maturity) is the rate of interest on the bond and indicates the cost of borrowing (or the opportunity cost of using internal funds). High interest rates will generally discourage investment activity while low rates can stimulate a large amount of investment demand.

3. Who's Left?

The remaining purchasers of an economy's output are the various levels of government and the foreign sector.

A government outlay is considered to be an expenditure, and hence a component of demand, only if it involves the actual purchase of a good or service from some firm or individual. This includes jet fighters, highways, sewer systems, dams, trash collection, and educational services, as well as the salaries to government workers who render direct services to the various levels of government. Excluded from the list of expenditures are *transfer payments*, cash grants to individuals. Transfer payments, such as unemployment compensation, social security payments, and income supplements to the poor do not involve the purchase of some good or service and are not counted as components of demand. These items are actually similar to taxes in the sense that they affect disposable or after-tax income, but of course in the opposite direction. Consequently they are classified as negative taxes.

In contrast to expenditures by businesses and households, government expenditures showed an increase in real terms between 1973 and 1974. Surprisingly, this increase was due solely to state and local governments, and the change was way too small to offset the expenditure reductions of the other sectors of the domestic economy. Government expenditures constitute an increasingly important component of aggregate demand, not only in terms of magnitude, but also in terms of the federal government's willingness to use its purchasing power as a tool for affecting aggregate demand.

Finally aggregate demand for a country's output is augmented when foreigners purchase domestically produced goods and diminished to the extent that locals consume foreign rather than domestic goods. The total impact of the foreign sector on aggregate demand is conveniently summarized by *net exports*—exports minus imports. This net figure is an extremely small share of the total demand for goods and services in the United States and thus is ignored in most analyses of aggregate demand. In 1974, for example, net exports amounted to $2.0 billion, which is equivalent to only one-seventh of one percent of GNP during that year. Even a quadrupling of this figure would have an insignificant impact on the total demand for goods and services in the economy. The 4-percent increase that did occur between 1973 and 1974 was certainly too small to have any perceptible effect on economic events. Foreign trade is, however, important in its own right, and there are reasons to believe that it has an impact on the domestic economy that far exceeds its relative magnitude. These considerations will be developed further in chapters eleven and twelve.

4. The Multiplier

The basis of interdependence among the four sectors is that one entity's expenditure is another's income. When there is an increased demand for motorcycles, for example, firms producing them will increase their employment of all factors of production—workers, capital goods, and land. Payment will now have to be made for the new inputs into the production process, and these payments constitute incomes for the various owners of the productive factors, the workers, capitalists, and landowners. Thus a given change in expenditure will generate income changes of equal magnitude except for the sums that are withdrawn by the government in the form of taxes and by firms in the form of retained corporate earnings (firm savings).

Now, recall our discussion of consumption behavior: the consumption level is likely to change if income changes. It is reasonable to suppose that only a fraction (possibly a large one) of income changes will be respent. A family experiencing $1000 increase in annual income may choose to spend anywhere from, say, $100 to $900 of that increase depending upon whether the increase is expected to be permanent or temporary, how it affects the family's relative income position, the time they have to adjust to the new income level, and a host of other psychological factors. In any case, changes in disposable income will cause changes in consumption. The fraction by which consumption changes in response to a change in income is called the *marginal propensity to consume.*°

Combining these two notions, we can see that a given change in expenditure by one sector of the economy can cause a multiple change in the total level of expenditure made by all sectors combined. Suppose there is a drastic reduction in the demand for investments in residential housing, as occurred in 1974. Construction firms, suffering a reduction in housing demand, cut back first of all on the number of workers and reduce the volume of supplies ordered from construction-materials producers. The laid-off workers have less income and cut back on their consumption correspondingly. This in turn reduces the demand for workers in various industries—food, clothing, entertainment, and so on—that were supplying goods to the construction workers, and workers in these industries are laid off causing a further reduction in aggregate demand. Likewise, the industries supplying construction materials to the housing industry cut back on output and employment, and the unemployed workers in these industries cut back on their consumption demands. The circular nature of the expenditure and income flow causes the initial reduction in housing demand to have a multiple impact on the level of aggregate demand in the economy.

5. An Hypothetical Example

Perhaps we can be more precise about the magnitude of this multiple contraction or expansion of the economy. Suppose that households spend 90 percent of any income increases and add the remaining 10 percent to their savings. To keep things simple for the time being, let us also suppose that all income ends up in the hands of households. That is, there are no taxes (a blissful assumption) and no savings or retained earnings by corporations.

Now assume that a $100 million order is placed by American Airlines for a

---

° The marginal propensity to consume is equal to the change in consumption divided by the change in income. For example, if a $1000 income change causes a $600 consumption change, the marginal propensity to consume is 600/1000, or .6.

fleet of Boeing 747s. Boeing immediately hires new workers and places new orders with suppliers, and the $100 million begins to flow through the system. The initial $100 million is used to hire new workers, either directly by Boeing or by its suppliers. Assemblers, stampers, electricians, engineers, truckdrivers, managers, and stockholders all receive portions of the $100 million until it is exhausted. These individuals respend the income they receive, according to our assumption, at the rate of ninety cents out of every dollar earned. Ninety million dollars in new, second-round expenditures on food, housing, clothing, recreation, services, medical care, and so forth are generated, and this $90 million also ends up in the hands of various individuals in the economy. Again 90 percent of this income or $81 million is respent, generating once more an equal increase in household incomes. And so on.

The total expansion in aggregate demand is some multiple of the initial expenditure. Furthermore the extent of this multiple expansion depends upon the rate at which new income is respent. In this example we have our original increase in demand of $100 million plus $90 million in increased consumption in the second round, $81 million in the third round, $72 million in the fourth round, and so forth. This was based on the assumption that 90 percent of all new income is respent as consumption. If the marginal propensity to consume were lower, a smaller fraction would be respent in each round, and the multiple expansion would be smaller.

Summing the increases in aggregate demand at each step, we can see that the total increase in aggregate demand in the above example approaches $1000 million—ten times the amount of the original expenditure by American Airlines. There is a *multiplier* on the American Airlines investment expenditure equal to 10, meaning that, for every dollar increase in investment expenditures, aggregate demand will ultimately increase by ten dollars. With a lower marginal propensity to consume, the size of the multiplier would be correspondingly lower. Suppose that only 75 percent of new income was respent. The initial $100 million expenditure would generate secondary increases in demand of $75 million, $56 million, $42 million, $31.6 million, and so on, for a total increase of $400 million. The ultimate increase is four times the size of the initial expenditure, or, in other words, the multiplier in this case would be 4.

6. A Not-So-Hypothetical Example

Because there is some blatant unrealism in this example, the multiplier on investment expenditures may not be 10, even though the marginal propensity to consume is pretty close to 90 percent. This impression needs some qualifications.

First of all the multiplier effect described above will sustain itself only if there are continuous injections of $100-million-dollar expenditures into the system. If the American Airlines purchase is just a one-shot deal and if no other orders are forthcoming, Boeing and the other subcontractors will have to start laying off workers once the order is filled. Once the effect of the single $100 million expenditure has worn off, we will be back at the same employment and income level we started with. Only a temporary expansion of jobs and incomes occurs.

One should also recognize that some fraction of income increases do get taxed away by the government and some portion of expenditures are raked off by corporations for the purpose of financing new investment projects. Taxation and corporate saving extract approximately 45 percent of every expenditure dollar, leaving only fifty-five cents out of every dollar's expenditure as household disposable income. Ninety percent of this amount, or about fifty cents is respent as household consumption. With an ultimate respending rate of only 50 percent, the value of the multiplier is only 2. The higher the rate of taxation and the greater the tendency of corporations to retain profits, the lower will be the respending rate and consequently the lower will be the multiplier.

The 45 percent rate of taxation and retention of corporate earnings and the 90 percent rate at which disposable income is consumed are all based on estimates employed by the economic advisors to President Kennedy.[1] These figures were the basis for the investment-expenditures multiplier upon which policy proposals were based. While the implied value of this multiplier is 2, they recognized that time must elapse before the full effect of the multiplier is realized. These same advisors estimated that about half of the response to the initial impetus would be felt within six months, and this too was crucial to the policy recommendations offered during the 1960s.

By this time the concept of the multiplier had been around for some time, although it had not seen use as a policy tool. John Maynard Keynes, the British economist who provided the theoretical foundations of the multiplier analysis, had advanced this concept during the 1930s, and the power of his reasoning had swept the economics profession within years of the publication of his ideas. His impact on the field of economics has been great enough to warrant labeling the resulting transformation "The Keynesian Revolution." Policy makers were slower to subscribe to the Keynesian heterodoxy, and it was not until the sixties that the implementation and testing of the theory behind the multiplier could take place. The Kennedy and Johnson administrations were open to the ideas of their Keynesian advisors, and policy proposals based on the multiplier principle began to emanate from the White House. As we will see in the following chapter, Keynesian economics was actively employed to stabilize the economy during the sixties. This was the heyday of Keynesian economics, an era when the most unlikely individuals were to claim, "We are all Keynesians now."*

---

*This is a partial quote from a statement by Professor Milton Friedman, which appeared in a *Time* magazine story on Keynesian economics. It has been used to indicate the broad acceptance of Keynesian economics, since Professor Friedman is not usually identified with a Keynesian position on economic policy. However, it is worth giving Friedman's full statement, which more accurately reflects his position: "In one sense, we are all Keynesians now; in another, no one is a Keynesian any longer."

Discussion Questions

1. Assume that one-third of every income dollar is taxed away, that firms retain none of their profits, and that 90 percent of additional disposable income gets respent on consumption. Trace through the successive rounds of spending in the multiplier process, showing at each stage (a) the increase in consumption, (b) the increase in tax revenues, and (c) the increase in GNP resulting from an initial increase in investment demand of $100 million.

2. Why does the multiplier increase (a) as the marginal propensity to consume increases or (b) as the tax rate decreases?

3. It has been observed that black families living in black districts spend a smaller fraction of their incomes than do white families of comparable income levels. What theory of consumption behavior does this data support?

4. In early 1975 it was estimated that GNP was $100 billion below the level of GNP that would have prevailed at full employment. Assuming the multiplier on investment expenditure is 2.0, how much would investment demand have to increase to restore full employment?

5. What assumptions must hold for the multiplier process to have full effect in the manner described in this chapter?

chapter **4**

We Were All
Keynesians Then:
A Look at Fiscal Policy

There was a time, extending into this century, when the budgetary operations of the government were tiny in comparison with the private economy. In 1929 the receipts of the federal government and of state and local governments amounted to a mere 3.7 and 7.3 percent, respectively, of gross national product. *Fiscal policy*, the use of federal taxation and expenditures to influence economic activity, was as impractical as it was foreign to the prevailing principles of governmental finance.

World War II, the several wars since that time (two hot, one cold but persistent), and increased involvement in social problems have made the government what it is today: large and powerful in its impact on the economy. While we lag behind our European friends in this regard—in Sweden and France taxes account for 40 percent of total income generated—governments at all levels take in a large (32 percent) and growing (from 25 percent in 1957) share of gross national income. According to our own philosophies we may differ on the question of whether government in the United States is too large or too small, but there is no doubt that the government sector is sufficiently large to have a substantial impact on the overall economy.

While the total government sector in the United States is large enough to have substantial economic impact, there is little coordination between the budgetary activities of the various state, local, and federal branches of government. These levels of government do not act collectively, changing taxes and expenditures from year to year in a unified manner, so there is not a common

27

posture of the government sector in its impact on economic activity. It is actually only the federal branch that takes on the responsibility for seeing that its budgetary decisions respond to what is required for economic stabilization. This is appropriate since the federal government is the largest single economic decision maker around; its budgetary decisions are massive compared to those of any other level of government or any individual business firm. How economic activity is affected by federal budgetary operations and how fiscal policy has actually worked in the past are the primary subjects under discussion in this chapter. We will begin with that old bogeyman of fiscal responsibility—the national debt.

1. Superdebtor

In the early months of 1975 President Ford appealed to Congress to raise the limit on federal indebtedness to $600 billion dollars. At the time federal borrowing was rapidly approaching the existing limit of $500 billion, a debt of almost $2400 for every man, woman, and child in the country. Can national bankruptcy be far down the road?

Massive federal indebtedness is actually a fairly recent phenomenon. Traditional views on sound government finance dictated that the government's expenditures be kept in line with tax receipts, thereby balancing the budget in all but extreme circumstances. In 1902 the total debt of the governments at all levels amounted to a mere $2.8 billion, indicating that traditional ideas of budgetary soundness were well in hand. The exigencies of World War I required a departure from this record of fiscal purity, but we were soon back on the path of righteousness with a program of debt repayment. The $24 billion war debt was reduced by $10 billion by 1929, a landmark year in economic history. The following decade of depression gave rise to increasing indebtedness despite repeated promises and attempts to balance the budget. Finally, with World War II, lip service to budget balancing was stopped, and federal indebtedness soared to $269 billion by 1946. Reassured by the survival, and even apparent strength, of the economy in the face of such indebtedness and encouraged by economists that a large public debt was not an unhealthy thing, subsequent administrations permitted the debt to rise to its present level. Nor is there any suggestion that the level of indebtedness will be reduced.

The U.S. Treasury is forced to borrow funds whenever tax receipts fall short of expenditures. This may happen by intention or by chance. Attempts to balance receipts and expenditures can be frustrated, as Roosevelt and Hoover discovered, when an unanticipated downturn of the economy reduces incomes and hence tax revenues. A number of devout budget balancers have seen the virtues of public indebtedness when a depressed economy failed to yield tax revenues sufficient to match expenditures. Taxation is obviously only one means by which federal expenditures can be financed. The alternative is borrowing, either from private banks, firms, or individuals or from agencies of the federal government, notably the Federal Reserve Bank.°

The impact of any budgetary operation depends upon the method by which it is financed. Imagine that the Department of Defense purchases twenty new jet fighters costing a total of $1 billion, and suppose that the government chooses not to raise taxes to finance this acquisition. The purchase can be financed by borrowing money through the issue of government IOU's (Treasury bonds). To begin with, the government makes the purchase by writing a check on its account with the Federal Reserve Bank, and $1 billion of new money enters circulation among private firms and individuals. To square its account with the Federal Reserve Bank, the Treasury sells a billion dollars worth of Treasury bonds and deposits this money in the Bank. The deposit matches the withdrawal, and the Treasury's account with the Federal Reserve Bank is once again in order.

If the bonds were purchased by the public, $1 billion is removed from private circulation, exactly offsetting the initial injection of money resulting from the purchase of the jet fighters. The public must relinquish the money to the Treasury in order to purchase the bonds, so there is no net change in the supply of money in the hands of the public. In this case—with no change in the money supply—the operation is referred to as a *pure fiscal policy*. The supply of money does not change, but there is a billion-dollar increase in the level of federal expenditures.

If the bonds end up in the hands of the Federal Reserve Bank, on the other hand, there is a monetary effect as well as a fiscal effect from the operation. The funds are in effect borrowed from the Federal Reserve Bank, not from the public. The initial injection of money from the purchase of the jets remains in the hands of private banks and individuals, that is, the supply of money in circulation increases by $1 billion. Therefore, when an expenditure is financed through borrowing from the Federal Reserve Bank, such an operation has both a fiscal (the expenditure not matched by taxes) and a monetary (the creation of new money in the hands of the public) aspect. It is thus referred to as a *mixed policy*.

In either case the total indebtedness of the U.S. Treasury mounts. Any time tax revenues fall short of expenditures there is a budget *deficit*, and the Treasury is forced to borrow. In the opposite situation, when revenues exceed expenditures and a budget surplus occurs, bonds can be repurchased, and Treasury indebtedness declines.

There is considerable concern in some circles over the size of the na-

---

° As discussed in the following chapter the Federal Reserve Bank is an agency of the federal government, whose primary function is the formation and execution of monetary policies. One aspect of this is the purchase and sale of government bonds.

tional debt. Politicians—including presidents—have been particularly wary of mounting public indebtedness. But the reason for this concern is not obvious. According to public-opinion surveys the size of the national debt or the annual budgetary deficits is not an issue of enormous concern to the voters. Nor is it considered to be worrisome in the economics profession. However, some people are uncomfortable because their government has been spending beyond its means and faces the threat of bankruptcy. Every year a few kindly and patriotic souls contribute small sums to repay the debt, usually with an accompanying letter that suggests the government needs the money more than they do.

Usually these people are comparing government with family finances. Certainly a household that runs up debts excessively feels a financial pinch when an uncomfortably large portion of its income is drained off to make loan and interest payments. Also, no individual can increase personal indebtedness indefinitely while making no provision for repayment. But what is impossible or financially disastrous for a family turns out to be acceptable, and possibly desirable, for a government. One fundamental difference between the federal government and an individual family is that the former has an indefinite life span and an interminable capacity to generate income. The ability of the Treasury to raise funds is related to the aggregate level of income in the country. As long as incomes rise, taxes will rise, and the Treasury can comfortably increase its interest payments at the same rate. The Treasury can continue to issue new debt, and with the taxing power of the government as backing and sufficiently generous rates of interest as inducement, government bonds need never fail to find eager buyers.

To some concerned citizens this seems unfair to future generations. If the government of the present generation spends more than it takes in taxes, it will leave behind a large burden for the subsequent generation in the form of public debt. Even if that generation opts not to pay off the debt, it will still have to pay higher interest payments. So far this line of reasoning is entirely correct. However, we might ask to whom this interest is being paid. The marvelous thing about the national debt, and therefore the interest payments on it, is that we owe it to ourselves, and subsequent generations will also owe it to themselves. Too bad we cannot say the same for our Mastercharge bill.

Another source of opposition to a mounting national debt is the fear that deficits are inflationary. This is undoubtedly the case when budget deficits come on top of an already booming private demand for goods and services. But inflationary pressures are not likely to result from a large deficit when the private economy is slack. This amounts to an argument, not against the national debt itself, but rather against deficit spending at inappropriate (inflationary) times.

How do these arguments fit in with present circumstances? An examination of the growth of the public debt since World War II indicates that things are pretty well in hand. At the end of World War II the federal debt stood at $279 billion, and annual interest costs on the debt were running close to $4 billion.

Gross national income for 1946, which serves as an indication of the revenue-raising capacity of the government, was $208 billion, actually smaller than the total debt outstanding. Since that time aggregate income has grown more rapidly than the national debt. By 1970, for example, gross national income was more than twice the value of the national debt. Also by 1970 interest payments to service the debt amounted to $14.6 billion, so that the fraction of aggregate income needed to service the debt had fallen from 2 percent to 1½ percent, and this in spite of the considerably higher rates of interest prevailing in 1970.

So we see that when put in perspective, the size of the public debt should not conjure up fears of national bankruptcy. However, this discussion does not suggest when, or even if, an increase in public indebtedness is a reasonable macroeconomic policy.

2. The Fiscal Prescription

By 1946 the national debt had risen to $269 billion, and yet the economy managed to survive. In fact it appeared to show signs of good health. It was converted to peacetime production, which after a brief recession, moved upward at a considerable rate. Fears of disastrous implications of a large public indebtedness were apparently misplaced. This realization freed the federal government from the constraint of budget balancing and permitted it to employ fiscal tools to achieve economic stabilization. When a conservative Republican president can recommend a budget that entails a deficit of $52 billion (President Ford, 1975), the old budget balancing orthodoxy is in for some very hard times.

The new orthodoxy calls for budget deficits or surpluses according to prevailing economic conditions, with the goal of economic stabilization. Medicine for a slumping economy is a budget deficit created through an increase in expenditures and/or a reduction in taxes. On the other hand, when aggregate demand is excessive, the government should counter this tendency by reducing expenditures and increasing taxes, thereby realizing a budgetary surplus. The magnitude of these budgetary actions should be geared to the extent of excessive or deficient demand prevailing in the private economy.

Returning to the example in chapter three, let us suppose that the government, rather than American Airlines, purchases $100 million worth of airplanes. If taxes are not raised to finance this purchase, the Treasury may choose to borrow from the public, making this a pure fiscal operation. Assuming the same rates of taxation and retention of corporate earnings (45 percent) and the same marginal propensity to consume (90 percent) as in the prior example, the multiplier for this expenditure is again 2. The initial $100 million purchase generates new disposable incomes of $55 million (55 percent of $100 million) which in turn induces new consumption spending of $50 million. This $50 million in new consumption generates $27.5 million in new disposable incomes, and this causes another $25 million increase in consumption. And so on until aggregate demand has increased by $200 million ($100 million from the initial expenditure plus $100 million in additional consumption expenditures resulting from the increases in income at each step).*

A $100 million tax reduction works in the same direction but with a slightly smaller impact. If individual income taxes are reduced by $100 million, disposable household incomes will increase by this same amount, and according to our assumed marginal propensity to consume, consumption demand will rise by $90 million. It is this $90 million initial increase in expenditure which is multiplied two-fold as it generates higher incomes and is respent as above. Therefore the total increase in aggregate demand is $180 million, which is more than the initial tax reduction but less than the increase in demand resulting from an expenditure of the same magnitude.

This certainly makes the formation of macroeconomic policy look easy. Once the taxation and respending rates are known, and once policy makers have determined the size of the discrepancy between aggregate demand and the full-employment level of output, it is a simple matter to compute the magnitudes by which taxes and government expenditures should be changed to balance demand with full-capacity output. Unfortunately, technical and political complications make fiscal stabilization policy considerably more difficult to implement.

3. What Made the Great Depression So Great?

The ideas presented above were around in some form or another prior to the onset of the Great Depression. In 1936 an elegant theoretical statement of these ideas was presented in *The General Theory of Employment, Interest and Money* by John Maynard Keynes. Yet in spite of the availability of a well-defined policy prescription for the ills of a seriously slumping economy, full recovery from the depression was not realized until the beginning of World War II. The total level of production in 1939 was just slightly higher than in 1929, the year prior to the Great Depression. Unemployment still averaged 17 percent over the year.

It is only fair to point out that the federal government, because of its relative size, was severely limited in its ability to affect the level of aggregate demand. At the onset of the depression in 1929 federal expenditures amounted to only 2.5 percent of gross national product and tax receipts accounted for 3.7 percent of gross incomes. In addition, the executive branch could not count on the Federal Reserve Bank to finance any part of a deficit, so that all borrowing had to be from the public. While budget balancing was not dogma to President Hoover and his advisors, there was some concern that government borrowing would spoil the market in investment funds for private businesses. In late 1931

---

*Notice that, as before, there will be a sustained increase in aggregate demand equal to $200 million only if there is a continuous injection of $100 million expenditures on the part of the government.

and early 1932 many banks failed, and money flowed out of the banking system. To prevent a worsening of the market for investment funds and further deterioration of business conditions, the Hoover administration acted in a manner exactly opposite to that recommended by our analysis of fiscal policy. Taxes were increased severely! In June, 1932 a tax bill was enacted that was to raise taxes by $900 million, a figure equal to one-third of the existing level of taxes. The corporate tax rate was increased, the personal exemption was lowered from $1500 to $1000, and the tax rate on the highest income groups was lifted from 25 percent to 65 percent in one shot. A massive tax increase was certainly not the Keynesian prescription for an economy with nearly one-fourth of its labor force out of work.

Nor can the Roosevelt administration be credited with implementing sound macroeconomic policy. President Roosevelt himself maintained very traditional attitudes toward budgetary policies, as suggested by this statement before Congress in March, 1933.

"Too often in recent history liberal governments have been wrecked on the rocks of loose fiscal policy.

"With the utmost seriousness I point out to the Congress the profound effect of this fact upon our national policy. It has contributed to the recent collapse of our banking structure. It has accentuated the stagnation of the economic life of our people."[1]

Roosevelt did not believe that fiscal policy was useful in stimulating aggregate demand, but he did believe in increased expenditures, particularly relief and public-works programs, for the sake of these programs themselves. He did not see that these expenditures could lead to a multiple expansion of demand through consumer respending. He viewed the depression as a structural problem, one of excessive competition and the inability of firms to plan and coordinate their activities. Thus the main thrust of his antidepression policies was to encourage cooperation among firms and prevent wages from falling to maintain purchasing power.

Some believe that Roosevelt's hands were tied by the attitude of the business community. Roosevelt consistently ran on a promise to balance the budget, and this could have been, at least partially, a concession to orthodox business sentiments. However, business opposition to budget deficits has never been strong. This opposition to Roosevelt's budgetary policies was more a function of the way in which the deficits occurred (increased spending) and the usual aftermath of budgetary deficits (increased taxation, particularly on businesses and the rich). The Revenue Act of 1935—the fifth tax increase in as many years—raised the tax rate on the highest income group to 75 percent and increased taxes on corporations. In the following year a tax on retained corporate earnings, which are used by the firms for reinvestment, was enacted. In light of such actions it is by no means surprising that the business community's confidence in the New Deal was low or that business investment activity was correspondingly low. By 1937 when real output had regained the levels that prevailed in 1929, private investment demand remained one-third below its 1929 level.

Fiscal policy during the Great Depression was unmistakably ill-conceived. There can be little doubt that the actions of both the Hoover and Roosevelt administrations aggravated the slump and frustrated the natural forces of recovery. We can look back on this unfortunate episode with our present understanding of macroeconomics, point to mistakes, and hope that present and future leaders will not repeat them. Unfortunately, however, this is only half of the picture. In the next chapter we will discuss the Great Depression from the point of view of monetary policy. There we will see that considerable evidence indicates that the errors in fiscal policy were minor in their impact when compared with the devastation of the economy caused by the policies of the monetary authorities.

4. The Keynesian Ascendancy

Between 1938 and 1962 the ideas of Keynes lay dormant as far as their influence on economic policy was concerned. World War II forced levels of expenditure that easily solved the problem of unemployment, and this was followed by periods of prosperity marred by a number of minor recessions. A major opportunity for the implementation of stimulative fiscal policy did arise during the recession of 1957–58, but the Eisenhower administration, anticipating that recovery would come about automatically, chose not to act. By 1960, an election year, the recovery had aborted with unemployment hovering around 5½ percent. Vice-President Nixon, the Republican candidate for the presidency, urged Eisenhower to unleash the stimulative powers of the federal budget. But Eisenhower had his mind set on leaving office with a balanced budget, his offering to the generations to come. With Eisenhower's failure to take countercyclical action, unemployment rolls were growing as election day approached. As Nixon later put it, "All the speeches, television broadcasts, and precinct work in the world could not counteract that one hard fact."[2] Nixon lost the election by a mere one vote per precinct.

Kennedy took office vowing to get the country moving again. In the economic sphere that was certainly a reasonable goal. Unemployment was rising toward 7 percent. It had not been close to the 4 percent level (often used as a benchmark of full employment) for three and a half years. The recession of 1960–61 was superimposed on a stagnate economy which had never fully recovered from the previous business slump. According to the economic advisors of President Kennedy, who were well steeped in Keynesian theory, the responsibility for the sluggish economy lay with the budgetary policies of the federal government. The early sixties provided Keynesian economists with the opportunity to bring their ideas into battle against the real-world problems of unemployment and economic stagnation. A key to winning this battle was the education of politicians—both the President and the Congress—and the public in the ways of Keynesian economics.

Kennedy's council of economists skillfully employed a trio of concepts to fight against the old superstitions of balanced budgets and passive fiscal policy. The Keynesian prescription called for either a tax reduction or an increase in government expenditures, in spite of the fact that the budget was already in the red. The Council of Economic Advisors pointed out that were the economy to operate at close to full employment the budget would realize a substantial surplus. An actual budgetary deficit prevailed only because the economy was operating below capacity. National income and hence the level of tax revenues were lower than they would be if full employment could be restored. The *full-employment budget*, which described the budgetary position of the federal government if full employment were realized, was thus advanced as evidence that fiscal policy should be more stimulative. If the economy were to move toward full employment in 1962, the Council estimated that a budgetary surplus of $11 billion would be generated. Such a surplus was likely to offset and frustrate any move that the economy made toward full-capacity output.

Furthermore, the Council reasoned that a growing economy tends to generate increasing tax revenues and that this automatic growth in the level of taxes exerts a drag upon aggregate demand. Every year the level of full-capacity output grows by about 3 percent—1 percentage point from natural growth in the labor force and 2 percentage points from increasing productivity. So in order to maintain full employment over time, output and incomes must grow by 3 percent each year as well. Now such a yearly growth in income will generate an increase in tax revenues of at least 3 percent per year, given the progressive nature of personal income taxes, and so with no change in the tax laws there will be an increasing tendency towards a budgetary surplus. Thus there is a natural long-run tendency towards *fiscal drag*, which could be eliminated by periodic reductions in tax rates, steady increases in government expenditures, or both. Not only would this be reasonable fiscal policy but also it goes hand in hand with meeting social goals people have set for the federal government, while reducing the tax burden. The tendency towards fiscal drag gives rise to the opportunity to declare periodic *fiscal dividends*, in the form of tax cuts or expenditure increases.

To cap their arguments and add some precision to their recommendations, Kennedy's advisors advanced the concept of the GNP gap—a measure of the discrepancy between the actual level of output and the level of output the economy was capable of producing. The difference between actual and potential GNP has often been quite dramatic, and it very effectively quantifies the waste that results from production at less than full employment. For 1961 the Council estimated that the gap amounted to $50 billion or 10 percent of existing gross national product. The science of gapology also indicates the appropriate size of a given fiscal-policy action. From the above estimate of the GNP gap in 1961 and the Council's best estimate of the multiplier on government expenditures at 2.0, a $25 billion expenditure increase would have been needed to bring the economy back to full employment.

While the Congress and the President were being educated in the doctrines of gapology and related matters, the economy was replaying the stagnation game. The recovery from the recession of 1960–61, like the recovery before it, was pooping out with unemployment still hovering around the 5½ percent mark. In June of 1963 Kennedy requested a $10 billion tax cut to eliminate the gap between potential and actual output, to increase economic growth, and to restore full employment. By the end of February, 1964, following repeated squabbles over the distribution of the tax reduction benefits among the population, this first active use of Keynesian principles became a reality.

The economy responded exactly as the Keynesian model predicted. Consumption expenditures soared as the reduced tax bill became translated into higher disposable income. In late 1964 the unemployment rate dropped below 5 percent for a considerable period for the first time in seven years. The gap between potential and actual output was more than halved from its 1962 level. Between 1964 and 1966 nominal GNP grew 17½ percent and real GNP over 12 percent, and by April of 1966 this growth in production had succeeded in reducing the unemployment rate below the 4 percent mark. Keynesian economics had successfully made the leap from academia to the real world of political economics.

5. The Government Giveth and the Government Taketh Away

Just as the orgy of self-congratulation began to break out among the Keynesians, a new problem began to rear its ugly head. Inflation, long suppressed behind a sluggish, stagnate economy, heard its cue with the call for increased military expenditures to finance the war in Vietnam. Coming on top of an economy which was by this time buoyant with consumption expenditures and government outlays for social programs of the Great Society, this increased expenditure severely taxed the economy's capacity to produce. The price level began to rise at rates mild by present standards, but appalling by the record of the early sixties. In the eight years since 1958 the consumer price index had not risen by as much as two percent in any year, but in 1966 consumer prices rose by 3.4 percent over the previous year. Finally by June 1968 with consumer prices increasing at the rate of approximately 4 percent per year, a 10 percent income surtax was levied on personal and corporate incomes. While this was in accordance with the Keynesian prescription, it came some thirty to thirty-six months after the Council's diagnosis of the problem. Convincing the President and the Congress to act on a forecast of inflationary pressures (in 1966) and in a manner potentially unpopular with the voters (increasing taxes) turned out to be considerably more difficult than persuading them to use stimulative fiscal policies.

Unfortunately the story does not end here. With the enactment of the tax surcharge in 1968, there was considerable concern in some circles that fiscal restraint had been overdone. There were some indications that the economy was already beginning to cool down, and a tax increase at that time might amount to fiscal overkill. Taking to heart these projections, the monetary authorities overreacted to the threat with the largest monetary expansion since the end of World War II. This expansion swamped the contractive effects of fiscal policy, and the consumer price index soared by over 6 percentage points between 1968 and 1969.

At this time another movement began to rise in prominence with the inflation of consumer prices. While Keynesian economics and the use of fiscal policy had been capturing the minds of observers of political economics, a small group of economists had been quietly accumulating massive evidence on the importance of monetary policies. The events of 1969 provided a public forum for their ideas, for their predictions that monetary expansion would swamp the effects of contractive fiscal policy were correct. No longer would monetary policy be relegated to a behind-the-scenes role. On top of this the potency of fiscal policy—in fact the underpinnings of fiscal policy in the multiplier analysis—were called increasingly into question.

6. Was Keynes a Keynesian?

One of the earliest critiques of simple multiplier analysis was provided by Keynes himself, such as in the following analysis of the multiplier stated in terms of employment rather than output.

"If, for example, a government employs 100,000 additional men on public works, and if the multiplier (as defined above) is 4, it is not safe to assume that aggregate employment will increase by 400,000 . . . . The method of financing the policy and the increased working cash, required by the increased employment and the associated rise of prices, may have the effect of increasing the rate of interest and so retarding investment in other directions, unless the monetary authorities take steps to the contrary."[3]

The several qualifications to the multiplier analysis offered by Keynes were disregarded by some of his followers and seriously downplayed by others, at least until some of their predictions went awry.

There are several reasons—some known to Keynes, some advanced since his time—why the simple multiplier analysis presented earlier may not be valid, and other reasons for believing that discretionary fiscal policy may not be all that it is cracked up to be. First of all there is the obvious problem of timing. The tax cut of 1964 came one and a half years after President Kennedy first recommended it to the Congress. The tax surcharge in the late sixties was enacted about two and one half years after such action was recommended to President Johnson by his economic advisors. These delays are problems inherent in our political system. Added to this are lags in policy action stemming from technical considerations: coming economic events must be reliably forecasted and with sufficient time to allow an appropriate response; decisions must be made on the method and degree of fiscal response. Whatever action is taken, its effects are realized only in the future because of delays in the response of the economic system to the initial stimulus.

This does not cast doubt on the theoretical basis of fiscal policy; it merely suggests that the timing of fiscal actions may not accord with the needs of countercyclical policy. Other criticisms of fiscal policy are more fundamental.

The previously quoted passage from Keynes might be the first statement of the phenomenon now known as *crowding-out*. In financing a deficit by public borrowing the government must compete with private corporations for scarce investment funds. A large deficit will absorb a significant fraction of the funds otherwise available for private investment. With a reduction in the funds available for private investment and a corresponding increase in the cost of these funds, private investment will be discouraged or "crowded-out." Unless additional funds are made available by wealth holders, banks, or the monetary authorities, private investment may be reduced sufficiently to offset entirely the expansionary effects of the budgetary deficit.

The use of tax policy to alter aggregate demand may also be ineffective if consumers are influenced by long-run expectations rather than current disposable income. In this case a temporary tax increase or reduction will have very little impact on consumption behavior. Tax changes may have a substantial effect on current disposable incomes, but consumers will not react strongly to these changes if they anticipate little alteration in their long-run income levels. Frequent changes in tax laws will have little impact on consumption demand under these circumstances, and the effective multiplier with respect to tax changes will be considerably smaller than the value indicated by crude re-spending rates.

In light of these comments it is not surprising that we can cite a number of episodes in which fiscal policy exhibited little effect on economic conditions. The events of 1968–69 we have already discussed. Also the inflation of the Korean War was accompanied by a rising budgetary surplus. When the surplus was reversed in 1952 and 1953 inflation subsided. Similarly, a tax cut in 1948 was followed by recession in the following year. Certainly this evidence cannot be taken as a systematic critique of the efficiency of fiscal policy, but it does indicate that other forces, often more powerful than the budgetary actions of the federal government, are at work.

DISCUSSION QUESTIONS

1. A reduction in tax rates will stimulate the economy in two ways. Identify these two effects and explain how they lead to an increase in GNP.

2. If taxes are increased by $1 billion at the same time that government expenditures increase by $1 billion, will GNP increase, decrease, or remain unchanged? Think carefully about the flow of incomes and expenditures before answering.

3. Use the theory behind fiscal policy to explain why the economy is always expansionary during wars. Is it necessary that a wartime economy always be expansionary? Is a war necessary to have an expanding economy?

4. During the inflation of 1974 many families experienced substantial increases in their money wages, but because of rising prices they were no better off in terms of real purchasing power. However, their rise in money wages pushed these families into higher tax brackets and increased their tax payments. How did this change the full-employment budget? What does this indicate about the full-employment-budget concept as a measure of discretionary fiscal policy?

5. In 1974 the federal government component of aggregate demand was $116.4 billion. Total expenditures of the federal government that year amounted to $298.6 billion. What accounts for this difference? Does the extra $182.2 billion not considered a part of the government component of aggregate demand have no effect on total demand? Explain.

6. Is a large deficit necessarily inflationary? In answering this consider (a) the cause of the deficit, (b) the possible existence of idle resources, and)c) the method of financing.

chapter **5**

Money Makes the
World Go 'Round

Money oils the wheels of business; and in that sense it makes the world go around. Because it is essential in a market economy, the volume of money in circulation has an important influence on economic affairs. Before considering it further, however, we must determine what exactly is money?

1. What Is Money?

Money has certain characteristics. It must, first of all, serve as a means for making payments, or in the economist's jargon, it must be a *medium of exchange*. The essential ingredient which gives any object this attribute is the user's belief that it can be exchanged. You accept payment for your work in the form of funny green pieces of paper because you know that everyone else in the country will accept them from you in exchange for goods and services. There is no intrinsic value in those dollar bills, but they are acceptable payment because everyone believes they are acceptable. Here tradition is a wonderful thing, as we can best appreciate by examining incidents in other countries where currency lost its medium-of-exchange quality (see chapter 7).

Money also has the attribute of being a vehicle for storing purchasing power over time. This is undoubtedly one reason it is acceptable as a means of payment, for people would be reluctant to accept money that wouldn't be worth as much when they tried to spend it. In fact in those incidents in which a currency lost its ability to serve as money, the reason was its inability to store purchasing power.

To be concrete we might ask what objects in our society possess these basic characteristics. Currency and coin certainly do. Also checking deposits satisfy the basic requirements, at least if you have a valid I.D. Actually checks are employed in financing a much greater number of transactions than is currency, so the membership of checking accounts in the money club cannot be denied. Beyond this, however, the definition gets a little fuzzy. Savings deposits in commercial banks are, strictly speaking, not available as a medium of exchange. However, the ease with which savings deposits can be changed into checking deposits or currency has convinced some that savings deposits should fall into the money category also. But what about accounts at savings and loan associations and marketable assets that are also readily convertible to cash?

Apparently a number of assets possess some of the attributes of money without strictly serving as means for making payment. It would be difficult finding someone who recently used a U.S. Treasury Bill° to buy something, but Treasury Bills do serve as a store of value over time and they are easily convertible into money. Assets which can be converted into money at very little cost are referred to as *liquid* assets. Conceivably the ownership of liquid assets can affect an individual's or firm's behavior in the same way that money would. If you have $200 in your savings account and you want to buy a ten-speed bike, the fact that your wealth is not in a form that you can use in direct payment will make little difference to you when deciding whether or not to make the purchase, for you know that the savings can be easily converted into cash or a checking account. On the other hand, if your $200 is in the form of land, a car, life insurance, or corporate stock that is expected to increase in value in the near future, the temptation to convert to cash may be thwarted by the costs you are likely to incur in selling one of these *non-liquid* assets.

The problem at this point is one of definition, but later on it will have practical policy implications. We must decide on an appropriate definition of money. This may exclude certain assets which are very similar to and very good substitutes for, some of the assets included in the definition. For the time being let us, in agreement with the government, the financial press, and the economics profession, define money to include only those assets which are, strictly speaking, usable as a medium of exchange: currency in circulation and privately held checking deposits.

According to this definition the supply of money in the United States at the end of 1974 was $283.8 billion. In order to finance the sale of the $1397 billion worth of goods and services produced and sold in that year, the money supply needed to turn over approximately five times. The rate at which money turns over (the monetary value of total output divided by the money supply) is sometimes referred to as the *velocity* of money. The bulk of this money supply consists of checking deposits; only about one-fifth of it is currency. If we included savings deposits at commercial banks in our definition, the figure for

---

°Treasury Bills are certificates of indebtedness of the U.S. government (bonds) with extremely short maturities.

the money stock at the end of 1974 would increase to 613.9 billion dollars. Adding deposits at savings and loan associations and similar institutions makes the figure $955 billion.

2. Monetary Instability of Earlier Years

Today's banking system grew out of the monetary disasters of the past. Prior to the establishment of the Federal Reserve system in 1914 the volume of money in private circulation was determined by a combination of chance and emotion. Some would claim that things are little different today, but that's a story for later on.

One factor that has made banking particularly profitable is that people are willing to leave their money with the bank in return for the privilege of writing checks on their accounts. Since only a fraction of the deposits outstanding are likely to be withdrawn in any given period of time, the bank uses a substantial part of the money deposited. The bank loans money to firms or individuals in the expectation that depositors collectively will not demand their money back before the loans are repaid or new deposits flow in from other sources. To insure that banks can meet normal demands for deposit redemptions, legal limits have been placed on the degree to which a bank may extend itself in this way. Banks are legally required to hold *reserves*, assets (such as cash in the vault) that may be used to cover withdrawals. A certain amount in reserves has to be held for every dollar of deposit claims against the bank. These conventions are the basis of modern commercial banking operations today, much as they were during the nineteenth century.

Prior to the Civil War, however, uniform national banking standards or practices did not exist. With the exeception of two short-lived nationally chartered banks, all banks in the United States had state charters and were subject only to state regulation. Some states imposed reserve requirements at a variety of levels and other states had none. In many cases the only effective limitation on the lending activities of a bank was the practical necessity of holding some reserves to meet anticipated withdrawals. When banks underestimated this demand, bank crises and financial panic resulted.

Usually a banking crisis started with the failure on the part of a bank or group of banks to satisfy their depositors' demand for withdrawals. These banks would then be forced to close their doors, and they would be declared insolvent, that is, unable to meet their obligations. In many instances the insolvent banks would be in debt to other larger banks, and the initial bank failure would threaten the financial position of the creditor banks. The financial deterioration of the larger bank would be aggravated by the deposit withdrawals of its customers, who may have gotten wind of the bank's insecure position. Runs on larger, more prominent banks would thus occur, and those banks would also be forced into insolvency. With considerable interdependence among banks in the system and with a large number of banks overextended in their lending activities, the collapse of a single bank could have widespread repercussions on the banking system as a whole. The only protection a bank could have against insolvency was the maintenance of adequate reserves.

Reserves at this time consisted of bank holdings of gold and U.S. Treasury notes, the latter being paper currency issued by the federal government to finance budgetary deficits. These assets were universally accepted means of making payments and thus provided a basis for the entire monetary system. Those assets which serve as bank reserves and currency in private circulation constitute a *monetary base*, which supports the whole system of bank notes and deposits. Banks would issue their own bank notes guaranteed exchangeable for gold or Treasury notes, and the bank notes would also serve as media of exchange with a range of circulation depending upon the issuing bank's reputation. Originally banks issued notes only if they were backed by holdings of gold or Treasury notes of equal value. With 100 percent backing there was never any danger of not being able to redeem any quantity of bank notes, outstanding. However, banks soon began to recognize that the rate at which bank notes were redeemed was sufficiently slow that this 100 percent backing was unnecessary. Banks could, and of course did, issue bank notes well in excess of their holdings of reserve assets, and thus the supply of money in circulation was some multiple of the size of the monetary base. However, a combination of legal and societal demand that banks hold some reserves in the form of gold and Treasury notes imposed a limitation on the entire supply of money outstanding at any time.

This limitation could be exceeded through the use of various unorthodox banking practices. One favorite scheme involved pooling the reserve assets of several banks and carrying these combined assets from bank to bank just ahead of the arrival of the banking inspector. Another practice was to locate the main office of a bank somewhere as far as possible from centers of commerce. Loan offices, where the bank notes would be issued, were conveniently located in the center of town. But holders of the notes would discover that the notes were redeemable only at the main office. This would permit the bank to create a tremendous volume of bank notes without fear of redemption. Unfortunately such practices could lead to an overextension of the banking system, resulting in an inability to meet withdrawals, and a subsequent banking crisis as described above.

A number of such crises did occur before the establishment of the Federal Reserve system. One of the most serious occurred after the demise of the Second Bank of the United States, the second federally chartered bank in our history. By its size and prestige the Second Bank had been able to influence other banks toward more conservative banking policies. Its twenty-five branches throughout the country followed a policy of presenting the bank notes of other commercial banks for redemption promptly, thus, severely restraining the banking system's tendency toward excessive bank note creation. Political pressure by advocates of easy money and opponents of a strong federal government caused termination of the Bank's charter in 1836, and loose banking practices again became the order of the day. Banking abuses were followed by a rash of bank failures in 1837 and one of the most severe economic contractions on record. One-quarter of the banks went out of business, and the stock of money fell by one-third. Episodes of widespread bank failure and financial panic were repeated in 1890 and 1907.

Each of these incidents was partly the result of banking practices, but a driving force behind nearly every severe contraction of the monetary system was international gold flow. Since the monetary base consisted largely of gold, gold flows in and out of the country would cause expansions and contractions of the monetary base. Legal and pragmatic considerations restricted the volume of bank notes that could be issued against a given money base. Consequently a contraction in United States gold holdings would force a contraction of the domestic money supply, and vice versa.

Unfortunately gold discoveries and international gold flows could not be counted on to accommodate the needs of the economy for exchange media. In fact throughout the pre-Federal Reserve period there were several prolonged monetary contractions that can be traced to the failure of gold discoveries to keep pace with the growth in real production. From 1869 to 1879 the money stock declined at an average rate of 2.7 percent per year while production rose at the rate of somewhere between 4.3 and 6.8 percent per year. With less money available for the purchase of a greater volume of goods and services, prices had to fall; there was a halving of the price level during the fourteen-year period prior to 1879. While this was a period of prosperity in terms of output growth, the strong downward trend in prices took its toll in terms of financial uncertainty, inequitable impact upon the debtor classes, and banking failures resulting from the inability of debtors to pay off their debts. This period also gave rise to the various forms of the easy-money movement, culminating in the nomination of William Jennings Bryan as the Democratic candidate for president on a platform of bimetalism—the use of both gold and silver as the basis for the money supply. By including both precious metals in the monetary base, the size of the base and hence the total supply of money would have been increased.

Partly in response to the uncertainties associated with the bimetalism movement, gold flowed out of the country in the early 1890s, causing a severe contraction of the money supply and a sharp contraction in real output between 1892 and 1896. Ironically, after 1896 (the year in which Bryan was defeated by McKinley), the goals of the easy-money forces were realized as the result of substantial gold discoveries in South Africa, Alaska, and Colorado and the development of the cyanide process, which permitted the recovery of some low-grade ores. These events led to a sharp expansion in the world's gold supply, no small part of which flowed into the United States. The long period of price stagnation was reversed, and prices rose by 50 percent from 1896 to 1913.

The final contraction in the pre-Federal Reserve period came in 1907, again the result of gold flowing out of the country. There was a serious financial panic in October and an 11 percent reduction in output between 1907 and 1908. This incident provided the final impetus for reform of banking and the establishment of the Federal Reserve system. Recurring crises and dependence on the vagaries of gold discoveries could no longer be tolerated. The Federal Reserve system was established to end our dependence on unpredictable, uncontrollable phenomena.

3. The Money Tree

Put yourself in the shoes of your friendly neighborhood banker. You are interested in extending loans and attracting deposits to make the greatest possible profit from your business.

The first decision to be made is whether or not to join the Federal Reserve system. Joining will force you to adhere to the rules set down by the heads of the Federal Reserve system, often nicknamed the Fed. These rules include, in particular, the amount of reserves you must hold as backing for your outstanding deposits. In spite of this constraint, banks accounting for about 80 percent of checking deposits in the country have joined the system because of the benefits they receive in the form of borrowing privileges and check-clearing facilities. Let's suppose you succumb to convention and join the club.

The first thing that will be impressed upon you as a member of the Federal Reserve system is that your bank is required to hold a certain quantity of bank reserves, depending upon the amount of deposits your bank has outstanding. Reserves are, from your point of view, a complete nuisance, for you are legally allowed to count only cash in the vault and deposits your bank has made with the Fed—both sterile or nonearning assets. Your reserve requirement is a percentage of the deposits outstanding against your bank, with the percentage ranging from 8 to 18 depending upon how large your bank is. Let's suppose the average reserve requirement is 15 percent and that your bank is typical in this regard. Now when someone deposits money in your bank, you can loan 85 percent of this money, thereby earning interest on it, while still meeting the regulations of the Fed.

There are a number of alternative assets that your bank may hold. Banks hold cash in the vault and deposits with the Fed as reserves, as was just mentioned. You will be interested in minimizing these holdings for they earn no income. Then your bank can put most of its money into loans to businesses or to households, say, for real estate purchases or consumption expenditures. It may also acquire bonds from the government, that is, make loans to the Treasury; these assets have the distinct advantage of being quickly redeemable for cash because of the active market in government securities, as well as providing a nice interest income. If yours is a typical bank, these various assets will compose the bulk of your holdings.

Changes in the composition of a bank's assets can alter tremendously the loan and deposit operations of the bank. Suppose, for example, that some wealthy individual deposits $100,000 in the Octopus Banking Trust. The Octopus Bank has additional deposits of $100,000, but it also has an extra $100,000 in vault cash, only $15,000 (.15 × 100,000) of which must be held as reserves to back the new deposit. The remaining $85,000 can be loaned out. Suppose the Octopus Banking Trust lends all $85,000 to Gerald's Meat Market for the purchase of a new store. Gerald gives the money to Randall's Construction Company, which then deposits the money in its bank, the Capitalist's National. This bank now has $85,000 in new deposits, only $12,750 (.15 × 85,000) of which must be held as reserves on the new deposit. This leaves $72,250 that can be loaned to Ann Johnston who wants to buy a new home. This $72,250 also finds its way back into the banking system, and the bank receiving this deposit can lend 85 percent of it, or $61,412.50, and still meet its reserve requirement. And so on, until ultimately a total of $666 thousand in new deposits is generated from the initial injection of $100 thousand in new deposits into the banking system. The banking system manages to create $666 thousand in money (checking deposits), given only $100 thousand to begin with.

The maker of this feat is the fractional reserve requirement. If banks were required to hold reserves equal to 100 percent of their outstanding deposits, there would be no capacity for deposit-and-loan expansion beyond the first deposit made. But since each bank is required to hold only fractional reserves, each is free to create additional loans and deposits up to the limit imposed by the reserve requirement. Furthermore the lower the reserve requirement, the greater the deposit-creation capacity. In the previous example if the reserve requirement had been only 10 percent, each bank would have been able to loan out 90 percent of the new money deposited. This would obviously lead to a greater total expansion of deposits and loans than before.

Because checking deposits are the major component of the money supply, the fractional reserve system gives the Fed control over the supply of money. The Fed first determines the legal minimum reserve requirements and thus limits the potential expansion of deposits that can take place from a given increase in bank reserves. Adjustment of this requirement can change the total supply of money without any change in bank reserves. Reducing the reserve requirement, for example, frees reserves formerly held to meet the legal stipulation. These reserves are loaned out, and new deposits will be created correspondingly up to the new limits of monetary expansion.

More commonly the Fed changes the level of reserves through the sale and purchase of government securities on the open market. This is referred to as an *open-market operation*. If the Fed purchases bonds directly from commercial banks, the banks' reserves are augmented by the amount of the purchase. The banks give up some of their bond holdings, which are not counted as reserves, in exchange for cash or an increase in their deposits with the Fed, which do count. Conversely the sale of government securities to commercial banks will reduce bank reserves. Given either of these changes in reserve levels, a multiple expansion or contraction in bank deposits will occur along the lines previously illustrated.

Finally the Fed may exercise some control over the level of reserves by offering to lend to commercial banks on more or less favorable terms. If the Fed will lend on easy terms, banks will reduce their reserves to a bare minimum because unanticipated deposit withdrawals can be offset cheaply by borrowing. If banks expect such borrowing to be costly, they will be a bit more cautious and hold reserves in excess of the legal minimum. The terms on which the Fed will lend to member banks is indicated by the *discount rate.*°

Using any or all of these tools, the monetary authorities can influence the supply of money in private circulation. We use the term *influence* rather than *control*, because independent actions on the part of the banks or the public can frustrate the intentions of the Fed. For example, if the Fed attempts to expand the money supply by increasing the level of bank reserves, banks may choose to hold on to the extra reserves rather than increasing their volume of loans and deposits. Also private individuals may increase their holdings of currency, thereby cutting down deposits in the banking system and offsetting the reserve increase initiated by the Fed. The extent of the Fed's control over the money supply is a subject of considerable controversy among students of monetary and financial institutions.

4. Money and Income

This whole discussion would be academic except that the supply of money can greatly influence the level of economic activity and prices. Exactly how money influences the economy is somewhat uncertain and thus a matter for useful research. Considerable evidence indicates that the money supply does influence business activity and the price level, but how? There are several views.

According to the Keynesian framework the link between changes in the money supply and in business activity is the rate of interest and its effect on firms' investment behavior. By supplying the banking system with abundant reserves, the Fed encourages banks to lend out their reserves. As we have seen, this initial injection of reserves into the banking system leads to a multiple expansion of checking deposits or money in circulation. Corporations and individuals find themselves with more money than necessary to make their day-to-day transactions. They will put some of this extra money into stocks, bonds, or some other interest-bearing assets by offering the funds to firms at favorable terms. A decrease in the cost of borrowing, increases the level of investment demand. (Conversely, an interest rate increase reduces investment

---

°Discount rate is just a fancy name for the particular rate of interest on loans from the Fed to commercial banks. The name has its origin in the process of "discounting paper." The "paper" refers to a loan certificate establishing the indebtedness of some firm or individual to the bank. This paper has a value, say, $1000, based on the amount which is owed to the bank. The Fed extends money to the bank in exchange for this loan certificate. However, the value of the paper is "discounted" to $950 (by 5 percent), for example, and only this amount of money is loaned to the bank. The entire $1000 must be paid back to the Fed, so this procedure establishes an implicit interest rate on the loan.

activity.) This increased investment activity, because of the investment multiplier, leads to a multiple expansion in output and income.

According to this view the effect of monetary actions by the Fed on the level of business activity depends on the responsiveness of investment demand to changes in the rate of interest. The initiating force is the change in the terms at which funds are lent. The impact on aggregate income depends on the responsiveness of investment demand to this change. Some early studies of investment behavior indicated that the cost of borrowing did not play much of a role in the firm's investment decision, and this led a number of Keynesian economists to conclude that monetary policy was relatively impotent in influencing aggregate demand. Some disagreement with the Keynesian position persisted, and alternative statements of the channels of monetary influences were advanced.

One such view is that the supply of money can affect expenditures directly without working through the interest-rate/investment mechanism. Households hold their wealth in a variety of assets, including money, bonds, stocks, and consumer durables—goods such as cars and houses, which provide a flow of services over a period of time rather than just at the moment of acquisition. When money holdings increase, households attempt to correct this imbalance by purchasing bonds, stocks, and, most importantly, consumer durables. Thus there is not only the indirect effect from the increased demand for financial securities as in the Keynesian view, but also a direct effect on expenditures through the purchase of consumer durables.

A further extension of this view holds that any increase in wealth will lead to a similar expansion of consumer-durable purchases. With an increase in the money supply, wealth holders increase their purchases of bonds and stocks. This increased demand for stocks and bonds will increase the prices of these assets, and every household with stocks or bonds will experience an increase in the face value of their financial wealth. This increase motivates them to spend more, particularly on durable goods, and once again there is a direct effect on expenditure levels that does not operate through the investment/interest-rate mechanism.

These alternatives imply a greater potency for monetary policy than is suggested by the Keynesian view. One of the important issues in macroeconomic policy today is the strength of monetary policy. These arguments advance the possibility that monetary actions have important effects on business activity, but evidence on this point will have to await the discussion of several historical episodes.

5. What Made the Great Depression So Great?—Revisited

We have already seen that monetary disturbances had repercussions on business activity in the pre-Federal Reserve period. The establishment of the Federal Reserve system was supposed to insulate the economy from monetary disruptions caused by either variations in the gold stock or banking crises. Unfortunately in one of its first important tests, the Great Depression, the Fed failed abysmally. The system, designed to protect us from banking crises, stood by while 20 percent of all commercial banks in the country folded in the midst of repeated financial panics. The system, empowered to generate a monetary expansion in line with the needs of business activity, permitted the domestic money supply to contract by one-third. The economy of the thirties had to buck not only the blunders of fiscal policy,° but also the ineptness of monetary policy.

The preceding decade, the Roaring Twenties, had been the Fed's finest hour. Following a sharp contraction of business activity in the first years of the decade, a period of moderately stable expansion set in. The money stock grew fairly steadily from 1923 to 1928, a period which provided the Fed with ample opportunity to demonstrate its effectiveness in counteracting gold flows and in fighting minor recessions with appropriately expansive policies. Real national income also grew steadily, and, contrary to the common image of this period, there was no price inflation (wholesale prices declined by one percent per year from 1923 to 1929). The only bothersome economic happening of the late twenties was the stock market boom. To curb what they considered to be an unhealthy stock market speculation, the monetary authorities restricted the growth of the money supply. For sixteen months the money supply did not grow, and then in August 1929 as a result of this restraint, the growth in industrial production was arrested.

From August 1929 to March 1933—the bottom of the depression—real output fell by one-third. Real per capita income during this year was at the same level it had been during the depression year of 1908. More than two decades of economic growth were wiped out by this contraction! The financial collapse that accompanied the business contraction was by no means unavoidable. Following the stock market crash in October 1929, Federal Reserve policy started out on the right foot with an immediate injection of reserves into the banking system, and for the first year of the depression banking conditions remained stable and sound. In spite of the stock market crash and weakening business conditions, there was no sign of insecurity on the part of the banks nor distrust of the banking system on the part of the public. For the year from October 1929 to October 1930, people actually increased their deposits relative to currency, a move which, by itself, leads to an expansion in bank reserves and the money supply. At the same time banks were not increasing their reserves much above their legal requirements—evidence that there was no reluctance on the part of the banking system to extend loans. Had the Fed moved throughout this period to increase bank reserves through open-market purchases of government bonds, the contraction of the money supply and business activity might have been arrested by the end of 1930.

But this was not to be. During the first year of the depression the money

---

°Details in chapter four.

supply shrank as the result of a billion-dollar decline in Federal Reserve lending. This decline occurred in spite of a reduction of the discount rate from 6 to 2.5 percent, a policy which the Fed interpreted to be expansionary. However, with the slump in business activity and consequent reduction in loan demand, interest rates on bank loans plummeted even more sharply. There was little incentive for banks to borrow from the Fed when the interest they would have to pay exceeded the interest rate they could receive from their loans. Relative to other interest rates, the discount rate was actually too high, as shown by the sharp reduction in the volume of borrowing from the Fed.

October 1930 saw the onset of the first banking crisis, and this event altered the attitudes of the public and the banks themselves towards the banking system. It cannot be said that the Federal Reserve system caused this first banking crisis, but neither did the Fed undertake policies to prevent it. During the first nine months of 1930, bank reserves declined in spite of the Fed's power to prevent it. The deteriorating business and financial climate combined with the weakened reserve position of the commercial banks to cause the banking crisis of 1930.

The reaction to widespread bank failure was predictable. The public began to withdraw their money steadily from the banks, further lowering bank reserves. Meanwhile the banks, seeing their competitors fail, began to accumulate reserves in excess of the legal requirements. Without offsetting action from the Fed, the volume of deposits had to continue to fall. Other banking crises followed, culminating with the Banking Holiday of 1933—a countrywide closing of bank doors to stem the flood of withdrawals.

Meanwhile, except for a four-month period in 1932, the Fed stubbornly refused to add to bank reserves through open-market operations. Their reluctance was based, first of all, on a belief that Fed policy was already sufficiently expansionary, judging by the very low discount rate and yields on government bonds. But for banks suffering from realistic concerns about their ability to meet withdrawals, a low discount rate was not really much of an inducement for monetary expansion. The system needed additional reserves, not merely the opportunity to borrow temporarily at favorable rates. A major error of the Fed was to concentrate on the discount rate as the indicator of monetary policy to the exclusion of other policy measures, such as money-supply growth.

A second error was the belief that an expansion of bank reserves would simply lead to an increase in the bank reserves above the legal requirement, with little additional lending activity on the part of banks. While the accumulation of excess reserves in the period after the initial banking crises may have supported this position, it is difficult to see how this belief could have been supported prior to October 1930. In any case the fear was that the creation of excess reserves would weaken the Fed's control over monetary policy. Banks holding reserves in excess of the legal requirement would be in a position to expand deposits and lending activity at their own discretion, regardless of which direction the Fed might wish policy to move. Thus the control of monetary policy would be in the hands of the commercial banks rather than the Federal Reserve Bank. Given the way that the Fed used its control, perhaps that would have been a desirable state of affairs!

A third problem was the innate conservatism of the leaders of the Federal Reserve at this time. Their big fear was "easy money," and at times they even expressed concern over the dangers of inflation. The only period of aggressive security purchasing was between April and August of 1932, when a fear of "radical" action on the part of Congress induced them to act. Never very enthusiastic about this program from the outset, the Fed quickly terminated its purchasing program in August, when Congress adjourned. It is appalling to read, in the accounts of Federal Reserve Board meetings and in the testimony of economists, about their concern with inflation—at a time when the economy was moving towards a 25 percent unemployment rate and a 33 percent reduction in the price level.

By 1933 the economy had bottomed out. From then until 1937 the money supply grew at the rate of 11 percent per year and real output at an annual rate of 12 percent. The business expansion went hand in hand with rapid money-supply growth, which occurred despite a totally passive Federal Reserve policy. Gold flows into the United States, resulting from the political uncertainty in Europe connected with Hitler's rise to power in 1933, were largely responsible for the growth in the United States money supply. However, recovery was by no means complete; unemployment was still high (above 10 percent) and per capita income was still below its previous peak level.

Then, for the first time in four years, the Fed felt impelled to engage in an active monetary policy. By 1936 commercial banks had accumulated reserves far in excess of their legal requirements, a wise policy in view of the financial crises of the previous seven years. But the Fed saw this accumulation of excess reserves as a threat to their control over the banking system and enacted a series of reserve-requirement increases, which doubled the legal requirement in the 1936–37 period. These reserve-requirement increases eliminated $3 billion in excess reserves—an amount equal to one-fourth the existing monetary base. Contrary to the Fed's belief that this action would simply trim the volume of excess bank reserves with no repercussions on the supply of money, banks attempted to rebuild their reserve positions by calling in loans and reducing deposits. In the last half of 1936, following the first increase in reserve requirements, the rate of growth of the money supply slowed abruptly. Further increases in reserve requirements in early 1937 caused the stock of money to decline over the subsequent year—a phenomenon which is only associated with the most severe business contractions. This period was certainly no exception. The four-year business expansion terminated in mid-1937. The subsequent contraction was one of the sharpest on record, topped only by two other episodes in the post-Civil War period.

The connection between Federal Reserve policy actions, the abrupt halt in monetary expansion, and the subsequent business contraction is too close to be discarded as coincidental. Then the resumption of economic expansion in June 1938 followed closely on the heels of the reduction of reserve requirements. The subsequent return to rapid growth in the money supply reinforces the impression that monetary policies during this episode had substantial effects on business activity. The recovery from the depths of the depression had suffered a serious setback as the result of inept Federal Reserve policy; the return to full employment was consequently delayed until well after the start of World War II.

Hopefully we have increased our understanding of economics in general and monetary effects in particular to avoid the repetition of anything like the Great Depression. It is hard to imagine contemporary monetary authorities permitting the money supply to shrink by one-third or standing by while many commercial banks are forced into bankruptcy. Still, great myths persist about this episode of our history. In light of the previous discussion it is ironic that the Great Depression has been taken as evidence by some that the private economy is inherently unstable and by others that monetary phenomena have relatively minor influences on business activity.

6. Money Makes It Happen

Although a long-lasting decline in the money stock certainly goes against the historical trend, the decline in the money supply that accompanied the Great Depression was typical of severe economic contractions. For the period from the end of the Civil War to World War II, the supply of money tended to rise during both expansion and contraction phases of the business cycle. However, the most severe business contractions were accompanied by absolute reductions in the stock of money. The contractions of 1873–79, 1892–94, 1907–08, 1920–21, 1929–33, and 1937–38 were the only ones showing an actual decline in the money supply; furthermore these contractions were the most severe of any during this entire seventy-five-year period.[1] The correspondence between monetary disturbances and business contractions is too prominent to be dismissed.

The association between these variables does not necessarily mean that monetary disturbances *cause* business cycles. It is possible that business contractions lead to monetary contractions with no significant influence running the other direction. It is also possible that some third factor causes the decline in both money and income. However, in each of the above episodes, the monetary disturbance arose out of factors other than the business contraction. In the first three periods listed above, banking panics led to a restriction of the money supply. Generally these banking panics were caused by a drying-up of bank reserves as gold flowed out of the country. The monetary contraction of 1920–21 was due to an increase in the discount rate initiated by the Fed, and the monetary contraction of 1937 came about as the result of a doubling of reserve requirements by the monetary authorities. The episode of 1929–33 has already been discussed in considerable detail. In each case there can be little doubt that the business contraction aggravated the decline in the money stock, particularly by causing banking panics and failures. It is also apparent that the monetary contractions developed out of independent forces—generally Federal Reserve actions or gold flows—which preceded the business contraction. History thus supports the monetary interpretation of business-cycle activity.

Any alternative explanation would have to say (a) why the business contraction occurred when it did and (b) why each severe contraction was accompanied by a decline in the stock of money. To our knowledge no other explanation can do this consistently over the above seventy-five-year span of time.

The monetary view can also account for incidents of severe inflation. The inflation of 1896 to 1913 was the result of a surge in the world and United States money supplies following gold discoveries in Colorado, Alaska, and South Africa. Our most recent inflation can be traced to expansionary policies enacted by the Fed over the last several years. From early 1972 to mid-1974 the money stock grew at the rate of 8.5 percent per year, building up an excess of aggregate demand, which resulted in an inflation of 8.8 percent in 1973 and 12.2 percent for 1974.

7. Policy Predicaments

This record of monetary policy certainly leaves something to be desired. The blame for many episodes of depression and recession can be laid at the door of the monetary authorities. The inflations of recent years can also be attributed to monetary actions. Why do the monetary authorities persist in these calamities? A partial answer lies in the political forces (to be developed in the following chapter) that influence the course of monetary policy. Another part of the answer involves technical problems of policy implementation. Before we cast too many stones at the Federal Reserve Bank, we should imagine ourselves faced with the Fed's problems of monetary control.

The first problem is that we may be asking the Fed to achieve ends which are unattainable. Sometimes we ask that the Fed meet two incompatible goals at the same time. The insistence that the Fed attempt to lower the rate of inflation while simultaneously preventing a rise in unemployment leads to a lot of disappointment and very little effective policy with respect to either goal. Forcing the Fed to concern itself with keeping interest rates high so that money does not flow out of the country, while demanding that monetary expansion be geared towards the stimulation of business activity is also a schizophrenic position. More sophisticated critics may focus on single policy objectives, but they also may pose unattainable or unsustainable objectives. A favorite of modern-day populists in the Congress is low interest rates, a policy for winning favor with active borrowers among the ranks of small businesses and households.

Why can't the Fed simply increase the rate at which money is growing (by supplying lending institutions with excess funds that they will be eager to lend at low rates)? At first glance this seems like a feasible goal. But this ultimately leads to an increase in the aggregate demand for goods and services. The greater demand induces firms to increase their investment activities and acquire more funds for investment. This increase in the demand for funds bids up the rate of interest toward the higher level at which we started. But this is not the end. If the Fed compensates for this interest-rate rise by further increases in the growth of money, inflationary pressures will materialize as the growth in aggregate demand outstrips the growth in the economy's productive capacity. With inflation building, people and financial institutions lending money will begin to ask for an interest rate that includes an inflation premium—some bonus to compensate them for the deterioration in the value of their money between lending and repayment. Thus the intermediate and long-run effects of an expansionary monetary policy, initially designed to lower interest rates, are *increases* in the cost of borrowing. Monetary actions may temporarily reduce interest rates, but this is an accomplishment which cannot be sustained for very long.

Leaders in the Federal Reserve have tended to focus on the level of interest rates as an indication of whether monetary policy is tight or easy. This was one part of the problem during the Great Depression. However, as we have just demonstrated, a monetary expansion brings about an initial decline in interest rates followed by a rise, as the result of an increased demand for funds and inflationary tendencies. Likewise a contraction will cause rates to go up initially, only to be followed by a decline as reduced investment activity and diminishing inflationary pressures lower the cost of funds. The signal that we read from the interest rate indicator, therefore, depends upon the stage in the operation at which it is observed. High or rising interest rates are just as much associated with easy money as they are with contractive policies, depending upon when you look.

Take the first several years of the Great Depression. The discount rate, that rate of interest charged by the Fed for loans to commercial banks, fell from 6 percent at the time of the stock market crash to 1.5 percent by the middle of 1931. The Federal Reserve authorities took this as evidence that monetary policy was quite loose. In the meantime the stock of money in circulation shrank by 9 percent indicating that the Fed was not in fact acting aggressively enough to increase the volume of bank reserves.

The picture becomes even more complex when we recognize that there are a number of different interest rates, and that they need not always move in the same direction. During this same episode, while the discount rate was falling, interest rates on corporate bonds rose sharply. During this time of financial insecurity, individuals lending to corporations naturally demanded a risk premium in the form of higher interest. In the light of these circumstances, which interest rate should one have taken as the correct indicator of the direction of monetary policy?

In 1974, the slowing of growth in the money supply led to a rise in interest rates to record highs accompanied by screams of outrage against the Fed. Most interest rates reached their peaks in August 1974 and then declined—some precipitously. However, this drop cannot be interpreted as an easing of monetary restraint, for the supply of money actually grew at a lower rate in the second half of the year when interest rates were declining than previously. Instead, interest rates dropped because of the business contraction that developed with increasing severity during the second half of the year, and this in turn was the result of the same monetary restraint which pushed interest rates to their place in the Guinness Book of World Records. Were the monetary authorities to interpret the fall in interest rates as evidence of stimulative monetary policy—as did their counterparts in 1930 and 1931—and consequently hold back from reasonable monetary expansion in 1975, the likely result would be a persistence of the business slump and an increase in its severity.

During this same period a number of Senators have taken notice of the importance of the money supply in determining business activity. The head of the Federal Reserve system, Arthur Burns, has been called repeatedly before committees in Congress to defend the actions of the Fed, particularly with respect to the erratic growth in the money supply in recent years. The problem is, according to Burns, that the Fed simply does not have as great a control over the supply of money as others would like to believe. Some aspects of this have already been mentioned: private individuals can reduce bank reserves by withdrawing money, and banks can hold reserves in excess of the legal requirements, thereby reducing the volume of deposits outstanding. On the other hand, the Fed has the power to engage in an expansionary government securities purchase program that would more than offset the contractive actions of banks and the public. During the Great Depression, for example, recurrent financial crises caused people to hold unusually large amounts of currency while banks were also holding large reserves in excess of the legal requirement. Statistically speaking the decline in the supply of money during the first four years of the Depression can be traced to the increased demands for currency and reserves. However, it certainly was within the Fed's power to increase the supply of currency and bank reserves by more than enough to offset these forces and cause the money supply to grow.

A second problem is that not all banks are members of the Federal Reserve system, so the Fed's control of commercial banks is not complete. However, almost 80 percent of all deposits outstanding are in member banks. Also, it is reasonable to suppose that nonmember banks behave much like member banks. As long as nonmember bank behavior is related in some stable fashion to the creation of bank reserves, this lack of control is not likely to be serious.

8. Timing

The most serious problems of monetary policy probably are those having to do with timing. Policies enacted today will have most of their impact some time in the future. Time—perhaps considerable time—must elapse before businesses and individuals respond fully to monetary changes. Because of the lag between policy action and its impact on business activity, we must have accurate predictions of business activity over the immediate future. Unfortunately the track record of economists and government officials on this course has not been inspiring. The inflation of 1968 surprised the fiscalists,° who were fearful of recession; the severity of the inflation in 1974 was not anticipated by any school of economists. Many contradictory or inaccurate forecasts could be recounted to show the difficulty of this task. The unfortunate result of this state of the science—state of the art, you may prefer to call it—is that policy actions are delayed until the problem, inflation, recession, or whatever, is upon us.

Policy action initiated to alleviate a problem already at hand may not have its strongest impact until the problem is well on the way to a cure. In fact if the lag between policy actions and their impacts is extremely long, say one year or more, then policies intended to be countercyclical will actually aggravate the business cycle. Contractive policies enacted during an inflation could begin to have the most effect after inflationary pressures had cooled and the economy is moving sluggishly. Stimulative policies enacted in the midst of a recession may have their greatest impact after recovery is well on its way. Countercyclical policies can be mistimed and actually worsen the swings in business activity from boom to bust and back again.

Considerations of this kind have led a number of people—Senators as well as economists—to recommend that the Fed attempt to induce the money supply to grow at a fairly even rate over time. The historical evidence shows that a number of important economic disturbances can be traced to monetary actions that were inappropriate for the time. Adherence to a constant-rate-of-growth rule would have prevented the 30 percent reduction in the money supply during the Great Depression. Also, the erratic changes of policy during the late sixties and early seventies would have been avoided if the Fed permitted money to grow at some constant rate. However, policy makers are concerned with the immediate problem, and they continue to use interest rates as a measure of monetary-policy directions, which has caused some serious business cycle problems during the Federal Reserve's existence. It may be that once again we are asking too much from monetary policy.

9. The Fiscalist-Monetarist Debate

There can be little doubt that monetary policy is a potent force in the economy. The discussion in the previous chapter suggests that fiscal policy is an impor-

---

°Fiscalists are those who believe fiscal policy is a powerful force.

tant force as well. There is some question, however, about the potency of fiscal policy as an *independent** influence on business activity.

The theoretical considerations behind the fiscalist and monetarist positions are these. The monetarists believe that government expenditures, financed by public borrowing, divert funds from the private sector and discourage private investment demand sufficiently to offset the public expenditures. Thus fiscal policy is likely to have little impact. Fiscalists, on the other hand, contend that during a recessionary period there are idle money balances that can be used to finance increased government spending with no corresponding reduction in private investment demand. Furthermore the relative weakness with which investment demand responds to interest rate changes suggests that monetary policy is likely to have little impact. To this the monetarists counter that money supply changes can have direct and powerful impacts on household spending which supplement the effects on investment. Both positions are carefully reasoned, and individually each is logically consistent. Theoretical reasoning alone will do very little to settle the question, so we must turn to some historical evidence.

The bulk of evidence for the monetarist position has been cited earlier in this chapter. The history of severe contractions during the seventy-five-year period between the Civil War and World War II supports the monetarist position. At the same time we have encountered a number of incidents which are consistent and supportive of the fiscalist arguments: the use of inappropriate fiscal policies during the Great Depression; the tax cut of 1964; and the inflation resulting from the failure to implement a tax increase in 1966–67. Most episodes of fiscal expansion coincide with periods of monetary expansion, and vice versa. When both policies move in the same direction, it is difficult to determine which policy was the dominant force. There do exist, however, a number of episodes in which monetary and fiscal policies were working in opposite directions.

The fiscalist explanation of the economic boom of the early sixties lies in the expansionary fiscal policies enacted during that period, beginning in 1961 with a tax-incentive program to stimulate investment demand and culminating with the tax cut of 1964. These policies reversed the stagnation that had persisted as the result (in the fiscalist view) of fiscal drag and burdensome full-employment surpluses. But what was happening to monetary policy at this time? The fifties was a decade of monetary stability which turned into stagnation at the end of

---

*Budgetary decisions affect business activity through their impact on monetary changes. A large deficit will tempt an interest-rate-conscious Fed to expand the money supply. Large-scale Treasury borrowing tends to bid up the interest rate on funds for investment. To avoid this the Fed can help finance the deficit by increasing the supply of money in an attempt to hold down interest rates.

the decade. From early 1952 to mid-1961 the money supply averaged an annual growth rate of less than 2 percent per year; from the beginning of 1959 to the end of 1960, the money stock did not rise at all. The stagnation at the end of this decade is entirely consistent with what a monetarist would expect. Then in 1961 an acceleration of money growth began, the timing here corresponding to the uptick in business activity. For the next five years the money supply grew at the rate of 3.4 percent, marking an abrupt departure from the monetary stagnation of the previous years.

In the second half of 1966 there was a leveling off of the money supply. From April 1966 to the end of the year, the money stock did not grow at all. The result was a mild retardation of business activity—the so-called minirecession—when real output failed to grow for the first quarter of 1967. Notice that this occurred at a time when fiscal policy was strongly expansive, with the full-employment budget moving towards a large deficit as the result of increased expenditures on the Vietnam war. We are thus provided with our first example of contradictory policies.

Continuing from 1967 to 1969, the monetary stagnation of the late sixties was reversed and money grew steadily for two years at the tremendous rate of 7.3 percent per year. One reason for this policy was to offset the restrictive fiscal policies—particularly the tax surcharge of 1968—which were moving the full-employment budget back toward a massive surplus ($8 billion for 1969 as opposed to a $12 billion deficit in 1968). And offset fiscal restraint they did! This massive two-year injection of money into the economy generated an inflation which peaked at a 6.1 percent annual rate in the second half of 1969. The tax surcharge hardly made a dent in consumption expenditures, which soared with the growth in the money supply.

In 1969 monetary policy joined fiscal policy in a period of restraint. Money growth slowed to a 4.7 percent rate from January through July and to a 1.5 percent rate from July 1969 to February 1970. The result, not surprisingly, was a recession that lasted throughout 1970.

From 1971 to 1973, there was a period of recovery marked by an episode of wage and price controls. The inflation rate, which had reached its peak in the last half of 1969, was beginning to come down under the pressure of excess capacity and idle labor resources. By the first half of 1971, inflation was reduced to a fairly livable 3.8 percent rate. Not satisfied with this performance, the Nixon administration enacted a program of wage and price controls, designed to ease the path to adjustment to full employment while maintaining price stability. Assuming the problem of inflation to be well in hand with the enforcement of controls, the forces of monetary and fiscal expansion were unleashed. In the one and one-half years from January 1972 to July 1973, the money supply grew at the horrendous rate of 8.5 percent. The full-employment budget moved into the red in 1972 and remained in a deficit position until mid-1973. The result: inflation rates of 8.8 percent 1973 and 12.2 percent during 1974.

The business contraction, which really became severe towards the end of 1974 and early 1975, was precipitated by a slowing of the money-supply growth coupled with the increased need for more money as the result of inflation. A greater volume of money was needed to finance the same volume of real transactions, just because the monetary value of each transaction had risen with inflation. A 12 percent increase in the money supply was needed just to keep even with the growth in prices.° The reduction of the rate of monetary growth below this level together with a large full-employment surplus in late 1973 and 1974 combined to produce recession.

One cannot say conclusively that money matters and fiscal policy does not. However, empirical evidence—both historical and recent—does support the position that monetary policy is an important determinant of business cycle activity. The episodes cited in support of fiscal policy, such as the economic boom of the early sixties, turn out to be entirely consistent with a monetarist interpretation. In those episodes in which fiscal and monetary policies were at odds, monetary factors appeared to be the dominant force.

The Keynesian revolution in economics pushed money into the background for a considerable period of time. A misreading of the evidence from the Great Depression convinced many that monetary policy was a very weak tool, and the experiences with fiscal policy during the early sixties showed others the importance of fiscal policy. Thus discussions of policy during the sixties focused primarily on budgetary changes, leaving to monetary policy a purely subsidiary role. Today, re-examinations of the historical evidence and the lessons from the most recent economic disturbances have converted many to the view that the emphasis has been misplaced. Monetary events are now seen to play a very important, sometimes disruptive, role in economic activity. Much remains unknown about how money influences the economy, the timing of monetary influences, and the best way to implement monetary policy. But it is doubtful that monetary forces will ever again be ignored or discounted in discussions of macroeconomic policy.

———————

° There is one other episode in this period for which it is necessary to analyze the growth in the money supply in relation to inflation: in 1968 the growth in the money supply more than offset the 4.7 percent inflation rate to sustain the expansion into 1969. In 1969 the slowing of money growth was reinforced, as in the 1974 period, by the 6 percent inflation of that year.

DISCUSSION QUESTIONS

1. What exactly is the difference between money and income?

2. Explain how each of the following issues is important in the debate on the relative strength of fiscal and monetary policy:
   a) The responsiveness of investment demand to interest rate changes.
   b) The mechanism by which monetary actions affect GNP.
   c) The extent to which non-money assets (other bank deposits, treasury bills) serve as substitutes for money.

3. Develop a theory, other than the one presented in this chapter, which could explain the remarkable coincidence between major business contractions and reductions in the stock of money.
   In the debate between discretionary monetary policy and reliance on fixed rules about monetary growth, present the arguments on both sides of this controversy.

4. Fiscalists contend that the appropriate measure of budgetary effects on the economy is the full employment deficit or surplus. If the most important aspect of the budget is how it is financed, as the monetarists contend, is the full employment budget still the most appropriate indicator of fiscal actions? What is? Explain.

chapter 6

The Political Economy of the Free Lunch: The Economics of Political Decision Making

Up to this point we have been discussing, from a fairly narrow perspective, government actions that relate to spending, taxing, and creating money. We have been concerned with how these actions affect aggregate demand and how they can be used to stabilize the economy around a full-employment growth path. But there are a multitude of motives for pursuing government programs. Economic stabilization is only one consideration, and in many cases it is not the primary one.

Most government expenditure programs are motivated by goals more immediate than keeping the economy on an even keel. The tens of billions of dollars spent by the military every year aren't justified primarily on the basis of economic stabilization. The same is true of expenditures for interstate highways, aid to education, medical research, dams and irrigation systems, and just about any other government program you can name. In each case the program is considered important in its own right.

Although we are interested in government activity primarily because of its effects on aggregate economic activity, it will be useful to survey the motives behind government programs. Only in the broader frame of reference can we appreciate some of the practical problems that surround the formulation and implementation of government economic policy.

1. Making Everyone Pay

The primary justification for many government programs is the ability of the government, through its collective power, to provide desirable services that wouldn't be provided through the private market. National defense and flood control are good examples. As valuable as these services may be, private entrepreneurs could not be expected to go into the national-defense or flood-control business. Once a dam or levee is built, for example, denying its service to those who don't pay is next to impossible. Therefore, it would be an extremely difficult task getting anyone to pay voluntarily for the benefits they received, and private firms would have little motivation to provide flood control. Consequently flood control is usually provided by the government, which, through its power to tax, has the ability to make everyone pay. Obviously, the same rationale applies to the provision of national defense by the government.

Many projects display these characteristics to some degree. For example, college admission can be denied an individual quite easily. But there are certain benefits from having a highly educated population that extend to everyone in society, and these benefits can't be selectively distributed. The same is true, to some extent, of museums and art galleries, cultural and sporting events, fine restaurants, plastic surgery, and underarm deodorants. All of these things will be provided by the private market simply because the direct beneficiaries can be excluded if they don't pay. However, because some benefit goes to those who don't pay, it can be argued that these goods and services will be inadequately provided by private enterprises. Therefore, should the government become involved and make everyone pay for these and other goods?[1] Often the justification for or against government activity in a given area is unclear.

2. Who Benefits and Who Pays?

Government expenditure programs are justified because of the benefits they provide, and it would be difficult to think of a government program that didn't benefit someone. However, government programs also have costs. These programs are paid for through either taxation or borrowing, both of which divert purchasing power away from the private sector and into the public sector.° Of course, there are costs associated with the production of any good or service. But when items are provided through the private market, there is normally a close correlation between those who receive the benefits and those

---

°Government expenditures are also financed through the creation of money, an activity over which, as we saw in the previous chapter, the government has a great deal of control. While this doesn't necessarily take money out of the private sector directly, it often adds to inflationary pressure in the economy, which indirectly transfers purchase power from the private to the public sector.

who pay the costs. This is often not the case with goods provided by government programs.

Many government projects benefit a relatively small group, but everyone pays for them through taxes. The concentration of benefits on a relatively small group may be due to the geographical location of the project, the influence of business interest, or the attitudes and tastes of the public. In the first category we find federal matching funds for water-treatment plants and federally financed irrigation projects. As desirable as such projects might be, it's hard to argue that much benefit is received by those outside a given geographical area.

From government projects, benefits accrue to everyone in the country, but these benefits are valued differently by different people. National defense is a good example. There are obvious advantages to living in a country with the ability to protect itself against foreign powers. But it is also obvious that some people see national defense as more important than do others. Generals, defense contractors, and workers in military installations are very likely to see large benefits associated with an expansion of the military budget. Their enthusiasm will not be matched by the bulk of the people in the country, although we are all picking up the military tab.

This observation can also be made for expanding aid to higher education. Again, there would be widespread benefits associated with such an expansion, but they will be valued variously. A retired couple trying to live on a fixed budget may associate little value with more aid to higher education. A couple trying to find a nice public-supported college to send their children to will see much more value in such aid. Of course, neither of them will appreciate the crucial importance of this aid as much as a professor whose income and job security are enhanced by an expanding system of higher education.

Any time you find a program for which the costs are spread over the general population and the benefits are concentrated on a small group, you can expect some enthusiastic supporters for the program. Although those receiving the benefits also have to pay through their taxes, their share of the total cost will be minuscule in comparison with the benefits they receive. This can explain a great deal of the enthusiasm.

There is another side to this story, of course. If a large share of the tax dollar is going for programs that provide general taxpayers with little benefit, there will be a certain amount of resistance to the many programs that concentrate benefits on a few, but draw on the taxes of many. This no doubt explains why there has been so much discussion of the impending taxpayers' revolt. It's reasonable to suppose that people will, through our democratic processes, exert strong pressure on political decision makers to eliminate certain programs and reduce taxes.

Yet a brief look at the growth of government budgets, federal, state, or local, shows little evidence that the taxpayers' revolt has gotten off the ground. If anything, it's losing ground. In 1950, for example, government outlay at all levels was 21 percent of GNP. By 1970 this percentage had grown to 31 percent, and by 1974 it was 33 percent. There are, no doubt, many reasons for this. But an important insight into the impotency of the revolt comes from an understanding of a rather paradoxical situation. The political process often operates in such a way that small groups are able to exert much more influence on important decisions than large groups can. Our democratic process often caters to the interests of the few at the expense of the many.

3. Taking the Free Ride

The motivation for a group to become politically active is often obvious. By pushing for a given piece of legislation or expenditure program, a group can hope to get everyone to support a project that benefits it. But any group that attempts to organize for effective political action faces some difficulties.

The major source of difficulty comes from the fact that once favorable legislation is enacted, everyone in the favored group will normally receive the benefits whether they worked for the legislation or not. From the point of view of an individual member of the group, there are good reasons not to sacrifice much for the passage of the beneficial program. If an individual thinks that everyone else in the group is going to push to get the program through, he or she can sit back and get the benefits for nothing as a free rider. On the other hand, the same individual realizes that if no one else makes an effort on behalf of the legislation, any effort he makes will probably be in vain. Therefore, from the individual's point of view, the best thing to do is nothing. It is this phenomenon that explains much of the apathy and let-George-do-it attitude that prevails in many groups.

The problems of organizing a group can be overcome, of course. It is easy to think of organizations that pursue common goals effectively through voluntary action. But in this regard we should expect more success from small groups than from large ones. The smaller the number of people involved, the easier it is to assign and coordinate the activities of each person. Also, in a small group the social pressure for each member to carry his own weight is greater than in large groups. Added to these advantages is the greater incentive to each member of a small group. With the benefits of successful action spread over a small number of people, the benefits that each member can expect from his individual effort will be greater. Although the free-rider syndrome will occur in small groups, it will be less of a problem. In some cases the benefits that a few individuals will receive from achieving the goals of the group will be sufficient to motivate vigorous effort on their parts, even though others are neglecting their responsibilities.

Specific examples of this type of group are numerous. Firms in concentrated industries such as the automobile, steel, and pharmaceutical industries find it relatively easy and useful to organize for the purpose of influencing legislation. Professional groups such as physicians and lawyers have been effective at pursuing specific legislative objectives through their professional organizations. The military establishment is another example of a group that makes up a very small percentage of the population but has been very effective over the years at obtaining a large share of public funds.

Things are quite different in large groups. In addition to the great difficulty of organizing, there is little incentive for anyone to attempt to organize. With the benefits, even if substantial, of successful group action spread over a large number of people, the individual's return will often be tiny. Few, if any, will be motivated to incur any personal expense on behalf of the group objective. The let-George-do-it attitude will prevail. Certainly this explains the overall ineffectiveness of the consumer movement and the difficulty of mobilizing the taxpayers' revolt.

4. Favorable Treatment For Special Interests

The implications of the distinction between large and small groups explain the tendency of government spending programs to expand and for legislation to favor small groups. Most proposed programs will have the support of a relatively small group: those who will benefit substantially. Members of such a group actively lobby for the desired program. Elected representives, who directly determine which programs will be funded, will hear a great deal from those supporters. These representatives know that their votes will be carefully noted and remembered, particularly at the next election, by the supporting group. There can be little doubt that this influences a representative's decision.

The influence exerted by those in favor of a program is accented by the limited activity from the general taxpayer who, because of cost-benefit considerations, is opposed to the program. Even extremely expensive programs or legislation, such as tariff protection that results in higher prices for everyone, will not cost any particular taxpayer and voter much. In most cases the money saved by preventing an expenditure program wouldn't justify the expense of writing a congressman. Couple this with the belief of each individual that his or her effort will have little impact and that organizing such a large and diverse group as voting taxpayers is next to impossible, and political apathy is not hard to understand. Most taxpayers are not even aware of the vast majority of expenditure programs and special-interest legislation that are passed into law by legislatures. Few constituents know how their elected representatives have voted on the programs they are paying for. The only programs most voters notice are those that will benefit them at the expense of the general public. The taxpayers' revolt hasn't materialized largely because the potential revolters are too busy pushing for special programs that others will have to pay for.

Therefore in deciding how to vote on most proposals for expanding government spending, elected officials will hear predominantly from those in favor of the proposal, not those against it. Although a lot of lip service is given to government economizing and public-interest legislation, when it comes to specific proposals, almost all the pressure is for more government spending and legislation to favor special interests.

5. It's Smart to Be Ignorant

Related to the problem of influential small groups is that of a voting public uninformed and apathetic about political issues and processes. National surveys conducted by the AIPO (American Institute of Public Opinion) have consistently shown that adults know little about their elected representatives. In 1945 only 35 percent knew the names of both U.S. Senators from their state. In 1954 only 31 percent had this information. In 1947 only 38 percent could name the U.S. Congressman from their district, and 43 percent in 1965. Following the 1958 Congressional elections a survey research center poll found that 59 percent had neither heard nor read anything about either candidate, and 46 percent of those voting admitted they had never heard or read anything about either candidate. The Gallup poll in both 1965 and 1970 indicated that only 20 percent of the adults knew how their congressmen had voted on any major bill.

However, this is no reason to take a condescending attitude toward the average voter. As we will see, there are sound reasons from the individual's point of view for remaining inactive and uninformed on political issues. But, as a result, the job of elected officials is much easier than it would be otherwise.

An important part of our elected representative's job is to formulate and enact programs to solve problems, problems best solved collectively through government action. A key element in the democratic process is an informed electorate that will keep elected representatives diligently and effectively at their task. To the extent that a representative's constituency is poorly informed, it will exert less pressure. The representative will be able to impress the voters by advocating and supporting policies that give the appearance of solving problems, whether they are effective or not. Actually solving problems normally requires tough measures and sacrifices; solutions seldom come cheap. It is always tempting for political decision makers to avoid the real, but painful, solutions by advocating "easy" remedies, ones that seldom do any good and often do much harm. This temptation is easier to yield to when the electorate is uninformed. So from society's point of view there are strong reasons for desiring an informed body politic.

But the question is: why are we, who make up the electorate, largely uninformed about our elected representatives and important political and economic issues? After all, we are the ones who would benefit from an informed citizenry. In answering this question let us look at the benefits and costs of becoming politically informed, from the individual's point of view.

There are definitely benefits to the individual from being politically informed. Most of us get a certain amount of satisfaction from knowing something about what's going on in the world. Much conversation revolves around political events, and the individual who wants to be included and to contribute something enjoys knowing about these events. There is also the advantage of being able to vote for those candidates and programs that will enhance your well-being. It is the collective realization of this benefit that political philosophers see as guiding the democratic process in desirable directions.

But from the individual's perspective there is little to be gained from voting intelligently. Each individual knows that his vote will probably have no effect on the outcome of an election. In national elections where millions of votes are cast, the probability of any one voter determining the results can safely be considered zero.* While this is less true for state and local elections, the probability of one voter deciding an election is still extremely small. Being politically informed provides certain benefits to the individual, but the ability to swing elections isn't one of them.

What are the costs of being politically informed? A certain amount of political information is easily obtained. People acquire some political information from news programs, reading the newspapers, conversations with friends and acquaintances, and campaign rhetoric from political candidates. This information is usually interpreted within the context of an accepted political party or ideological position which eases the task of deciding among candidates and proposals. One of the primary reasons for the existence of political parties is to provide voters with political information at very little cost. The Democratic or Republican endorsement is all many need in order to decide who is the best candidate.

Of course, to be really well-informed about the effect of different candidates and political proposals on your well-being requires a lot more than casual reading and listening to campaign slogans. Because of the complicated nature of many issues, one would need to develop expertise in complicated fields and converse with a wide assortment of experts in order to make an informed judgment. In order to judge the views and abilities of a candidate, one needs to know more than the party affiliation and the fact that he or she believes in "balanced" growth, "conserving" our resources, world peace, stable prices, full employment, and lower taxes. Reviewing voting records, reading past position papers by the candidates, becoming informed on candidates' past activities, questioning them personally, as well as acquiring a great deal of technical information, are some of the things the extremely conscientious voter would need to do.

Obviously, the cost to the individual of obtaining all this information would be high. When the cost is compared to the meager benefit from applying this information at the ballot box, it isn't surprising that most voters are uninformed and apathetic. While it can be argued that collectively we would be better off if all eligible voters became informed participants in our democratic process,

---

*In the 1972 national elections 77,681,461 votes were cast in the presidential contest.

from the individual point of view there is little motivation to do so. Each individual knows that he will benefit from the good decisions of others, whether he becomes informed or not. On the other hand, he also realizes that if others fail to become informed his expertise will have little or no influence on political decisions. No matter what the rest of the voters are expected to do, from the individual perspective it's smart to be ignorant.

At this point we should emphasize that while the above discussion does a lot to explain voter apathy, it shouldn't be taken to imply that everyone is politically uninformed and unconcerned. Obviously this isn't the case. Some people are strongly motivated to become informed and politically active, especially in support of particular issues or candidates. As was discussed earlier in this chapter, many political proposals concentrate substantial benefits on relatively small groups while spreading the costs over society at large. Individuals in such groups have a clear incentive to become informed on the proposals they favor and to organize politically. In so doing they can magnify their influence over what their relative numbers could exert at the polls by prevailing on key political decision makers to see issues their way.

Unfortunately, political awareness motivated by these considerations is not the type of citizen participation we normally have in mind when we think of the democratic process responding to the wishes of the majority. When citizen groups become politically aware and active it often leads to political actions which ignore the interests of the majority in order to convey benefits on a minority.

6. On a Clear Day You Can See Until the Next Election

So far we have seen why the general electorate does not cause political decision makers to give as much weight to broad social interests as to the interest of small minorities. A major macroeconomic-policy implication of this is the tendency for benefit considerations to outweigh cost considerations in the formation of government policy and, hence, a bias toward expanding government programs. Even when the costs of a program have to be paid immediately, politicians are apt to hear little from the apathetic taxpayers footing the bill. This is even more true when the cost of a current political action will not be noticed until some future date. Many political decisions require weighing current benefits against future costs or undesirable consequences. Or similarly, sometimes future benefits can only be had by accepting current costs and inconveniences. While it would be desirable if politicians took a long-run perspective in weighing the costs and benefits of different programs and policies, there are reasons for pessimism.

The fact that few voters are motivated to become thoroughly informed politically allows the politician to concentrate on the short-run impact of policy decisions without fear that he or she will be blamed for the long-run repercussions. It is not always easy to trace unfortunate future happenings back to their source, and few voters are likely to know whose political actions were responsible. Identifying the politicians responsible for short-sighted policies is further hampered by the fact that the political selection process rewards those who are most adept at taking credit when things are going well and shifting the blame when problems arise. So politicians don't have to be overly concerned about the long-run consequences of their proposals. Proposals that convey short-run benefits will appear attractive even though the eventual costs may be severe. Proposals that require immediate sacrifices will be avoided even though the long-run benefits are substantial.

The implications of this for election-year politics are obvious. Considering a policy in an election year, politicians will be strongly tempted to judge its merits on the basis of its preelection impact. Less importance will be attached to postelection ramifications. Notice that we aren't saying that all our elected representatives will yield to political expediency. We are simply saying that the temptation is there, and we shouldn't be surprised if it has some influence on those in the political arena. After all, even the most forthright politician, strongly feeling he is working for the social good, can rationalize the urgency of being reelected.

An obvious place to look for the impact of political temptation of the type just described is in the area of monetary and fiscal policy. Ever since the beginning of the Kennedy administration in 1961, our presidents have been conscious of the capability of expansionary monetary and fiscal policy to stimulate the economy. They also know that an expanding economy during election time is extremely helpful in a reelection bid, while a sluggish economy is a major liability. Of course, expansionary policies can lead to inflation, but this problem doesn't surface until sometime after the more immediate and favorable effects on output and employment are realized. Therefore, we shouldn't be too surprised to find that every presidential election year since 1960 has witnessed expansionary economic policies.

In 1964 a major tax cut was enacted to stimulate the economy. Politically motivated or not, this tax cut was followed by approximately two years of impressive economic growth with only mild inflation. However, before the next presidential election, in both 1967 and 1968 large federal deficits were planned, and this was after the effects of inflation were beginning to be felt. The enactment of the tax surcharge in 1968 didn't prevent a large deficit in that year, and any impact it did have was more than offset by an expanding monetary policy. With hindsight we now know that the long term impact of these expansionary policies was the beginning of an inflation that we have yet to control. An expansionary economic policy was followed under the Nixon administration during 1971 and 1972, with the effects of inflation being disguised with a program of price controls. When the controls were phased out after the 1972 election, a substantial inflation ensued. At the time of this writing the policies for 1976 can only be guessed. But according to the *Economic Report of the President, 1975* the largest federal deficit in history is projected for 1976.

7. Telling It Like It Is

The discussion in this chapter hasn't been very flattering to the democratic process. We have seen that political decision making will most likely be dominated by special-interest pressures and short-sightedness. One shouldn't infer from this that we are anxious to replace the democratic process. There are strong reasons for supporting collective action as an appropriate means of providing certain types of economic goods and solving some economic problems. Given this, we must have some mechanism for making collective decisions, a mechanism that balances as equitably as possible the diverse desires found in the society. Considering the alternatives to democracy, it is our feeling that some form of the democratic process is the desirable way for making collective decisions.

Given our preference for the democratic process, we are tempted to view this process as it should work. This can easily lead us to engage in moralizing about how others should behave when we see behavior that prevents the actual from realizing the ideal. Unfortunately (or fortunately), such moralizing seldom affects behavior, even the behavior of those doing the moralizing (practicing what you preach is preached more than it is practiced).

Since we are primarily concerned with the macroeconomy as it actually operates, we must look at the democratic decision process realistically. The formulation of our macroeconomic policies, as well as other government policies that have direct effects on the performance of the macroeconomy, occurs in the context of our democratic process. Without a realistic view of how this process operates we will be severely handicapped in our understanding of the performance of the economy. And, as much as we may deplore the fact, it is true that a lack of political awareness and concern on the part of the public makes it easier for political decision makers to yield to the temptation of taking short-sighted positions. In so doing they can avoid the real, but often unpleasant, solutions to pressing problems by applying pseudo-solutions that often do more harm than good. It is also true that the political activity and awareness we do find demonstrated by citizens is often used to influence the legislative process in favor of special-interest groups and at the expense of the wider interests of the public.

In the light shed by the discussion in this chapter, many of the problems and policies that will be discussed in the remainder of this book will be better understood. This is certainly true of the topic of inflation, to which we turn our attention in the next two chapters.

DISCUSSION QUESTIONS

1. Assume that a technical breakthrough made it feasible to deny individual landowners the flood protection provided by a levee. Can you see any advantages in using this breakthrough to allow properties to flood unless their owners pay for flood control services?

2. One means of reducing the influence of small interest groups or the political process would be to require a 90 percent affirmative vote before government expenditure programs could be approved. While there would be benefits to such a proposal there would also be costs. Discuss these benefits and costs.

3. Governments regularly use tax money to support such things as sports arenas, ballet companies, and art museums. The justification for this support is that these things convey benefits to everyone in society. How strong do you feel this justification is? What type of abuses can practices such as this encourage? What would you think of this justification if it were applied to fine restaurants, deodorant soaps, and sexy dresses?

4. Some argue that there are advantages to be had by having the government increase its control over productive and allocative decisions. Based on your reading of this chapter can you cite some disadvantages of such a policy?

5. The contents of this chapter have implications for judging the probable success of legislation designed to protect consumers against abuses from big business. What are these implications, and do they call for optimism or pessimism regarding the effectiveness of consumer protection legislation? Can you think of any reasons why consumer protection legislation might do more harm than good?

chapter **7**

Inflating Away Unemployment

Few people have to be told what inflation is. In the last few years every corner of the world has experienced it. We are painfully aware that inflation means spending more money to purchase the same bundle of goods today than a year ago. Because of inflation, our standard of living can be decreasing even though our income is increasing. We talk about it often and read about it in the papers. Yet, there are many misconceptions about inflation, about its causes and effects, and about the type of policies needed to deal with it.°

1. The Representative Bundle of Goods

Inflation can be defined conveniently as a general increase in prices. But to say that "most prices" are increasing doesn't give us much information. What do we mean by most prices? Even during periods of rapid inflation not all prices are going up, as anyone who has priced electronic hand calculators recently can tell you. At all times, some prices will be going up and others will be coming down. So how do we measure inflation?

Inflation is commonly thought of as an increase in the cost of living. This idea gives us a clue to how inflation is measured. Your cost of living is determined by

---

°Although it may seem surprising to the present-day observer, who has experienced nothing but inflationary tendencies since the late 1950s, episodes of deflation (a general decrease in prices) have been experienced in our history. The decade of the 1930s saw dramatic decreases in prices. From the end of the American Civil War in 1865 until about 1897, the trend in prices was definitely downward. In terms of contemporary social issues, however, inflation is of more concern than deflation.

the cost of that bundle of goods which you find desirable to consume. By multiplying the price of each commodity you consume by the amount used, you can determine your cost of living. Obviously it can be going up even though the prices of many of the items you buy are going down.

To measure inflation, or the increase in the cost of living, for the entire economy, a similar approach is used. But not everyone consumes the same bundle of goods. Consequently, measuring your bundle of goods may give little or no information on what is happening to my cost of living. To get around this problem an effort is made to select a representative bundle of goods, one that would be used by the "average" American family. Without going into a discussion of the selection process, it should be clear that the choices are somewhat arbitrary. But hopefully, with the use of such a representative bundle of goods a reasonable measure of inflation can be obtained.

Once a representative bundle of goods is chosen, the current cost of purchasing it is determined. This becomes the base-year cost of living, and for convenience it is indexed at 100. The following year the cost of purchasing this same bundle of goods is figured. If, for example, the cost has gone up by 5 percent, then the index for that year is 105. If in the next year it costs 12 percent more than in the base year, the index will be 112. These index numbers, by measuring the increase in the cost of living, provide us with a measure of inflation. When we hear that the rate of inflation was 12.2 percent in 1974, this means that the *consumer price index* was 12.2 percent higher at the end of 1974 than at the beginning.°

The usefulness of a representative bundle of goods as a measure of the bundle consumed by the average American family diminishes through time. As tastes, technologies, and incomes change so does the composition of the typical consumption bundle. Because of changes in tastes in men's hair styles, we find more being spent on "Dry and Natural" hair spray and less on "Butch Wax." Because of improving technology in the electronic field, aspiring engineers are using electronic calculators rather than slide rules. And as people become more affluent, they spend a smaller percentage of the income on food and a larger percentage on entertainment.

From time to time different goods have to be chosen to represent the consumption patterns of society. When this is done, a new base year is selected, and the cost of living in that year is indexed at 100. We are currently working with 1967 as the base year. At the end of 1974 the consumer price index was 155.4, which means that it then took $155.40 to buy the same bundle of goods that would have cost $100.00 in 1967.

To the extent that we are consuming a different bundle of goods now than we

---

°There are other price indexes, such as the *wholesale price index*, designed to give information on the changes in wholesale prices. However, it is the consumer price index that measures the rate of inflation that consumers are most interested in.

were in 1967, our measure of inflation is flawed. But even if our consumption patterns haven't changed, we should still be somewhat skeptical of the figures on inflation. While we might be consuming the same type of commodities as we did in 1967, the quality of these commodities has not remained the same. Certainly the quality of medical care has been improved. There is evidence that the quality of housing has been improving over the years, and there can be no doubt that the color television you buy today gives a better picture and is more reliable than the one you would have bought in 1967. With more and more clothes being made from synthetic fibers that hold their shape better and are easier to care for than traditional fabrics, it is safe to conclude that the quality of clothing has improved since 1967. However, quality improvements are not adequately taken into consideration when the inflation rate is figured. The result is that the consumer price index tends to overstate the actual increase in the cost of living.

2. Increasing Prices Not Necessarily Inflationary

Most people are quick to see increases in the prices of important commodities, such as agricultural products or energy products, as being inflationary. As we will see, such price increases are never the initial cause of inflation. Normally they are the symptoms. But it may be that many prices are going up, some dramatically, and yet there would be no inflation. In fact, even in the absence of inflation, we can be sure that some prices will be going up.

Prices do much more than provide a means of measuring the cost of living. They give us information on the value of additional units of one good relative to all others. Such information is indispensable in our world of scarcity. When a commodity comes into short supply, possibly because of increased demand for it or reduced availability, we can expect its price to increase relative to the prices of other goods. This tells producers that additional units of the commodity are now more valuable and that more should be produced. At the higher relative price the producing sector will find it attractive to sacrifice some of the output of other products in order to increase the output of the more valuable commodity. The higher price also motivates consumers to use the commodity more sparingly. When a product is in short supply, it is desirable that it be consumed only in its most valuable uses. In response to changes in relative prices, consumers conserve goods that have become more valuable by substituting products that are relatively less valuable.

It is essential to have a large measure of flexibility in prices if economic decision makers are to respond intelligently to the changing supply-and-demand conditions that characterize any economy. A common mistake is to see increases in some prices, not as useful signals on relative values, but as inflation. The fact is that individual price increases are not necessarily inflationary. If the government is pursuing an effective policy of maintaining a growth rate in aggregate demand that is no greater than the growth rate in the economy's real output, then price increases in one area of the economy will be offset by decreases elsewhere.

3. Trying to Buy More Than There Is

A guaranteed way to cause an inflation is to increase the public's purchasing power at a rate faster than the increase in the output of goods and services. This really isn't surprising. What would you do if you found that your money income had doubled? Although you probably wouldn't spend all the additional money you found at your disposal, there can be little doubt that much of it would be spent. And what's true for you is also true for just about everyone else. If everyone found their money incomes doubled, they would want bigger homes, more automobiles, more extravagant clothing, more airline trips, better stereo equipment, and so on.

But there is a problem here. Everyone may be attempting to buy more goods and services with their extra money, but unless there is more to buy, they will not be successful. In their attempt to buy more than is available, consumers will spend more money on what is available. The only way to spend more on the same quantity of goods and services is for the prices of those things to increase. If purchasing power, in money terms, is growing faster than the supply of goods and services, inflation will be the result.

The fact is there has never been a major inflation that wasn't preceded by a rapid increase in the money supply, and therefore a rapid increase in consumer purchasing power. And there have been some spectacular inflations. Inflations have been particularly prevalent during wartime. Traditionally, governments have been reluctant to finance war efforts completely through taxation, which would have reduced aggregate demand in the private sector.° Borrowing from the private sector, which also has the effect of reducing aggregate demand in that sector, has been another means of financing war efforts. But most wars have been financed to a considerable extent simply by the government creating additional money. This increases the purchasing power of consumers at a time when the supply of consumer goods and services is being reduced as the result of diverting resources into the military effort.

During the Civil War the cost of living in terms of United States currency, as opposed to Confederate currency, increased at the rate of 25 percent per year. Things were even worse in the Confederacy. The South was not able to borrow much from foreign sources to finance their war effort. Also, their tax revenues were restricted, since most taxes were in the form of import duties which were substantially reduced because of the blockade on Southern trade. As a result, the Confederacy financed the bulk of its expenses by issuing large

---

°Federal tax receipts amounted to only 24 percent of federal expenditures during the Civil War. During World War I, tax receipts amounted to 30 percent of federal expenditures, and World War II, saw tax receipts equalling 45 percent of expenditures.

amounts of currency. The predictable result was rapid inflation. In January 1861 the commodity price index for the South was set at 100. By April 1865 this commodity price index was 9210. In just a little more than four years, the cost of living in the South had increased by a factor of over ninety-two. In terms of the Confederate dollar, it was over ninety-two times as expensive to live in April 1865 than it had been in January 1861. It is easy to understand the feeling of the unidentified Southerner who said during the Civil War, "We used to go to the stores with money in our pockets and come back with food in our baskets. Now we go with money in baskets and return with food in our pockets. Everything is scarce except money!"

But when it comes to spectacular inflation, the Confederate South doesn't have much to brag about. In 1939 the commodity price index in Hungary was at 100. As the result of simply printing money to support its involvement in World War II the commodity price index had reached almost 5,500,000 by January 1946. And that was merely a modest beginning. By July 1946 the price index was equal to 20,000,000,000,000. In other words it took 200 billion times as much money to buy the representative bundle of Hungarian goods in July 1946 as it had in 1939.

Other countries, such as Germany, Greece, and Russia, have also had episodes of extreme inflation, or *hyperinflation*. During the sixteen months from August 1922 to November 1923, the price level in Germany rose by a factor of slightly over 10,000,000,000 (ten billion) in response to a 7,320,000,000-fold increase in the hand-to-hand money supply. In November 1944 the price level in Greece was 470,000,000 times greater than it had been in November 1943, as a result of a 3,620,000-fold increase in the hand-to-hand money supply. A 33,800-fold increase in the Russian money supply from December 1921 through January 1924 was accompanied by a 124,000-fold increase in the price level.

Once such an inflation gets started, it tends to feed on itself. Not only does the supply of money increase dramatically but the rate at which money is spent and respent also increases rapidly. With inflation quickly decreasing the value of money, no one wants to hold on to it for very long. The smart thing to do is exchange money as soon as possible for real goods and services. During the Hungarian inflation, between January and July 1946, what consumers didn't buy one day would cost over 20,200 times as much twenty-four hours later. During hyperinflations workers have been paid several times a day; their wives picked up the pay as soon as it was received in order to spend it immediately.

The eventual result of hyperinflation is that the monetary system breaks down completely. With money depreciating rapidly, people become unwilling to accept it as a means of exchange, and it effectively ceases to be money. Exchanges have to take the form of barter—goods are exchanged for goods. Unfortunately, barter is very inefficient; both parties to a trade must have exactly what the other person wants. Without money, a commodity that everyone desires, it is very difficult to make mutually advantageous exchanges. Because of this inconvenience and inefficiency, a breakdown in a monetary system is normally followed by the appearance of another monetary system, which once more facilitates exchanges.

While hyperinflations are spectacular and make interesting examples, they aren't typical of most inflations. Most are more pedestrian. From 1967 to the end of 1974 prices increased by 55.4 percent in the United States. The biggest increase during that period occurred during 1974 when prices went up by 12.2 percent. Even some of the 30 to 100 percent annual inflations that are fairly common in many Latin American countries look quite mild when compared with hyperinflation. But whether we are talking about a hyperinflation or a sustained inflation of 2 or 3 percent per year, the underlying cause is the same. Any time there is a sustained increase in the general price level, aggregate demand, in monetary terms, is growing more rapidly than the output of goods and services. Because the government is the only entity that has any control over aggregate demand, through its fiscal and monetary behavior, the government bears the responsibility for inflation.

4. A Relationship Between Inflation and Unemployment

There seems to be a negative relationship between unemployment and inflation. The higher the rate of inflation, the lower the rate of unemployment, and vice versa. Although there has been an awareness of this relationship for years, it wasn't until 1958 when English economist A. W. Phillips presented supporting data that this relationship received much attention.* Since that time this relationship, referred to as the Phillips curve, has been the topic of much discussion among economists.

Before discussing whether there are macroeconomic policy implications to be drawn from the Phillips curve, let us consider the economic rationale behind such a relationship. Recall from chapter two that a substantial amount of recorded unemployment is the result of people moving between one job and another. This frictional unemployment is the desirable consequence of people shifting jobs in response to changing preferences, demands, and technologies. When an individual is searching for a new job, he or she normally has in mind the type of job and the salary that are acceptable. This salary expectation will depend largely on such things as what this person was making before, the increase he or she expects in wages and prices, as well as what other workers with comparable skills are receiving. A salary expectation that is too low, while resulting in rapid reemployment, will mean forgoing the more attractive salary that could have been obtained with just a little more patience. On the other hand, too high a salary expectation will result in an extended period of unem-

---

*Actually Phillips's argument considered the relationship between the rate of increase in wages and the unemployment rate. Most of the subsequent work motivated by the Phillips article, however, has attempted to establish a relationship between the rate of increase in prices and the unemployment rate.

ployment. Even though the high expectation may eventually lead to a higher paying job, this gain will be more than offset by the loss of earnings during the longer job search.

As indicated earlier, the rate at which prices and wages are expected to increase is an important consideration when an unemployed worker is determining salary expectations.° For example, if the inflation rate is expected to be 3 percent, the worker, in his attempt to maintain his real standard of living, will expect a wage that is growing 3 percent faster than if prices were stable. Now assume that the inflation rate increases from 3 percent to 6 percent. In most cases it can be assumed that such a jump in the inflation rate will be largely unanticipated.† Being unanticipated, the higher inflation rate will not be taken into consideration by unemployed workers when they are deciding on the wages they expect to receive in their next job. In other words, job seekers will not immediately revise upward their acceptance wages in response to the increase in the inflation rate.

On the other hand, employers, though they may not be aware of the general increase in prices, will rapidly notice that they are receiving more for the product they are selling. As a result, employers will be willing to pay higher wages in order to expand their work force and take advantage of what they individually see as increased demand for their product. Workers looking for employment will quickly find job opportunities that pay their acceptance, or expected, wage. Because of the unanticipated increase in inflation, workers are in effect fooled into accepting employment too quickly.

Therefore, one of the effects of the increase in the rate of inflation is to reduce unemployment. This is consistent with the Phillips curve relationship: increasing the inflation rate reduces the unemployment rate. It is also true that an unanticipated drop in the inflation rate will increase the rate of unemployment. Unemployed workers, unaware of the decrease in the inflation rate, will not adjust their acceptance wage accordingly. But employers, again not necessarily aware of any change in the inflation rate, will see that the prices of their products are not increasing as much as they had anticipated. The result is that

---

°One can expect a fairly well-defined relationship between the increase in wages and the general price level. Over the long run we can expect wages to increase at a rate equal to the increase in prices plus the increase in labor productivity. In other words, if the inflation rate is 3 percent per year and the increase in labor productivity is also 3 percent per year, the tendency will be for the increase in the wage rate to be 6 percent per year. What this means is that the increase in real wages will, in the long run, be determined by the increase in the productivity of labor. If, for a given input of labor, the value of goods and services increases by 3 percent per year, we can expect that real wages will also increase by 3 percent per year. That is, the increase in wages will be such that workers will be able to consume 3 percent more goods and services each year.

†If the inflation rate holds at, say, 3 percent for a while, then that 3 percent becomes an anticipated inflation rate, and decision makers begin making plans based on that rate. A sudden increase to 6 percent would be unanticipated. However, if the inflation rate remains at 6 percent it will not take long for this rate to be anticipated.

employers will moderate the wages they are willing to pay, and those looking for jobs will be either unsuccessful or successful only after a prolonged period of unemployment. Once more the situation is consistent with the Phillips curve relationship. Reducing the inflation rate increases the unemployment rate.

5. Inflating Away Unemployment

Some economists have seen the Phillips curve relationship as a constraint on macroeconomic policy. While everyone would agree that full employment along with stable prices, (a zero inflation rate) would be nice, a strict interpretation of the Phillips curve relationship makes these goals incompatible. Rather than hoping to have both full employment and stable prices, we may be forced to trade one of these desirable goals off against the other. If we decide that we want a lower rate of unemployment, we will have to live with a high rate of inflation. And conversely, if we are serious about reducing the inflation rate, we must be willing to have more people out of work. In this view, the economist's job is to recommend the appropriate policies, monetary and fiscal, for achieving that combination of inflation and unemployment which the society feels is desirable, given the constraint imposed by the Phillips curve relationship.

Suppose it is decided, presumably through the political process, that the inflation rate is too high and that lowering it a few percentage points would be worth the extra unemployment that would result. In this case the economist would recommend monetary and fiscal policies that were less expansionary, the intent being to slow the growth in aggregate demand enough to reduce the inflation rate. However, in another situation, society may feel that it would be desirable to get more people to work even at the expense of increasing inflation. This situation would call for more expansionary policies. The intent here is to eliminate some unemployment with the help of some more inflation.

6. The Shifting Phillips Curve

The idea of a policy trade-off between unemployment and inflation is usually thought of in terms of a stable Phillips curve relationship. If the relationship between between inflation and unemployment changes frequently, then basing policy decisions on a trade-off between these two factors becomes somewhat tenuous.

The evidence indicates that if there is a negative relationship between inflation and unemployment, it isn't very stable over time. Assuming a Phillips curve existed in 1953, for example, it went through the point indicating 1 percent inflation and 3 percent unemployment, the inflation and unemployment rates actually experienced in 1953. A Phillips curve for 1968 would have gone through an inflation rate of a little more than 4 percent and an unemployment of 4 percent. Obviously the Phillips curve for 1953 could not be the same one that existed for 1968, since 1968 had a higher rate of both inflation and unemployment. The only way for the same relationship to have existed in both 1953 and 1968 would be for a positive relationship to exist between inflation and unemployment. Of course, such a positive relationship is inconsistent with the idea of a Phillips curve. Moving up to 1974 we find that the inflation rate was 12.2 percent and the unemployment rate averaged 5.6 percent. Therefore a Phillips curve for 1974 would have had to pass through that combination of inflation and unemployment rates. Once more we find that the Phillips curve has passed through higher rates of both inflation and unemployment than it did in previous years. The trend since the mid-1960s seems to be that the Phillips curve is shifting and shifting unfavorably (by an unfavorable shift we will mean passing through progressively higher rates of inflation and unemployment).

To the extent that the Phillips curve is shifting unfavorably, the policy trade-off that is often discussed between inflation and unemployment is becoming less and less attractive. The trade-off in 1953 might have required going from a 1 percent to a 2 percent inflation rate in order to lower the unemployment rate from 3 percent to 2.5 percent. In 1968 reducing the unemployment rate from 4 percent to 3 percent might have taken an increase in the rate of inflation from 4 percent to 6 percent. Certainly the alternatives in 1968 weren't as attractive as those of 1953. But compared with the possibilities in 1974, the policy options in 1968 look extremely pleasant. In order to have reduced the unemployment rate in 1974 from 5.6 to say 4 percent, it might have required accepting an inflation rate of 16 percent instead of the 12.2 percent rate that actually existed.

What could cause the Phillips curve to shift in this unfavorable way, making the achievable combinations of inflation and unemployment less and less attractive? Recall that an explanation for the Phillips curve relationship had to do with an unanticipated increase in the inflation rate. This results in a reduction in the amount of time workers between jobs remain unemployed and therefore a lower unemployment rate. Likewise, an unanticipated reduction in the inflation rate, or even an unanticipated reduction in the rate at which inflation is increasing will increase the unemployment rate. But if the inflation rate persists it will not be long before people begin to expect and adjust to the new rate. From the point of view of our discussion, unemployed workers will soon be taking the new inflation rate into consideration when determining their acceptance wage. In the case of an increase in inflation, for example, they will soon cease being fooled into accepting employment too soon and taking too low a real wage. So what we find is that in spite of the higher inflation rate, the unemployment rate, although temporarily reduced, tends back to the natural rate. In effect what has happened is that the Phillips curve has shifted unfavorably, going through a point that represents the same rate of unemployment as before, but which is associated with a higher inflation rate.

It may still be possible to reduce the unemployment rate, but in order to do so it will take another increase in the rate of inflation, an unanticipated increase. One might conclude that an effective way to keep unemployment very low is to follow a policy of increasing the rate of inflation year after year. The problems are, first of all, that we would soon face an extremely high inflation rate. Secondly, such a policy would not work; it would not lower the unemployment rate for very long. Just as people will learn to expect a higher rate of inflation after it has existed for awhile, so will they learn to expect a given increase in the inflation rate once that increase has been observed for a period of time. Workers will anticipate the inflation increase by a certain amount each year and adjust the acceptance wage accordingly. So unemployment rate will remain at, or near, the natural rate. There will be an increasing rate of inflation with no reduction in the unemployment rate.

From this we can understand how the Phillips curve can shift unfavorably, passing through higher rates of both inflation and unemployment. Pursuing policies to reduce an existing inflation rate, or even slow down its rate of increase, will cause an increase in unemployment until workers begin adjusting their acceptance wages to be compatible with the changing inflation rate. The result is both high inflation and high unemployment.

Once an inflation becomes severe, putting the brakes on will invariably cause a high unemployment rate, at least temporarily. Unfortunately, "temporarily" can be a painfully long time. This explains why there is often much resistance to the type of restrictive monetary and fiscal policies that are needed to bring an accelerating inflation under control. Long before such policies have restored stable prices, they will have resulted in serious unemployment problems.*

There can be little doubt that a high unemployment rate is a problem that political decision makers cannot afford to be complacent about, not if they expect to remain political decision makers. Consequently, there is a strong temptation to give up the fight against inflation in order to attack unemployment. This means pursuing a more expansionary policy, which will, after a certain period of time, aggravate the problem of inflation. Once an inflation starts rolling and becomes expected by economic decision makers, applying the brakes is a painful process because it involves sacrificing employment and output. Therefore the battle is often fought with a notable lack of enthusiasm or with policies that give the appearance of attacking the problem without actually doing so.

Although fighting inflation will have an undesirable effect on the unemployment rate, this impact will be temporary. One of the primary reasons reducing the rate of inflation increases the unemployment rate is that economic decision makers have learned to expect a higher inflation rate. But if the inflation rate is reduced to a constant level, possibly zero, and maintained, that inflation rate will eventually become what is expected. Once this happens,

---

*In the next chapter we will discuss the time lags that exist when either restrictive or expansionary policies are pursued. These policies influence the unemployment rate and the real output rate of goods and services, before they affect the inflation rate.

those looking for work will be basing their wage expectations on more accurate information about employment and wage possibilities. With job seekers basing their decisions regarding how long to search for a better job on a realistic understanding of the labor market opportunities, we can expect the unemployment rate to move back toward the natural rate.

7. The Long-Run Vertical Phillips Curve

Regardless of the rate of inflation or the increase in the rate of inflation, once it becomes expected the unemployment rate will move toward the natural rate. This observation has motivated some economists to refer to a long-run Phillips curve. This curve is a vertical line at the natural rate of unemployment. It shows that, once expectations catch up with reality, unemployment will be equal to the natural rate no matter what the inflation rate is. There can be any number of short-run Phillips curves passing through the long-run curve, each showing a negative trade-off possibility between inflation and unemployment. These short-run curves demonstrate that, at any inflation rate, an unanticipated increase in the inflation rate can *temporarily* reduce unemployment, and vice versa. But no matter what inflation rate is eventually reached, if it is maintained we will find unemployment tending toward the natural rate.

This indicates that there isn't any stable Phillips curve trade-off that will allow policy makers to make permanent choices between a little more inflation for less unemployment, or vice versa. Any hope that unemployment can be lowered permanently below the natural rate by accepting a little more inflation will eventually be frustrated. The long-run Phillips curve tells us that the most we can hope for from such a policy is the natural rate of unemployment with a higher inflation rate. What we will eventually get from a policy that attempts to inflate away unemployment is an unacceptable rate of inflation that can be reduced only by accepting an unemployment rate that is temporarily (which can be several years) well above the natural rate.

An analogy between inflation and narcotics isn't entirely inappropriate. Starting off with stable prices and the natural rate of unemployment we can get the thrill of an even lower unemployment rate by taking a small dose of inflation. Unfortunately, once the dose is expected, the thrill is gone, and unemployment goes back to the natural rate. In order to continue getting a high on subnormal unemployment, a stronger dose of inflation has to be taken. Of course, the large dose will soon become expected, and so larger and larger injections of inflation must be taken if the euphoria of low unemployment is to be maintained. Unfortunately, too much inflation causes severe problems for the economic body. There have been cases of economies that have actually overdosed on inflation. (The economic machinery of Germany, Hungary, and other countries has been halted by hyperinflation.)

Because of the drastic consequences of continuing with larger and larger doses of inflation, it will eventually become imperative to take the cure. But any cure that will eventually get the economy entirely off inflation will be agonizing. Once the economy is used to heavy doses of inflation even the natural rate of unemployment depends on maintaining these heavy doses. A cold-turkey policy of extremely restrictive monetary and fiscal policy would probably be unbearable. To reduce the growth in aggregate demand severely enough to quickly eliminate inflation from an inflation-ridden economy would painfully increase the unemployment rate to very high levels. Even the less extreme treatment of tapering off by slowly reducing the inflation will cause economic discomfort as employment and output are reduced. Only if the economy sticks with the cure long enough to bring the inflation rate back to zero and allow this to become the expected rate can sound economic health be restored. Although relentlessly staying with the anti-inflationary cure can be long and painful, it is the only way that the economy will ever get back to stable prices and the natural unemployment rate after a bout with inflation.

We now turn to some slightly different aspects of inflation and its effects on the economy. In the next chapter we will discuss some of the effects of inflation on different sectors of the economy, as well as some of the policy approaches that have been used and suggested to deal with inflation.

DISCUSSION QUESTIONS

1. If the demand for beef liver increases dramatically in response to a scientific discovery which indicates that liver consumption increases life expectancy, we can be sure that there will be a sharp increase in its price. Explain why this increase in price is not inflationary.

2. Recall that the consumer price index is based on the change in the dollar cost of purchasing a bundle of goods that is representative of the consumption patterns of society. Assume that such a bundle is chosen, and in the ensuing years the prices on half of the goods in the bundle increase substantially while the prices on the other half remain the same. Do you think the consumer price index based on this bundle of goods will overstate or understate the impact of inflation? Why?

3. Assuming that denomination sizes on paper money remained the same, explain how hyperinflation could effectively remove the threat of counterfeiters.

4. During hyperinflations why would you expect the price level to increase more rapidly than the growth in the money supply?

5. Explain why the idea of a trade-off between unemployment and inflation is of little value from an economic policy point of view. Can you support the position that if this trade-off were taken seriously it could lead to unfortunate results?

6. Like any analogy, the one between inflation and narcotics has its weaknesses. In what ways do you feel drawing parallels between inflation and narcotics addiction is stretching reality?

chapter **8**

Inflation: The Hidden Tax

Inflation is considered undesirable almost universally, especially when it reaches the rates we have been experiencing in recent years. In this chapter we want to examine some of the economic effects of inflation, particularly its effects on the output of the economy and its impact on the distribution of this output between groups. Then we will turn to remedies and suggestions. Unfortunately, there are high costs to fighting inflation with the only approach that is sure to work. This is the traditional approach, slowing down the growth of aggregate demand to bring it in line with the growth in real output. Here, we will be extending the discussion on inflation and unemployment which occupied much of our attention in the last chapter.

Because of the costs incurred when the problem of inflation is approached with the traditional tools for moderating aggregate demand, political considerations become important in determining how these tools will be used. There is also the hope of finding painless solutions to inflation. This hope has motivated a number of suggestions about ways of reducing the cost of the traditional solution. It has also resulted in suggestions for inflation-fighting alternatives to the traditional approach. Some of these suggestions will be discussed in this chapter.

1. The Economic Effects of Inflation on Real Output

We know what inflation is and that most people don't like it, but what effect does it actually have on the economy? We first ask ourselves what the impact is on the output of goods and services.

It has been argued by some that a little inflation is a good thing because it stimulates real output. Others have argued that inflation is disruptive to the economy, causing resources to be diverted from productive uses and stimulating excesses which lead to recession. Unfortunately, it is difficult to tell who is correct. There are arguments and evidence to support both positions.

From the view that a little inflation causes real output to increase, we find several propositions. It is argued that during inflation the prices of goods and services increase sooner than wages and other costs of production. This increases profit margins and stimulates business to increase output and employment. Output is also stimulated because people work more to maintain their real purchasing power in the face of inflation and because current purchases increase since people expect prices to be higher later.

Although these arguments are subject to severe criticism, evidence indicates that output normally does increase during inflations. We quickly point out, however, that the simultaneous occurrence of increased output and inflation doesn't necessarily establish cause and effect. There are also cases of rising prices and falling output (as recently as 1975) and falling prices and increasing output (the periods 1879–1897 and the decade of the 1920s in the United States). Although there are reasons for believing that inflation can stimulate increased employment and output temporarily, inflation certainly isn't necessary for an expanding full-employment economy.

The arguments supporting the contention that inflation motivates economic growth should be looked at carefully. One of the crucial points is that wages lag behind output prices during an inflation. This may be true in the early stages when the inflation is unanticipated. But once the inflation becomes expected there is no reason to believe that workers will continue accepting jobs at lower real wages. Since World War II, wages in the United States have risen rapidly during periods of inflation. The only wage lags have been temporary ones during quick bursts of unanticipated inflation. The ability of wages to keep up with output prices is typical throughout Western industrialized countries.

As a matter of fact, during the period of recurring inflation 1950–71, the percentage of national income going to wages and salaries actually increased from 61 to 67 percent, while the percentage going to corporate profits decreased from 15.7 to 9.5 percent. Most of this shift from corporate profits to wages and salaries occurred during the three periods of greatest inflation: 1950–52, 1955–57, and 1965–71.[1] The argument that inflation stimulates employment and output by increasing profits at the expense of wages and salaries seems dubious on empirical grounds.*

There are also reasons to be skeptical about the other arguments supporting inflation as a business stimulant. It's true that people may work more in order to

---

*The above information on the shift from corporate profits to wages and salaries during inflationary periods probably understates the shift. This is because reported profits have tended to be overstated during periods of inflation. Without going into a technical discussion of why this has been the case, let us simply say that it has to do with the way business inventories have traditionally been valued for accounting purposes.

maintain their purchasing power during an inflationary period if their wages lag behind the rise in prices. But as we have seen, the evidence indicates that this lag, even when it exists, is a very temporary phenomenon. It's also true that if people expect prices to increase, they may buy now rather than pay higher prices later. This increase in current purchases will have the effect of stimulating current output. However, additional current purchases are likely to mean a reduction in future purchases. To the extent that inflation stimulates output today, it may lead to a reduction in aggregate demand and a corresponding decline in output tomorrow. Actually if wages are keeping up with prices, much of the motivation to increase current purchases to avoid higher prices later is lost because the real cost of goods and services will not be going up.

While looking critically at the idea that inflation acts as a stimulant to output, we have anticipated some of the arguments supporting the view that inflation reduces output. One such argument is that inflation tends to set up an economic situation that precipitates recession. In this view any current increase in output caused by inflation will be more than offset by the increase in unemployment and loss of output that will follow. As indicated earlier, the inflation is supposed to stimulate current purchases at a faster rate than can be maintained. This doesn't include consumer purchases only, but business purchases as well. In an effort to get the jump on price increases, business will accumulate large inventories. This accumulation is motivated by the age-old desire to buy cheap and sell dear. Unfortunately, this type of speculative buying cannot be maintained for long. Consumer purchasing will decline after the inflation-motivated spending spree. Also inflation can erode the value of consumer's monetary assets, which will moderate consumer spending. As a result firms will soon find that their inventories are too large. Their response is to reduce their demand for inputs and inventories, which causes a reduction in aggregate demand. This can precipitate a cumulative, or multiple, drop in aggregate demand and, therefore, output, because of the multiplier. The inflation is followed by an economic recession or, worse, a depression.

The empirical evidence on the validity of this point is both supportive and contradictory. It is easy to find examples of inflations, usually ones that are rapid in comparison to what the economy is accustomed to, that are followed by economic recession and substantial unemployment. The economic collapse in the United States following the inflation during World War I is a case in point. However there are cases that contradict the inflation-recession point of view. Since the Second World War the United States has experienced a fairly consistent inflation rate with only temporary interruptions in real-output growth. Brazil, which for decades has experienced a much higher inflation rate than ours, has also had consistent growth in real output. Japan has had a significant amount of inflation since 1950, but its growth in real output has been very impressive during this period. Also, in those cases when a recession does follow a period of inflation, it may well be that it is the attempts at controlling the inflation, not the inflation itself, that cause the recession. As we saw in the previous chapter, efforts at slowing down the rate of inflation can be expected to have recessionary consequences.

Finally, there is the argument that inflation upsets normal patterns of economic behavior, causing people to divert resources and effort away from productive employments. This is undoubtedly true of hyperinflations. Certainly issuing paychecks several times a day so that the money can be spent before price increases make it worthless diverts valuable resources away from productive activities. Also hyperinflations normally end up with money becoming worthless as a medium of exchange, forcing people to resort to barter, which is very inefficient. With exchange more difficult there is a tendency for the efficiencies of specialization to diminish as people produce personally more of the things they desire. This, along with the extra effort that is involved in exchange, effectively reduces the resources available for increasing real output.

But what is true for hyperinflations doesn't seem to be the case for milder ones. We have already discussed examples of substantial growth in real output and inflation coexisting. Of course we don't know, in these cases, whether or not real output would have grown even faster in an environment of stable prices. There is no clear evidence on either side of the question regarding the effect of moderate inflation on real output. We now turn to the effects of inflation on the purchasing power of different groups in society for a more severe indictment of the problem.

2. Inflation Gives to Some and Takes from Others

During an inflation those whose incomes increase faster than the inflation rate are better off in terms of real purchasing power, while those with less rapidly rising incomes are worse off. Asset holdings are also important in determining how inflation will affect the distribution of real purchasing power. Those who hold most of their wealth in the form of money or assets that increase slowly in price will be hurt by inflation. Those who keep little of their wealth in the form of money and a high percentage of their holdings in assets that rise rapidly in price will make out much better. Debtors can normally expect to benefit from inflation since they will be paying their loans off with money that is worth less than when they borrowed it.° On the other hand, it doesn't pay to be a creditor when an inflation springs up. If you are, you will be paid back with dollars that buy less than those you loaned.

When an inflation is expected, people will take actions to prevent losses to their real purchasing power if they can. Workers and labor unions will insist on higher wages in order to at least maintain their real wages. Businesses will be able to pay these higher wages since the prices of their products are increasing.

°This assumes that the interest rate on the loan doesn't reflect the inflation rate and that repayment is in fixed dollar terms.

During inflationary periods people will try to minimize their cash holding and move into assets whose monetary value will increase with the price level. Also people with money to lend will insist on higher interest rates or interest rates and repayment based on an increasing principal to be determined by the inflation rate. Borrowers will be willing to pay these higher rates because they realize that when inflation is taken into consideration the real cost of a loan hasn't increased.

Not everyone is equally capable of protecting his real income. Some people find themselves becoming worse off during an inflation, and there isn't anything they can do about it. Unfortunately, many of those who suffer the most are the ones least able to afford a reduction in their purchasing power. Old people are very vulnerable to the harmful effects of inflation. A large percentage of our elderly, often unable to reenter the labor force, depend on relatively fixed incomes and past savings. To these people inflation is worse than a thief. They can hope to stop the thief or recover what is stolen, but with inflation there's practically nothing they can do to prevent or recover the loss of their purchasing power. Fortunately, more and more people are retiring with retirement benefits that are designed to keep up at least partially, with, the cost of living. Social Security benefits, for example, have been adjusted upward to take into consideration the effects of inflation. But large numbers of our elderly are not protected in this way. Only 50 percent, approximately, of those over sixty-five receive significant benefits from Social Security, and even these people normally have to depend on other sources of income that are subject to inflation erosion.

There is also evidence that poor families have asset holdings that are much more exposed to the harmful effects of inflation than those of middle-and upper-middle-income families.[2] The poor have a hard time getting loans and, therefore, don't have much debt. They hold much of their limited wealth in the form of money. On the other hand, middle-income families are often heavily in debt for appliances, automobiles, homes, and so on, and hold a much smaller percentage of their assets in the form of money.

Inflation, even when it is anticipated, causes a redistribution of purchasing power among identifiable groups within the economy. The evidence indicates that this redistribution harms those who are already the most disadvantaged, our senior citizens and low-income families.

3. The Hidden Tax

Many people aren't aware that inflation has the same effect as an increased tax on their income and wealth. Inflation takes real purchasing power out of the private sector of the economy and transfers it to the public sector, primarily to the federal government.

The effects of inflation as a tax are the result of several considerations. First, the federal income tax is progressive. This means that the rate at which an individual's income is taxed increases as his income increases. With this in mind we see that even if your income is growing at the inflation rate you will experience a loss in purchasing power. Assume that the inflation rate during the year was 10 percent and your money income also increased by 10 percent. The first impression might be that you are just as well off as before. This would be true if your taxes also increased by 10 percent. But your increase in money income (you experienced no increase in real income) will have put you in a higher tax bracket. This means that your federal income tax will increase at a rate greater than your money income. Therefore your after-tax, or spendable, income will have increased by less than 10 percent, not keeping up with the increase in the cost of living. Your real purchasing will have decreased, some of it having been transferred to the federal government through an inflation tax.

As an example, personal income in money terms rose approximately 8 percent from 1973 to 1974. This increase was entirely due to inflation. (Real personal income went down during this period.) The result was that Federal receipts rose by 15 percent during this period. People were pushed into higher tax brackets even though their real incomes fell. This tax effect is relatively more pronounced on low income people. Individual exemptions, the low-income allowance, and the standard deduction are usually the only deductions that poorer families are able to write off against their income. These deductions are established by law and do not increase with inflation, except possibly after long lags. More affluent taxpayers find it to their advantage to itemize specific expenditures as deductions from their income before paying taxes. These deductions reflect price increases, and this moderates the increase in their taxable income in a way not available to the poor. This effect is documented in a study that appeared in the National Tax Journal, which investigated the period 1965–67. During this period nominal tax rates were unchanged, but the consumer price index increased 5.8 percent. As a result the effective tax rate increased on all incomes, but more so on low incomes. The study showed that the effective tax on real income increased 10.9 percent on incomes of $5,000, 5.8 percent on $10,000 incomes, and 1.9 percent on incomes of $40,000.

Inflation also acts as a tax on money holdings. Most of us hold a substantial amount of our monthly income in the form of money (currency and checking account deposits). We could put our paychecks in a saving account or bonds and convert these interest-bearing assets into money only as we needed it. For most of us, however, this is too much trouble, and we deposit most of our paychecks into a checking account where it can be conveniently spent. But during inflation the value of the money that we hold is being reduced by an amount equal to the inflation rate. In other words, if during the year you hold an average money balance of $1000, a 10 percent inflation will reduce the value of this asset by 10 percent. Once more inflation has taxed away some of your purchasing power. From your point of view this is no different than if there had been no inflation, but at the end of the year you had to write a check to the government for 10 percent of your average money holdings during the year.

The debtor-creditor posture of different groups in the economy is also important in understanding how inflation taxes away the real purchasing power of households, transferring much of it to governments. It happens that households have always been the major net creditor group in our economy, and governments have become the major net debtors in the last few decades.° In 1970 households were net creditors by approximately $658 billion, while governments, local, state, and federal, were net debtors by $326 billion (businesses owed the rest). Because of the advantage of debtors in inflation, here again purchasing power is transferred from households to the federal government.

4. The Temptation to Use the Hidden Tax

Before the 1930s and the Great Depression, the role of the federal government was relatively limited, and most people felt that this was the way it should be. But because of the hardships of the Great Depression, this view was seriously eroded. This experience, along with the proposals of John Maynard Keynes, gave popularity to the notion that the federal government should not hesitate to use taxes and expenditures to help stabilize the economy. This popularity was enhanced when large government expenditures on World War II succeeded in pulling us out of the depression. Although it is hard to argue that Keynesian policies were specifically used to effect economic growth until the early 1960s, there can be no doubt that government expenditures had a newly found justification and respectability by the end of world War II.

How important this has been in the rapid growth of government since the 1940s is hard to say, but it certainly didn't retard this growth. As discussed in chapter 6 there is constant pressure on political decision makers to increase government expenditures. Many groups stand to gain by pushing for increased government funding of programs that they feel are important. Increased respectability for government expenditures can only make the pressure to increase these expenditures more difficult to resist. This temptation to appease relatively small, but politically powerful, groups by increasing government expenditures often becomes irresistible because even expensive programs will not affect the tax payment of the individual taxpayer by much. Consequently, there is often little organized resistance to these programs.

However, the taxpayer is not completely ignored in the political process. Although taxpayers may not make themselves heard on a particular spending program, they are sensitive to the size of their tax bills. Organized resistance may not be necessary to make politicians responsive to the public's distaste for higher taxes. An increasing tax rate can cause a widespread feeling of "get the rascals out," which is a feeling that incumbent politicians like to avoid.

Based on this discussion we might predict that politicians will campaign on platforms of increased benefits for their constituencies and lower taxes. It's hard

---

°The indebtedness of the government is held largely by private individuals and corporations in the form of government bonds. Many may hold government bonds indirectly through pension plans and life insurance programs.

to imagine a safer prediction. Of course, we can't expect politicians to feel bound by such principles as "truth in advertising," and what we have experienced is both substantial increases in government expenditures and tax rates. But because of the political advantages of increasing expenditures and the liabilities of increasing taxes, politicians have been reluctant to finance all their expenditures by legislating tax increases.

When government spending exceeds tax revenues, deficits occur in the federal budget that have to be covered by borrowing. Of course, this increases our national debt. Although many commonly held fears about our large national debt are misplaced, it is true that a growing debt can result in inflationary increases in aggregate demand.

Just how much deficit spending increases aggregate demand depends on how the deficit is financed. If the government borrows from the public, money that might have financed private investment will simply be transferred into government projects. In this case the possibility exists that there will be little increase in aggregate demand arising from the deficit spending.° However, if the deficit is financed by borrowing from the Federal Reserve, the effect is to increase the amount of money in the economy; there is no offsetting decrease in the amount of money available for spending elsewhere. This increases the amount of demand in the economy. With a significant portion of the deficit being financed by borrowing from the Fed, it follows that much of the federal government's expenditures have been financed simply by creating money.† Part of the motivation for this may be explained by the Federal Reserve system's desire for low interest rates, and the fact that extensive borrowing from the public tends to increase the interest rates. This together with the temptation for political decision makers to spend more while giving the appearance of taxing less has to be seen as an important explanation for the rapid growth in our money supply.

The last fifteen years have seen the money supply grow much faster than real output, and as discussed in the last chapter this, is guaranteed to cause inflation. When it is recalled that inflation acts just like a tax on the purchasing power of the private sector of the economy, we have to conclude that our political decision makers haven't been as reluctant to raise taxes as the legislated tax rate would indicate. Rather than rely entirely on highly visible legislated taxes they have found it convenient to make use of the hidden tax, inflation.

5. Pay Now—Benefit later

The strong political pressures to increase government expenditures and finance some of these expenditures by borrowing from the Federal Reserve provides

---

°See chapter five.

†Between 1965 and 1974 the deficit increased by roughly $100 billion, of which approximately 40 percent was financed by borrowing from the Fed.

some explanation for the inflationary tendency our economy has exhibited in recent years. Another aspect of this is the reluctance of political decision makers to pursue anti-inflationary policies once inflation gets started. In order to understand this reluctance, we have to recognize the costs associated with the elimination of inflation. These costs are primarily the reduction in output and employment that accompanies the restrictive economic policies necessary to stop inflation. Our discussion in the last chapter spelled out the reasons for these output and employment reductions. What we haven't discussed is the fact that the benefits of restrictive policies are not felt immediately. It is only after a period of time that these policies have a restrictive impact on output and employment, and only after a longer time that they have moderating influence on the inflation rate. Because the costs of stopping inflation are high and also these costs precede the benefits, it is politically difficult to stick with an anti-inflationary policy until it has achieved its purpose.

When inflation has become habitual in the economy, producers and workers come to expect it and plan for it. Often, wage increases will be written into long-term contracts. When anti-inflationary policies begin to reduce the growth in aggregate demand, producers will find fewer buyers for their products at existing prices. Each firm will expect its production costs to continue going up as before and will therefore be reluctant to make price concessions to keep sales up. So the initial response of firms to anti-inflationary policy will be to reduce output, not prices.

With reduced output come reduced demands for factors of production, including labor. At first workers will not see the reduction in demand for their services as part of an economy-wide phenomenon that will slow up increases in the cost of living. Therefore, they will be reluctant to make the wage concessions necessary to encourage employers to maintain high levels of employment.

So we see that the first impact of economic policies designed to reduce inflation is the unfavorable one of reducing output and employment. It usually takes anywhere from six to nine months after the initiation of effective anti-inflationary policy before this effect on output and employment takes place. The benefits from the fight against inflation take longer to arrive. Only after a fairly long period of depressed sales and high unemployment is upward pressure on prices and wages reduced. Past experience indicates that the impact on prices may come anywhere from one to two years after a restrictive policy has been initiated. For example, the rate of inflation slowed in 1953 nineteen months after the rate of growth in the money supply peaked. In 1957 this lag was seventeen months, twenty-two months in 1960, only four months in 1966,* and ten months in 1969.[3]

Only after paying the price of depressed output and employment for a year or so do we begin to realize the benefits of a slowing inflation rate. The inflation

---

*The 1966 lag of only four months serves to remind us that wide variations can exist in these lags which make crystal ball gazing very difficult.

rate will continue to slow and eventually lead to general price stability if the pressure of anti-inflationary policy is maintained. The moderation in wages and prices that is reflected in the declining inflation rate is part of the adjustment that will push the economy back toward full employment. Sticking with the anti-inflation policy, while painful at first, will eventually lead the economy back to the healthy situation of full employment and a stable price level.

6. Fighting Inflation vs. Getting Reelected

While long-run economic considerations may call for an unrelenting fight against inflation, short-run political considerations may lead us down a different path. The public has come to expect the government to keep the economy running at, or near, full employment. When real output starts dropping and unemployment starts increasing, people get upset, and they are quick to place blame. Much of this blame gets directed toward their elected representatives in Washington, D.C. The probability of incumbent politicians getting reelected drops dramatically during recessionary periods. Therefore, long before an anti-recessionary policy has completed its job, politicians will be under enormous pressure to do something about the rising unemployment and falling output. And we can be sure that politicians will react to this pressure.

First they will blame the other guy: the other political party, big business, labor unions, foreign competitors or suppliers, and so on. One would have a hard time finding politicians who will acknowledge that the policies advocated by them and their party had any undesirable effects on the economy. Politicians will also respond to growing complaints over the weakening economy by switching from anti-inflationary policies to ones designed to stimulate aggregate demand. It may not produce long-run economic stability, but from the perspective of the politician who has to consider his chances in the next election it might make a lot of sense.

The short-run political advantages of switching to an expansionary economic policy are even greater than the above discussion might indicate. We discussed the reasons why an anti-inflationary policy would have the effect of reducing output and employment before it started to reduce the inflation rate. For similar reasons the first impact of an expansionary policy is to increase output and employment. Only after a further lag will the policy have the effect of increasing the inflation rate. When the lags involved in the anti-inflationary policy are coupled with those in the expansionary policy, we see that switching policies in midstream may lead to very attractive results for a short period of time.

Assume that the anti-inflationary policy is dropped for an expansionary one at the time the inflation rate is about to slow down. By the time the expansionary policy begins to increase output and employment, the effects of the previous anti-inflationary policy will be exerting downward pressure on prices and the rate of inflation will be coming down. The economic picture will look rosy at this point. Output and employment will be going up while the inflation rate is coming down. It will look as if the economy is finally moving in the right direction.

Political incumbents, particularly those in the party likely to get most of the credit for the state of the economy,° hope this improvement in the economy will be in progress during election time. Timing is important because the desirable combination of increasing output and employment and a declining inflation rate will be short lived. Within a year or so after the expansionary policy stimulates output and employment, it will start having an effect on prices. The inflation rate will cease to decline and, depending on how expansionary the policy is, may begin to increase. After a short period of optimism about the state of the economy, there will be another round of inflation.

We are not saying that political temptations will always result in switching from anti-inflationary policies to expansionary ones in midstream or that a gradual switch as the inflation rate is coming down will always rekindle the inflation. But these temptations do provide a plausible explanation for the sharp, and sometimes dramatic, shifts that have been observed in our economic stabilization policies.

In 1973 inflation increased the cost of living 8.8 percent and was an important issue, overshadowed only by the Watergate scandal. This inflation can be traced to expansionary policies initiated in 1970. By late 1973 anti-inflationary policies had been put into effect (mostly through monetary policies). From mid-1973 to February 1975 the average rate of monetary growth was 4.1 percent per year, as opposed to an 8.6 percent average from January 1972 to mid-1973. It should also be noted that with the high rate of inflation from mid-1973 through 1974, the rate of growth in the real-money supply (money growth rate minus the inflation rate) was negative. This made the 4.1 percent growth in money more restrictive than it would have been with stable prices. Predictably, this had no effect on prices during 1974. In fact the rate of inflation during 1974 increased to 12.2 percent. But the restrictive policies did have an impact on real output in 1974, and during the last half of that year both output and employment dropped sharply. In early 1975 almost all political decision makers were calling for policies to stimulate the economy. Pressure was exerted on the Federal Reserve Board to increase the money supply rapidly, and huge deficits in the federal budget were called for. As this was happening there were unmistakable signs that the inflation rate was coming down. This timing agrees with our discussion in the previous section. This change in policy emphasis before inflation has been stopped is also consistent with what we might expect given the existing political temptations.

For another example of this type of reaction, we go back to 1969-70. In response to an inflation rate of around 5 percent at the beginning of 1969, the

---

°This is normally the party that controls the White House, but not necessarily, especially when the opposing party dominates the Congress. In the latter case it depends on which party is best able to shift blame or take credit.

rate of growth in money supply was reduced. From a growth rate of 7.3 percent during 1967–68, we went to 3.1 percent during 1969. As might be expected, this had no impact on the inflation during 1969, which actually was 6.1 percent during the second half of that year. But industrial production peaked in September of 1969 and dropped sharply during the rest of the year. Also the unemployment rate was rising by the end of the year. In response to this economic contraction, and possibly with an eye on the upcoming congressional elections, there was a reversal in monetary policy. From February 1970 to January 1972 money grew at a 6.3 percent annual rate. This reversal in policy occurred in spite of the fact that inflation was still a serious problem, running at almost 6 percent per year during the first half of 1970.

Since the fall of 1966 when the Fed enacted a very restrictive monetary policy in reaction to rising prices (the inflation rate was 3.4 percent in 1966, up from 1.9 percent in 1965), the pattern of restrictive policies followed by expansionary policies has existed, particularly with monetary policy. The results have been a series of ups and downs in real output and employment with a dramatic upward trend in the inflation rate.

Inflation seems to be becoming a chronic problem even though the means of controlling it with monetary and fiscal policies is well known. What seems to be lacking is the political will to use the policies to fight inflation effectively. Being unprepared to pay the admittedly heavy cost of fighting inflation with conventional means, some economists and most politicians have embraced other means of carrying on the fight.

7. Making Inflation Illegal

According to some, an effective way of combating inflation without painful restrictive policies is to pass legislation giving the government the power to control prices. Then the government can dictate that prices will not rise and enforce this dictate with its police power. In effect this approach simply makes inflation illegal.

It's easy to understand the appeal of this approach. If rising prices are the problem, it makes sense superficially to prohibit people from raising prices. In fact, governments have been trying to control inflation by imposing price controls for centuries. Diocletian, the Roman emperor from 284–305 A.D., found prices rising to unacceptable levels around the year 300. Not being one to mess around, Diocletian issued an edict in 301 specifying maximum prices on about 800 different items and enforced the death penalty for those who charged too much. This price control program was soon discarded as unworkable. In the first place it was extremely difficult to enforce because people were very ingenious at getting around specific price controls. In the second place, to the extent these controls were policed, they resulted in inadequate supplies of goods and services. The program didn't accomplish its objective of insuring adequate supplies of goods at low prices. However, the price controls of

Diocletian were not the last attempt to outlaw inflation. Many other governments have resorted to price controls, but with little more success than Diocletian achieved. The price controls imposed in the United States in 1971, some of which are still in effect at the time of this writing, are no exception.

The trouble with price controls is that they treat the symptoms of inflation and do nothing about the underlying cause: purchasing power growing at a faster rate than real output. In fact experience indicates that, once price controls are imposed, government authorities feel that the problem is solved and expansionary policies can be pursued. The consequences are easy to predict with simple economic reasoning, and these predictions are consistent with the experiences of many price control episodes. To the extent that the price-control scheme is effectively enforced, the result will be shortages of valuable commodities and resources, wasteful use of these goods, and an increase in the amount of favoritism and discrimination practiced in the society. Because of these consequences there are strong incentives for people to violate the price-control policy, and cheating becomes widespread. While strong enforcement may reduce the amount of cheating, there is no reason to believe it can ever be eliminated. Even a quick-and-sure death penalty didn't prevent violations of Diocletian's price control program.

8. Shortages, Waste, and Self-Deception

There are literally millions of different prices in the economy. At any given time the prices of some commodities will be coming down to reflect such things as increased availability or reduced consumer interest. The prices of other goods will be increasing because of scarcity or growing demand. These relative price changes are extremely useful in motivating resource allocations toward the production of the more valuable goods and for encouraging consumers to economize on the use of these goods. Price controls invariably prevent these desirable changes in relative prices. Even when the price controllers attempt to permit flexibility in relative prices they will be frustrated by lack of information. The preferences of millions of individuals, the varying technologies that are available to the hundreds of thousands of producing units, and the relative availability of different productive inputs are just some of the things that determine the appropriate relative prices in the economy. It would be extremely naive to expect any government agency to maintain current information on all these considerations. Often even the pretense of doing this is discarded, and price control and price freeze (where all prices are frozen at specified levels) become synonymous.

When the demand for a product increases, as it will for many products during an inflationary period, a rising price for the product moderates the increase in the quantity demanded, motivates an increase in the quantity supplied, and tends to keep these two quantities equal. When the price is not allowed to increase, the quantity demanded will exceed the quantity supplied. In other words there will be a shortage of the product.

With people not getting as much of the product as they want at the existing price, some means has to be found for determining how to allocate the product among those anxious to buy. It is here that favoritism and discrimination may play a big role. The sellers of the scarce commodity will be in a position to bestow favors by letting certain people buy all they want at the controlled price. Of course this means that little or none will be available for others anxious to buy. When people are in a position to grant favors they don't convey them impartially. The apartment owner who prefers certain ethnic groups over others will be in a better position to exercise this preference if the rents he can legally charge are less than prospective renters are willing to pay. The butcher selling price-controlled beef is likely to be more generous with the gas station owner who sells price controlled gasoline but makes sure his friends get all they want.

During the 1973–74 energy crisis the price of gasoline was controlled below the market clearing price, and it was not uncommon for people to wait in line several hours for ten gallons of gas. During this time there was ample evidence that gas station owners gave preferential treatment to some of the customers. It would really take a calloused individual to make his "little old mother" wait in a long gas line. In order to stop this type of preferential treatment, the Federal Energy Office issued an order in early 1974 making it illegal for gas station owners to discriminate between customers. The order was unenforceable, and it was rescinded soon after being issued.

Price controls not only create shortages and encourage discrimination, they inevitably result in the waste of valuable resources. Unless prices can adjust freely to changing circumstances, owners of valuable resources have neither the information nor the motivation to direct these resources into their most valuable uses. The result is that resources will be carelessly used in one endeavor when their value would be much greater elsewhere.

Examples of this type of waste would exhaust the carrying capacity of a book this size, but one example which comes from post-World War I Germany is particularly vivid. In an effort to stem the tide of inflation, the authorities resorted to price controls. Butter was in particularly short supply, and its price was tightly controlled. Farmers could no longer sell the butter they produced for more than the controlled price. Other prices were controlled also, including the price of lubricating oil. However, at the controlled price for lubricating oil, a shortage quickly materialized. Many farmers found they could not get any oil without waiting in lines, doing favors for its suppliers, and so on. This, coupled with the fact that they couldn't sell their butter for much, led to a predictable, but extremely wasteful, practice. Farmers began lubricating their farm machinery with butter. Not a very desirable practice during a butter shortage but about what you should expect from price controls.

These examples point out another important aspect of fighting inflation with price controls. If the underlying cause of inflation continues, the prices that people would be willing to pay for items will exceed their controlled prices, and these controlled prices will understate the real cost of obtaining the items.

People spend much more to obtain price-controlled items than the prices on these items indicate. Spending time in long lines, providing favors to sellers, having to do without desired items, and being unable to depend on supplies impose much greater costs on purchasers than is indicated by the controlled price. Yet that price is used by officials to determine the inflation rate, not the real cost of purchasing a given bundle of goods. Naturally, the official statistics will show a dramatic decrease in the inflation rate because of the controls, when in fact the real cost of living continues to soar. Thinking that price controls stop inflation is a crude form of self-deception.

9. Rubber Bathtubs and the High Price of Toilets

Fortunately for the sake of wise resource use, attempts to enforce price controls have never been very successful. Even during World War II when there was widespread support for the wartime price-control program, countless violations took place. They occurred in spite of approximately 400,000 paid and volunteer price watchers. When people are willing to pay more than the controlled price, you can be sure that sellers can be found to accommodate them. In such a case both parties to the transaction enhance their well-being by violating the price controls. Governments have never successfully prevented such mutually advantageous exchanges.

Some violations of price controls are quite straightforward. Many times buyer and seller simply agree on a price that is illegally high and carry out the exchange secretly. These are referred to as black-market transactions. Although they are obvious violations of the law, they are normally so widespread that effective control is, for practical purposes, impossible.

Many other forms of illegal price increases are more subtle and harder to spot. Without increasing the monetary price of a product, the seller can increase its real price simply by lowering quality, providing less service, or enforcing stricter credit requirements. The shortages that will exist because of the price controls will allow the sellers to increase real prices in this way without having to reduce sales.

Another interesting way for sellers to raise the price of a product during price controls is with tie-in sales. As we have indicated before, even during an inflation some prices will be going down. Therefore, during price controls we can expect to find the market price for some commodities to be less than the controlled price. However, the seller of such a product may still be able to sell it at the controlled price by tying its sale to other products that are in short supply. In effect the customer is paying more for what he or she wants, but no laws have been violated.

For a specific example of tie-in sales, we go back to the United States price-control programs that went through various phases from 1971 to 1973. At one point toilets were in very short supply, causing the completion of houses to be postponed. At the controlled price for toilets, suppliers were unable to meet the demands of anxious customers. One supplier who was fortunate enough to have a good inventory of toilets was at the same time unfortunate enough to have a large supply of rubber bathtubs, which he hadn't been able to unload even at bargain prices. The toilet shortage was just the break he needed. He raised the price of rubber bathtubs to the controlled price and required that each toilet sale be accompanied by a rubber-bathtub purchase. Predictably, sales in rubber bathtubs soared. Without actually violating the price control laws, this supplier had effectively raised the price of toilets.

10. Reducing Those Expectations

Even the casual reader will have noticed that we haven't had much good to say about price controls. But if price controls are so useless and harmful, why have they been so popular throughout history? A partial explanation has to be that political decision makers, always anxious to impress their constituents with bold, decisive actions, find it politically attractive to support price controls. To the casual observer it looks as if price controls go quickly and effectively to the heart of the inflationary problem and help the little guy. So there is often political mileage in supporting price controls during periods of inflation and usually little to lose when they end up doing more harm than good. At that point, the politician can do one of those things he does best, blame someone else.

While we obviously don't feel that price controls are desirable from a practical point of view, there is a theoretical argument for a program of temporary price controls. As we saw in section six of this chapter, the first result of an anti-inflationary policy is to reduce output and employment. Only after the economy declines for a year or so will the inflation rate begin to fall. This slow response is caused by widespread inflationary expectations. Everyone expects costs to keep on rising and is, therefore, reluctant to adjust prices or wages downward. However, it is this temporary unresponsiveness to declining demand that results in reduced quantities of output purchased and increased unemployment.

It is theoretically possible that temporary controls on prices, or a price freeze, accompanying restrictive economic policies would eliminate the problem of inflationary expectations and ease the period of transition as these policies dampen inflation. Unfortunately, what is theoretically possible often isn't what happens. Several practical problems exist with the above strategy.

For one thing, if people anticipate the imposition of controls, their reactions will frustrate the intent of the controls. If businesses think controls are about to be imposed, they will increase stated prices and, if need be, make concessions to buyers in order to keep their real prices lower. To the extent that this happens, controls will establish prices that are higher than market prices and will therefore be ineffective.

Also, when producers anticipate an end to controls that have kept prices lower than they otherwise would have been, they will be motivated to keep their products off the market until controls end. This will aggravate the shortages that tend to exist under price controls.

Of course these problems wouldn't exist if the price controllers knew the proper level of prices and how to enforce these levels. But this is the Herculean task facing any attempt to control prices in a desirable way. The enormous amount of information that would be necessary to keep relative prices in proper adjustment makes the task impossible for practical purposes.

But even with the problems, wouldn't controls be worth the trouble in order to eliminate inflationary expectations? Then the deflationary fight could be carried on without so much unemployment and lost output. Maybe. Unfortunately there seems to be a strong tendency for political decision makers to forget the fight against inflation once controls have "solved" the problem. They think it safe to pursue strongly expansionary policies in order to stimulate rapid growth in output. This was certainly the case when the 1971 price freeze was imposed in the United States.

For a strictly theoretical perspective, there can be a justification for temporary price controls to eliminate inflationary expectations. But in actual practice, historical evidence indicates that they do more harm than good.

11. Pushing Up Inflation

So far we have been discussing inflation almost exclusively as a phenomenon caused by excess demand. This is often referred to as *demand-pull inflation* and occurs when the monetary demand for goods and services grows more rapidly than real output. However, we have seen that inflation can continue even after demand has subsided because of the lags that exist with anti-inflationary policies. During such periods wage rates and other input prices will continue going up, and these business costs will be reflected in rising output prices. This gives the appearance that prices are being forced up by costs and economists have coined the phrase *cost-push inflation* to describe the phenomenon of prices being forced up by increasing costs in spite of inadequate demand.

If one is looking for a nongovernment villain to blame inflation on, then the idea of cost-push inflation has appeal. Some have blamed inflation on labor unions. By pressuring for large wage settlements the costs of production are driven up, and these costs, being passed on to consumers, are supposedly the explanation for inflation. Not surprisingly, those who are sympathetic to organized labor don't see the problem in quite this light. They are more likely to see high profits as the cause of rising costs and inflation and wage increases as legitimate attempts to keep up with the cost of living.

No matter which variation of cost-push inflation you might pick as your favorite, the main idea is the same: inflation is caused by cost and is not dependent on excess demand. Those who feel that this is a legitimate explanation for some episodes of inflation are likely to be advocates of price controls.

While acknowledging that price controls fail to get at the source of the problem when inflation is caused by demand pull, some feel that by placing ceilings on prices and wages, costs can be controlled. Therefore, if inflation is being caused by rising costs in the face of inadequate demand, the feeling is that price controls will go to the heart of the problem. It is also pointed out that during periods of slack demand, shortages are not likely to be a problem so that some of the disadvantages normally associated with price controls will not be present.

It must be recognized however, that cost-push inflation can be at most only a temporary phenomenon. It is true, as we have seen, that prices can continue to rise even when demand is dropping back. But this certainly can't keep up indefinitely. No firm or labor organization can be completely insensitive to the demand for its product, and there is plenty of evidence to indicate that prices do not continue to rise independent of demand. Rising prices in the face of inadequate demand can be explained in terms of false expectations which are based on past inflations, inflations which invariably begin with demand pull. But whether one prefers to explain this phenomenon as expectational inflation or cost-push inflation, it cannot persist for very long. The only justification for price controls to combat cost-push inflation is that they can alter inflationary expectations.

Some have argued that cost-push inflation can persist, but only because the government validates it with expansionary policies. If, for example, labor unions push their wages above that justified by increased productivity, firms will increase their prices in response to their increased cost. But if the demand isn't adequate, firms will find that they are selling less at the higher prices and lay off workers as a consequence. But if the government is committed to full employment, it will respond with policies designed to increase aggregate demand. In this way products will find plenty of customers at the higher prices, and the higher wage rates will not lead to unemployment. If the government consistently acts in this way, there is little to restrain what may be referred to as cost-push inflation. But since this inflation can only be maintained by expanding demand, there is little to distinguish it from demand-pull inflation.

Even if there were no such thing as cost-push inflation, most people would believe there was. Regardless of why prices are going up, people will always see it as an increase in their cost, either their cost of living or cost of production. If you ever ask a merchant or manufacturer why he or she is increasing prices, you will be sure to hear that he or she really hates to do it, but it's necessary because costs are going up. No matter what the cause of inflation, to the casual observer it will invariably look like cost push.[4]

12. Indexing Inflation

We now turn to another proposal that has been suggested as a means of eliminating some of the undesirable effects of inflation and bringing it under control. This proposal is referred to as *indexing* and involves relating the number of dollars required to satisfy contractual agreements to changes in some agreed-upon price index. For example, assume that you bought a $1000 government bond that paid 5 percent interest. If after one year there had been no inflation as measured by the price index, the value of your bond would still be $1000, and you would receive a fifty dollar interest payment. However, if during the first year the inflation rate was 10 percent, the adjusted value of your bond would be $1,100, and your 5 percent interest would be fifty-five dollars. If upon the maturity date of your bond the price index had doubled, you would receive $2000 from the government, an amount equivalent in purchasing power to the $1000 you had loaned.

The idea behind indexing is to insulate contractual claims from the effects of changes in the purchasing power of money. A fully indexed economy would tie the following to a price index: all loan contracts (this would include saving accounts, pension plans, and insurance policies), unemployment compensation, social security, wage contracts, and tax payments. The indexing of tax payments would involve adjusting the tax brackets to make sure people weren't bumped into a higher tax bracket simply through inflation, and adjusting the level of exemptions.

The most widely accepted argument for indexing is that it would prevent many of the undesirable distributional effects of inflation discussed in section two of this chapter and protect creditors, old people, and the poor from inflation-induced declines in their real purchasing power. In fact, if the economy were perfectly indexed, it would operate as if there were a stable price level even during an inflationary period. So to the extent that inflation hampers the economy's growth in terms of real output, we would achieve another advantage from indexing. In response to these advantages from indexing some moves have already been made in that direction. Wage contracts are often linked to the cost of living as are social security benefits. In 1974 Citicorp, a large bank holding company, announced the issuance of interest-bearing notes whose returns would be linked to the cost of living.

Ironically, it is the advantages of indexing that provide what some feel is a strong argument against it. Some feel that taking the sting out of inflation will make it less likely that an effective fight will be mounted against it. The argument is that every time you shelter another group against the effects of inflation, you have eroded some of the public support so necessary if we are to carry through an effective anti-inflationary program.

Interestingly enough, the proponents of indexing argue that one of the big advantages of indexing is that it would increase the chances of a successful campaign against inflation. For one thing, it is argued that the advantage, from the government's point of view, of inflation as a hidden tax would be largely eliminated. With tax brackets and exemptions tied to the inflation rate, inflation would no longer transfer real purchasing power from the private to the public sector through the income tax. With government bonds indexed the large federal debt would cease to provide an opportunity for the government to use inflation to transfer real purchasing power to the public sector.

This last point deserves some amplification. We saw in section three of this chapter that households are major creditors in our economy and the federal government is the major debtor. And because of this, inflation, by reducing the real value of the money the federal government pays back to holders of government bonds, benefits the government at the expense of bond holders. Obviously this provides a temptation for inflationary policies.° Indexing government bonds would remove this temptation. It should also be pointed out that when government bonds are not indexed, there is an incentive not to reduce inflation substantially once it really gets rolling. Once inflation becomes widely anticipated, the government is going to have to increase the interest rate paid on its nonindexed bonds in order to attract purchasers. Therefore, a reduction in the inflation rate will result in an increase in the real rate of interest (the money rate minus the inflation rate) the government is paying on its bonds. If an inflation is of long standing, the interest rate on most outstanding government bonds will reflect an inflationary premium. In this situation reducing the inflation rate below the rate indicated by this premium would make the national debt a vehicle for transferring real purchasing power from the government to the private sector. A policy designed to reduce the inflation rate to zero could impose severe restrictions on the government's purchasing power; an important part of the hidden tax would be operating in reverse. This cannot help but discourage the government against effective anti-inflation policies. This disincentive would be eliminated if government bonds were indexed.

It has also been argued that if all wage agreements were indexed to the inflation rate, they would drop more quickly in response to anti-inflationary policies. Instead of waiting until expectations caught up to the lower inflation rate, wages would have to adjust immediately. This would be a desirable adjustment in terms of moderating the unemployment and lost output normally associated with such policies. Therefore, indexing might make it less painful to fight inflation. Indexing wage agreements would also prevent lags between the increases in inflation and corresponding increases in money wages. It would eliminate much of the temporary stimulation of employment that we have been able to buy with inflation. This makes the short-run Phillips curve trade-off less attractive and could reduce some of the temptations to pursue inflationary policies.

Just how effective indexing would be in moderating inflation is a debatable issue. The arguments just discussed are not persuasive to many. Also there

---

°The strength of this temptation is debatable. But it is difficult to see how the inflation-induced transfer from private sector to governmental coffers would discourage political decision makers from inflationary polities, particularly given the incentives to expand governmental spending.

would be difficulties setting up an indexing system. Choosing the acceptable price index would be no easy task. Also, with many long-term contractual agreements currently in force, the transition to an indexed system could cause temporary problems. But indexing is a possibility to consider in our frustrating fight against inflation.

13. Biting the Bullet Now or Swallowing It Later

We have taken the position that inflation is a problem and something should be done about it. Not everyone agrees. Some people feel that the costs of fighting inflations are just too high in terms of unemployment and lost output. Instead of fighting inflation, they feel that we should simply learn to live with it.

Unfortunately choosing to live with inflation is no guarantee that we will have full employment. As discussed in the previous chapter, you can buy a temporary increase in employment with inflation, but in the long run a high rate of unemployment is likely to be associated with a high rate of inflation. Countries that have experienced long-term and rapid inflation, such as Brazil, haven't always been successful in avoiding high unemployment.

So the choice is either to let inflation continue on its merry way with no long-term advantages in terms of employment or to accept the temporary costs of achieving a noninflationary economy. If the former is chosen, there will be a strong tendency for the inflation rate to continue upward. And the higher the inflation rate, the more costly will be an effective anti-inflationary policy. So unless one is willing to risk chronic inflation at increasing rates, the choice is one of when to take the medicine. Here, the longer we wait, the more bitter it will be. Biting the bullet now may be a lot more desirable than eating it later.

DISCUSSION QUESTIONS

1. Some politicians have argued that inflation would be brought under control if only consumers would be less extravagant with their money. Implicit in this argument is that consumers are responsible for inflation. How do you, as consumer, feel about this? Do you think that there is any hope that appealing to consumers to spend less will reduce the inflation rate? How is the problem of free riders important here?

2. Assume consumers did band together and collectively decide to spend less of their income in order to fight inflation. Would this increase or decrease the effect of inflation as a hidden tax?

3. Explain why inflation will transfer purchasing power from creditors to debtors only when it has not been anticipated.

4. Explain how the progressive income tax can result in taxpayers paying a larger percent of their income in taxes when their real income is going down.

5. Politicians who are very vocal in support of shifting the tax burden from the poor to the rich are often the same ones supporting larger deficits and rapid increases in the money supply. Explain the possible conflict in these two positions.

6. Based on the discussion of price controls in this chapter what do you think would be the effect of imposing rent controls as a means of providing renters with low-income housing?

7. How would you argue that allowing prices to be determined by free markets will discourage discrimination against minority groups?

8. Why would the issuance of government bonds which are indexed to the inflation rate encourage private borrowers to follow suit? How would the existence of indexed government bonds facilitate indexing elsewhere in the economy?

chapter **9**

Income Distribution:
The Inequality of
Equal Opportunity

The super-rich elite in America—those with incomes greater than $200,000 per year—receive 23 percent of all corporate dividends and 37 percent of all capital-gains income in the United States.[1] Yet this group consists of less than $\frac{1}{10}$ of 1 percent of this country's population. Ninety percent of their income is from the ownership of capital: income in the form of dividends, interest, rent, capital gains, and profit. Only 10 percent is income earned through their labor services.

In 1956 fewer than 2 percent of all taxpayers in America owned 32 percent of the private wealth and a whopping 82 percent of all privately held corporate stock.[2] They received approximately three-fourths of the country's income from capital gains and dividends.

To add insult to injury, 155 taxpayers with incomes in excess of $200,000 paid absolutely no income taxes in 1967.[3] On the 1974 tax returns the Treasury Department discovered that tax loopholes had enabled members of the over $100,000 income elite to avoid $7.3 billion in income taxes, an average tax savings of $45,662 per taxpayer in this group.[4]

Contrasting with the elite of this society are the 24 million Americans with incomes below the official poverty line—$4275 for a family of four in 1972. The families near and below the poverty line, constituting the poorest one-fifth of all families, took in about 5½ percent of the nation's total personal income. Although the number of people officially classified as poor has declined considerably since World War II, the relative share of income going to this bottom group has not changed perceptibly during this period.

These statistics are undoubtedly familiar to anyone who has heard the message of the New Left. Many who are aware of these figures have formed two general conclusions about inequality in America. First the distribution of income in America is extremely unequal and, furthermore, there is no indication that inequality is lessening over time. The other is that there exists an elite, a broad middle class, and a lower class in our society with very little mobility between the classes. There is widespread belief in a "vicious cycle of poverty" and strong barriers to entry into the upper echelons of society.

The primary task of this chapter is to examine carefully these two notions about American society. A useful starting point in this discussion is an analysis of the factors that determine individual incomes in a capitalist economy. Then we will move to a detailed description of the income and wealth distributions in the United States. Finally some ethical considerations will be mentioned before we turn in chapter ten to an analysis of policies designed to lessen inequality.

1. To Each According To . . . ?

In a pure market economy every person's income is a payment for services rendered in some productive activity. This is true for the capitalists as well as the workers; the difference is in the type of service rendered. Businesses are interested in making payment for a service only if that activity will lead to greater profits for their organization. Those individuals with the most to offer in the way of profit-making services for business firms end up with the greatest incomes.

The services offered to productive enterprises can take a number of different forms. The most common is labor. Somewhere around three-fourths of the total incomes received in the United States are payments for labor services rendered.

The income of capitalists comes from payment for the use of nonlabor factors of production: land and capital. By lending money to a business firm, capitalists enable that firm to acquire land, plants, and machinery, which are useful in the production of goods and services. Insofar as these resources are productive, firms are willing to pay an income to the capitalists in the form of rent, dividends, or interest. Some object to the fact that the capitalist receives income for offering services that involve no real physical effort, while the worker earns payment by the sweat of his brow.

However, in offering to hire some productive resource, a firm does not care about such moral questions as how much work is being expended by the owner of the factor of production. The firm just wants to know (a) how much will the use of this resource add to production and (b) how much will the added output increase profits?

The demand for a productive resource has an important influence on the price paid for it. A resource's price is also affected by its availability. The most highly paid individuals in a capitalist society are the owners of highly unique skills or assets: Muhammad Ali for his possession of fast feet and hands and a quick tongue; Joni Mitchell for her song-writing and singing abilities; Racquel Welch for her voluptuous charms; Dr. Land for his patent on self-developing film. In each case, if there were a large number of individuals with similar assets, competition among them would lower considerably the rewards they could expect for their services. The same principle applies to everybody: owners of unique assets instrumental in the production of goods and services greatly desired by society receive the highest incomes, while those possessing relatively abundant assets that are not highly productive of activities desired by society earn only low incomes. Whether these differences arise from diligence and ambition or just luck, this is how income differences are determined.

These principles enable us to recognize quickly why particular individuals and groups have relatively high or low incomes. Almost all of us have some savings, capital, or land, but only a few have sufficiently large holdings to enable them to live off this source of income. All of us possess some labor skills, but for most of us they are not sufficiently unique or productive to enable us to command a large labor income. Differences in productivity and uniqueness account for the fact that engineers are paid more than draftsmen, managers more than clerks, and skilled workers more than unskilled. Furthermore, these underlying determinants of income—productivity and relative scarcity—change as the result of technological advance and education. Any change that affects these determinants leads to a corresponding change in relative income positions.

One way to affect individual incomes is through investment in *human capital*, that is, the human embodiment of particular knowledge or skills that increase a person's productivity. Training in particular skills and acquiring a general education can enhance an individual's productivity and, thus, increase his or her income. Studies of economic growth in the United States have shown that a relatively small fraction of our past growth can be attributed to a physical increase in nonlabor productive factors. Professor Solow, for one, estimated that between 1909 and 1949 output per person-hour doubled, but that only 13 percent of that increase was due to increases in capital stock.[5] The remaining 87 percent must have been due to increases in the productivity of the physical resources, most likely to investments in human capital. The major source of the wealth of nations is a well-trained and educated humanity.

From this proposition many people have concluded that the key to income equality is education. They feel that educational advancement of particular groups, previously the disadvantaged, could lead to substantial gains toward income equality. Unfortunately things are not so simple. There are many factors accounting for differences in individual incomes, only one of which is inequality in educational background.

While there can be little doubt that the average income for people with a college education is higher than the average for people with just a high school diploma, there is still a tremendous amount of income inequality within each educational group. Educational credentials give people access to occupations

otherwise closed to them, but most income inequality exists within occupational groups. A comprehensive study of inequality in America by Christopher
Jencks and his associates revealed that equalizing everyone's education would
have practically no effect on the degree of income inequality.[6]

If differences in education do not account for the disparities in income, what
about other measurable characteristics, such as socioeconomic background
and cognitive abilities? Both of these factors relate to the question of social
mobility—the extent to which economic advantage or disadvantage is passed
on from parent to child in this society. Before getting into this, let's examine
in more detail the extent of inequality in the United States today, and how
this has changed over time.

2. The Division of the Pie

There are at least a couple of reasonable ways of looking at the division of
income among people in an economy. One is according to the type of income
received—income from capital, labor, and so on. Another is by percentiles of
the population arranged by income levels regardless of the type of income
earned.

When we divide income according to type of income received, the following
picture emerges: Seventy percent of all incomes generated today are in the
form of employee compensation; the remainder is income of self-employed
persons (12 percent) and property income consisting of interest, rent, and
corporate profits (16 percent). Since the turn of the century employee compensation has increased dramatically (from 55 percent of total income in the
first decade of the twentieth century), while the share of income accounted for
by the other two categories has declined. These persistent changes can be
attributed to a couple of long-term structural changes. First of all, the decline in
agriculture caused a severe shrinkage in the proportion of income going to
self-employed persons, and those who left the farms ended up on industrial
payrolls. Secondly, the accumulation of human capital can account for some
part of the increase in labor's share of income. This is, in fact, a common feature
of economic development in any market economy. We see a persistent relation
between the level of economic development in a country and labor's relative
share of income.

Most of the increase in the share of income going to employees as wages and
salaries has come at the expense of the income of self-employed persons.
Whether this trend represents a net gain for the working class depends upon
whether the income of self-employed persons is considered labor income,
capitalist income, or some combination of both. If the income of the self-
employed is primarily labor income, then the division of income between the
capitalist and working classes has remained fairly stable over the twentieth
century. If, on the other hand, a portion of the income of private entrepreneurs
is a return to capital, then workers have experienced a significant gain at the

expense of the capitalists. It is difficult to come to a definite conclusion here, but any interpretation of the data indicates at least a mild decline in capital's share over the past sixty years.[7]

While these figures on labor's and capital's share are interesting, they do not tell us directly whether incomes are becoming more or less equally distributed. Table one divides population into groups according to family income arranged from low to high. For the various years the percentages of total income received by each income group are given in columns two through four. This gives a fairly good picture of income inequality and how it has changed over time in the United States. You can see, for example, that in 1969 the richest 5 percent of the population made more than 2½ times as much income as the poorest 20 percent.

TABLE 1   Shares of Before-Tax Family Income[8]

Income Groups	Percent of National Income		
	1929	1947	1969
Poorest one-fifth	} 13%	5.0%	5.6%
Second one-fifth		11.8%	12.3%
Third one-fifth	14%	17.0%	17.6%
Fourth one-fifth	19%	23.1%	23.4%
Richest one-fifth	54%	43.0%	41.0%
Richest 5 percent	30.0%	17.2%	14.7%

A couple of general statements can be made about income inequality in the United States from these figures. First of all, it is apparent that incomes have become more equally distributed since 1929, with the richest fifth's share of income, for example, falling from 54 percent in 1929 to 41 percent in 1969. However, most of this reduction in inequality took place prior to 1947, and there has been little change since that time. The leveling in incomes that has taken place can be attributed to a number of factors, including the decline of agriculture, and the increase in the total share of income going to wage and salary earners. Since the figures refer to pre-tax incomes the increase in equality cannot be attributed to the progressive income tax, which has become fairly steep over this period. The changes in income distribution were due to structural factors which affected relative income shares before they were affected by government actions.

In spite of the tendency toward greater equality of incomes, the picture is still far from perfect equality. Rather than a comparison with theoretical ideals, however, it is probably more interesting to see how the United States stacks up against some of our allegedly more equalitarian counterparts in Europe.* A United Nations study of eight European countries, including the welfare states of Scandinavia, showed that in none of the countries studied did the share of income received by the richest fifth fall short of 40 percent.[9] In Germany and France the percentage of income going to the top fifth of the population was considerably greater than 50 percent, a percentage which the United States fell below long ago. Inequality is apparently no greater in the United States than in other industrialized market economies.

Furthermore, the degree of inequality tends to be overstated by the figures in table one. A substantial amount of the inequality depicted by such figures reflects the fact that they are based on observations of family incomes *at one point in time*. More meaningful measures of inequality would consider differences in lifetime incomes. These two measures differ considerably from each other because of the stages of work people go through in the course of their lives. Most people begin their working lives at the low end of the income scale, reach a maximum income level in middle age, and experience a sharp drop in income after retirement. By measuring the distribution of family incomes in a given year (as in table one), we will capture disparities that are due solely to these extremes in lifetime income range. For example, of the households earning under $5000 per year, 56 percent are headed by a person who is either under twenty-five or over sixty-five years of age.

Additional factors suggest that simple income distribution figures do not accurately depict disparities in individual well-being. The number of people in a family certainly affects the degree of comfort or discomfort provided by a given income level. Only 22 percent of the families in the $5000-and-less income category consist of more than two individuals. Furthermore some differences in income reflect a willingness to accept low income when compensated with some nonmonetary reward—greater leisure, job satisfaction, job security, or income stability. For all of these reasons income inequality is not as great as might appear from figures such as those of table one.

You might recall, however, that some of the most glaring statistics on inequality cited early in this chapter had to do with the ownership of wealth rather than the distribution of income. For example, 1.6 percent of the people own 30.2 percent of the country's personal wealth and 82 percent of the privately held corporate stock![10] Again, however, there are indications of a leveling of wealth over time, as there was for income. Looking at the wealthiest 1 percent of the adult population, their share of personal wealth declined from 32 percent of the total in 1922 to 26 percent by 1956. This still appears to show an extreme

---

*Developing countries, still characterized by a large agricultural sector, naturally show incomes to be much more inequitably distributed than industrialized countries. Agricultural economies nearly always feature masses of small property holders or tenant farmers and a few extremely wealthy landowners.

degree of concentration of wealth ownership in the hands of a small number of people. However, we are speaking of *personal* wealth—that held directly by individuals. What this statistic ignores are the tremendous holdings of wealth that are owned collectively and indirectly by the less wealthy individuals in society. The bulk of wealth holdings of many individuals consists of claims on private and government pension plans, such as social security. These claims can amount to considerable sums (current claims against the social security fund amount to about 2 trillion dollars), but they are not wealth in the individual's name; hence, these assets will be omitted from the previously cited data. The same is true of corporate stock. Some 35 percent of the stock in major corporations is held by financial institutions—pension funds, insurance companies, and so on—that are indirectly "owned" by individual policy holders. To say that 1.6 percent of the population owns 80 percent of the privately held corporate stock clouds the fact that a substantial portion is owned, in all but name, by small wealth-holders with holdings in financial institutions. Furthermore, the data on the distribution of wealth includes only financial wealth, or the ownership of physical capital. However, most personal wealth is actually of the form of human capital. Ignoring this aspect of wealth will seriously overstate the extent of inequality in wealth distribution.

This is not to say that wealth, or income, is not unequally distributed in the United States, but rather to point out that the degree of inequality can be easily overstated by many of the figures that are casually thrown around.

3. Mobility

Possibly more important than any of the above figures on income and wealth distribution is the question of accessibility to higher economic positions. Are high and low economic positions passed on from parent to child with little interclass mobility between generations, or are the Horatio Alger stories suggestive of real-world conditions in the United States? Some degree of income inequality may not be too bad if the prospects for individual movements up (and down) the economic ladder are significant.

The data concerning intergenerational mobility between occupational classes is quite revealing.* Thirty-seven percent of the sons of blue-collar workers end up with white collar jobs versus 69 percent of the sons of white-collar workers who stay in that occupational group.[11] Sons of white-collar families do have a better probability of ending up with white-collar jobs than do sons from blue-collar families. Yet there is substantial mobility between these two broad classes. Perhaps even more important is the chance of moving into one of the so-called elite professions of society. The elite professions employ roughly 11½ percent of all men, and the working class in the United States

---

*The authors do not wish to appear sexist in presenting data only on mobility for males, but unfortunately very little data is available on female mobility.

contributes only slightly less than its fair share of sons—10½ percent—to this high-status socioeconomic group.[12] Compared to Denmark, France, Great Britain, Italy, The Netherlands, Sweden, and West Germany, mobility is consistently higher in the United States. Your chance of making it into the elite of U.S. society from a working-class family is almost as great as it is for those coming from other socioeconomic backgrounds. The probability of a working-class son attaining elite status is nine-tenths as great as for the population as a whole.°

Perhaps it is more to the point to consider the extent to which a father's occupation or socioeconomic status narrows the income range likely to be attained by the son. Very little of the observed disparity in incomes is due to differences in the educational attainment or occupational status of the father. In fact, if we compare the incomes of sons whose fathers had the same socioeconomic status, we would find almost as much disparity in their incomes as for the population as a whole.[13] Considering only those families with the same socioeconomic background, the richest fifth of families would have average incomes equal to about 6½ times the average incomes of the bottom fifth. This compares with a factor of 7½ for population as a whole.[14] Less than 15 percent of income inequality can be explained by the socioeconomic class of the parent.[15]

This undoubtedly contradicts many impressions people have about the inheritability of economic status. The common assumption is that rich parents can pass on to their sons or daughters advantages that substantially improve the child's chances for success. This is undoubtedly true for the highly visible super-rich, such as the Kennedy's and the Rockefellers. However, it is incorrect to infer general conclusions from this small fraction of the total society. According to a 1960 survey of 3000 families, only 1 percent of the population received an inheritance of more than $25,000.[16] Even for this top percentage of the population, inheritance boosted their annual incomes by an average of less than $3000 per year. The inheritance of capital apparently makes a significant difference in income for only a tiny fraction of the population, and this can have very little effect on the overall distribution of incomes. In terms of less tangible assets, such as environmental and genetic advantages, there is little evidence that these have much effect on the overall distribution of income. In fact, if we could reduce all measurable inequalities between individuals to achieve the degree of equality of opportunity that exists between brothers, the extent of inequality would be reduced by only about 15 percent! The richest fifth of the population would still be making about six times the average income of the bottom fifth.[17]

There is considerable evidence here that the existing degree of inequality in America is not due to family background or socioeconomic class. Large per-

---

°Divide the percent of working-class sons that achieve elite status (10½%) by the percentage of the total population in the elite group (11½%), and this shows the degree of mobility from working class to elite relative to the population as a whole.

centages of people can and do move up and down the economic ladder. There is no denying that socioeconomic background has some effect on an individual's expected income. Race, age, sex, education, and occupation do account for some of the differences in individual incomes. However, the evidence shows that the extent of inequality existing in America today cannot be attributed to any great degree to measurable differences in individual backgrounds. Inter-generational mobility is high, while the ability of parents to pass along to their children the advantages or disadvantages of their own economic status is extremely limited. Economic success in our society depends much more on some peculiar set of traits—salesmanship, aggressiveness, or whatever—than on any asset transmittable between generations.

Most of the preceding discussion has assumed that inequality of income or wealth is a bad thing. Certainly most of us would agree that, all other things being equal, the society which generates a more equal distribution of income and wealth is the better society. But "all other things" are not generally equal. There are bound to be some implicit costs in any move toward greater equality, and these disadvantages will have to be weighed against the social betterment derived from equalization. We will take a look at some of these costs later, but first let us consider the dual nature of the factor pricing mechanism in a market system.

4. The Laborer Is Worthy of His Hire

As was pointed out in the first section of this chapter, the prices paid to the various factors of production in a capitalist economy depend upon their usefulness in producing goods and services of value to society. Resources which are unique and highly productive in some line of activity desired by society receive the highest return, while those resources which can contribute little to the output of goods most desired by society are paid a lower income. In this way, individual incomes are determined. This method of pricing factors of production also serves to direct resources into the socially most useful lines of activity. The relatively high incomes of engineers and managers provides the incentive for people to train and otherwise work to achieve these positions. High profits in certain industries motivate the movement of capital into these lines of production. Differentials in wages or rates of return to productive resources in general provide the information and the incentive for resources to shift voluntarily into their socially most useful lines of activity.

There are, of course, other methods for directing resources into their most valued pursuits—government decree or tradition are the two most widely used alternatives—but the market system of resource allocation has the advantage of being noncoercive. Resources are directed into various lines of activity in voluntary reaction to the incentives provided by differences in wages and profits. Two roles are played simultaneously by the market system of factor pricing—an allocative role and a distributive role. There is, however, no guar-antee that the distribution of individual incomes determined by the market process will satisfy any sort of humanitarian norms that society might wish to impose. The market mechanism may be very effective in channeling resources into the lines of production most desired by consumers in society, and yet it may fail abysmally in achieving any degree of equity in the distribution of incomes.

5. The Goal of Equality

We have, in fact, seen that substantial inequality in incomes does exist in this and other capitalist societies. Incomes are far from equal, and little progress has been made in the direction of equalization since the end of the World War II. Yet, outside academic circles, income inequality does not appear to be a topic of major concern for most people. This has undoubtedly been of considerable frustration to social philosophers who have taken the time to think seriously about such issues and come to feel that income inequality is one of the under-rated problems of our society. "The crucial problem today is that relatively few people view income inequality as a serious problem," writes Christopher Jencks.[18] So philosophers have attempted to advance a number of more or less objective arguments in support of an equalization of incomes.

One fairly convincing position is that income equality is a necessary prereq-uisite for political equality. A society that prides itself on equality before the law must first see to it that incomes are equal. Political influence and advan-tages in the halls of justice are only too clearly connected with financial means. This is an unfortunate state of affairs; but it is not clear that it provides, in and of itself, a weighty argument for equalizing incomes. If political equality is the fundamental goal of society, then it need not get entangled with the whole income redistribution debate. If this really is one of society's primary goals, then it can be achieved directly by changes in the financial arrangements behind political activities and the provision of legal services. Needless to say these changes would not be costless, but some institutional changes would move us toward political equality independent of individual incomes.

Another fairly old argument is based on the assumption that increases or decreases in a person's income are felt much more strongly by a poor person than by a rich one. If we are talking about a $100 change in income this would seem to be a much bigger deal to the man who otherwise earns $1500 than it does to the millionaire. From this position it is an easy step to the notion that if we take $100 away from the millionaire and give it to the poor man, the psychic loss experienced by the millionaire would be more than offset by the increase in satisfaction felt by the poor man. Generalizing this principle we easily end up with an argument in favor of perfect equality of incomes over the whole population. The only problem, of course, is selling the millionaires on the initial assumption.

The most interesting variant of the equality school is an argument advanced by John Rawls in his *Theory of Justice*, in which Professor Rawls attempts to ground his sympathies towards equality in a principle of "fairness." Rawls asks us to imagine a situation (called the "original position"), in which individuals choose principles for their society without any knowledge of their own personal attributes or the particular position in that society which they will occupy (under a "veil of ignorance"). The principles decided upon in this manner would then have the quality of "fairness," in that every person's decision would be independent of vested interests. Rawls concludes that people placed in such a situation would choose a society characterized by two primary principles of justice. The first principle involves equal access to basic liberties, and the second provides for the arrangement of social and economic inequalities so as to provide the greatest advantage to those otherwise least advantaged. Political, economic, and social equality emerge as the primary principles of a just society according to Rawls's notion of a fair decision. This is indeed an intriguing argument, causing one to consider whether or not the same principles of justice would emerge if the primordial decision makers had consciences other than Professor Rawls.

When dealing with matters of ethics, an economist's value judgment should not be given any special weight. Economics can, however, point out some of the costs of any particular value judgment, such as the goal of equality, so as to make clear some of the tradeoffs that must be accepted in considering alternative goals. Some of the preceding arguments in defense of equality may be appealing, but each of them is short on discussion of the sacrifices that must be borne in the realization of that goal.

6. Give Me Liberty Or Give Me Equality

The first thing to keep in mind is that there is a basic conflict between the goal of equality and that of individual freedom. Few people espousing economic equality are aware of this. In fact many political movements oriented towards equality also claim to be the champions of personal freedom. However, some consideration of the means for realizing an equalization of incomes exposes these two positions as incompatible.

To the extent that the allocation of resources is not based on a system of income differentials, society must rely on coercive methods. Consider, for example, a socialist system that provides equally for every member of society. After discarding wage differentials some alternative method for directing workers into appropriate lines of activity must be found. The government cannot expect individuals, by themselves, to have the motivation or the information necessary to direct themselves into the socially most useful lines of production. The only real alternative to a system of wage differentials is government decree, which necessarily involves a restriction of individual freedom.

Under a market system like ours, income equalization is supposed to take place, after resource prices have served their allocative role, through a progressive tax, which takes a higher percentage of income from the rich than from the poor. We wonder how far the tax system can go before the incentives are wiped out by taxes. But let us assume that a substantial degree of equalization can be achieved in this way. The taxation of individual incomes is necessarily coercive—you do not see people voluntarily contributing to their governments. It imposes limitations on the personal freedom to spend one's income as one desires.

For either system, socialism or capitalism, to the extent that society departs from paying rewards commensurate with a resource's contribution to production, coercion will be substituted for voluntary exchange. This is the unfortunate cost of the pursuit of equality from which there is no escape.

7. The Meritocracy

As an alternative to equalization of income, society seems to be willing to strive towards an equalization of opportunities to earn income, but as we have seen earlier in the chapter equal opportunity is a far cry from an equal distribution. With the removal of all forms of discrimination and all measurable differences in abilities and family background, we would still encounter almost as much inequality of incomes as we do today. Income differences would be due entirely to the distribution of those peculiar traits that account for economic success in a market economy. The genetic or environmental makeup that produces the strong arm of a fastball pitcher, the controlled voice of a singer, the aggressiveness of a salesman, or the judgment of a corporate manager would be the determinants of income inequality in the society of equal opportunity. Equal opportunity produces a *meritocracy*, a society that rewards its citizens with economic, social, and political status solely according to individual abilities. It is not clear why we should consider people blessed with those special traits any more deserving of economic advantages than the people who are rewarded under alternative hierarchical systems. Is rewarding the individual who inherits a strong need for achievement, for example, ethically more justified than rewarding the son of nobility? It is not clear that we can defend one system or the other in terms of fundamental value judgments.

8. Where Do We Stand?

The preceding discussion should dissuade anyone from attempting to ground his or her attitudes about income distribution in economic analysis. Economics can point out some of the implications of alternative forms of economic organization, but it will not indicate which is best in an ethical sense. For the answer to this question, you must turn to your own sense of values.

Judging from the results of political actions, however, it does appear that American society has taken certain well-defined positions on these issues. Society is not, first of all, willing to let incomes be determined entirely within the marketplace. In 1975, governments in the United States were disbursing transfer payments—funds granted to individuals for which no service was provided in return—at the rate of $156 billion per year, a figure which was equal to 20 percent of incomes earned from wages and salaries.[19] The question we might ask as students of economics is whether or not this massive expenditure coupled with the existing tax system is giving society its money's worth in terms of income redistribution. Society also appears to be concerned about achieving a greater degree of equality in opportunity. This is certainly one motivation behind expenditures on education and job training programs as well as anti-discrimination legislation.

The following chapter takes a look at some government programs and private institutions designed to equalize the distribution of incomes. The system of taxation, welfare programs, social security, and the activities of labor unions will be examined from the point of view of their effectiveness in achieving an equalization of incomes and an equalization of opportunities.

DISCUSSION QUESTIONS

1. Is the income of the capitalist class earned or deserved? What sacrifices or costs are incurred by a capitalist in lending money to a business?

2. Does a certain degree of upward mobility necessarily imply an equal degree of downward mobility? Explain.

3. What is the difference between social mobility and income mobility? Which is more comprehensive? Give an example of data on each.

4. Discuss the pros and cons of a confiscatory tax on inheritance in terms of (a) ethical considerations, (b) the effect on savings, and (c) the anticipated effects on income equalization.

5. Starting from Rawls's "original position" and given a "veil of ignorance" about your role in the society to be, what principles of justice would you establish for society? Are they comparable to Rawls's? Can such a conceptual experiment be performed, in actuality, given our conditioning in a particular society?

6. What justification, if any, can you advance in support of a governmental role in the determination of income distribution? Why is government action necessary at all when private charities exist to carry out such activities on a voluntary basis?

chapter 10

The Pursuit of Equality

A number of programs and institutions in our society are purported to serve the goal of income redistribution. It is the suggestion of their supporters that these policies and institutions redistribute incomes from the rich to the poor, although in some cases there is reason to doubt that such is their actual effect. This chapter focuses on a limited number of government programs—the tax system, Social Security, and the welfare program—and a single private institution—labor unions—to see if these are effective in (a) equalizing incomes and (b) reducing inequalities of opportunity. Many other redistribution programs exist but the selection here is intended to isolate the programs and institutions that appear to dominate the redistribution policy in this society.

1. Unions and the Interest of the Worker

It is practically gospel that trade unions have been effective in raising the worker's standard of living. Just compare the income level of today's laborer with the subsistence wage that once was earned for grueling labor under deplorable conditions and long hours. No one really believes that the avaricious capitalists conceded to the working class this improvement in welfare out of the kindness of their hearts. Only through collective bargaining with the working-man's position strengthened by the threat of strike could a fair share be extracted from the profits of the owners.

Is this the way things actually evolved? Is there really any evidence that the improvement in the workers condition is due to the bargaining strength of labor unions? How much can a labor organization expect to accomplish for the working class in the realm of labor markets?

The number of workers hired by a business depends on the wage that must be paid. At an extremely high wage it may be unprofitable to undertake any production at all. With wages somewhat lower a few workers may be hired who would contribute sufficiently to production to cover their wage costs and secure a profit for the firm. At a relatively low wage the business can profitably hire a large number of workers, each contributing little to the firm's output, but each providing sufficient revenues to the firm to warrant their employment.

In the face of this proposition, what can a labor union expect to achieve for its members by demanding an increase in wages? The firm's immediate response to a change in wages will probably be an attempt to pass this cost on to the buyers of its product by increasing prices. If the firm faces strong competition from other firms not faced by the same labor situation, it will not be able to raise prices without losing a substantial share of its market. Likewise an industry which faces strong competition from closely related products will not be able to get away with much of a price increase without losing a substantial share of its market. Likewise an industry which faces strong competition from closely related products will not be able to get away with much of a price increase without cutting sales drastically. In either of these two situations, we would expect the union's ability to extract large wage increases from employers to be quite weak. Hefty wage increases in either of these two cases would lead to a reduction in output and employment that would be harmful to the worker's economic position.

On the other hand, we have unions organized over entire industries that face little competition from alternative products. These unions tend to be relatively successful in securing wage increases for their members. Building trades unions and the United Mine Workers prior to the widespread use of natural gas have been among the strongest unions in the country for this reason. It has been estimated that these unions have succeeded in raising the wages of their members some 20 percent above the wages they would have faced without unionization.[1]

Given the apparent effectiveness of some unions in securing wage increases for their members, the obvious question is at whose expense does this wage increase occur? The first place we might look is at the income of capitalists, for the basic claim of organized labor is that the wage increase comes at the expense of capital. If this position is correct, we should observe a substantial reduction in the share of income going to capitalists and an increase in labor's share in those periods of greatest union growth. The data, however, suggests just the opposite. The greatest growth in organized labor occurred between 1936 and 1953 when union membership grew from 7.4 percent to 25.5 percent of the total labor force. Union membership has held at about one-fourth of the labor force since that time. Yet in spite of this growth there has been comparatively little change in the shares of income going to labor and capital. From 1936 to 1953, the share of national income represented by compensation to employees rose slightly from 66 percent to 68½ percent, while the share of income from interest, rent, and corporate profits also rose a bit, both gaining at the expense of the income of unincorporated enterprises. There is no evidence here that labor gained during this period at the expense of capitalists' income. While the percentage of income going to labor as compensation to employees did grow during this period, this was simply a continuation of the long-term trend that has been taking place for decades. The massive accumulation of human capital over time and the decline of agriculture have both contributed to the growth in labor's share of national income. These effects are apparently much more important than those stemming from union activity. Considerably more dramatic increases in labor's relative share occurred between the turn of the century and 1936, when compensation to employees rose from 55 percent of income to 66 percent—all at a time when union membership comprised a very small and slowly growing component of the labor force.[2]

If, through unions, wages go up but the share of income going to workers stays the same, then union workers aren't gaining at the expense of capitalists. Therefore it must be at the expense of non-union workers. This can come about in two ways. First of all, an increase in wages in unionized industries will be passed on to consumers in the form of higher prices. But who are these consumers? Most of them are workers, and in fact most are non-unionized workers. Price increases resulting from union-imposed wage settlements lower the living standard of non-unionized workers.

There is a second, more direct way that non-unionized workers are affected by wage settlements in unionized industries. An increase in wages can only be realized through some reduction in employment. This may not show up as an absolute reduction since most industries are experiencing long-term growth but there will be a reduction relative to what would have prevailed if the wage increase had not occurred. Firms will attempt to pass wage increases on to consumers, but this will ultimately lead to some reduction in sales and, hence, employment. Firms will also be tempted to substitute capital for the increasingly costly labor resource, and this directly reduces the level of employment in such an industry. The result of these two occurrences is a diversion of workers away from unionized industries and into the non-unionized sector of the economy. The supply of workers in the non-unionized sector is thus greater than it otherwise would be and competition for jobs forces wages in this sector below the levels that would otherwise prevail. The non-unionized workers get hammered from both sides: first, their wages are forced down by competition from the greater number of workers in their sector; then they must spend their relatively smaller paychecks on goods made more costly by union wage agreements.

Not all unions are guilty of exploiting their brothers and sisters because not all unions are effective in achieving wage boosts in excess of the normal increases warranted by productivity gains. Strong unions will be found in industries facing relatively weak competition from other sources. In addition, the unions themselves must effectively protect their members from direct competition with non-union labor. The effectiveness of a union depends upon limiting competition, not only indirectly from competing products, but also directly from competing workers.

A number of practices have been employed by unions to lessen competition for their members' jobs. One of these is minimum wage legislation.[3] If workers are legally barred from offering their services at less than the legally established minimum, non-union workers lose their competitive edge in the market for labor. It is no surprise that organized labor consistently provides the major support for legislation to broaden minimum wage legislation.

A particular example of minimum wage legislation that has the effect of protecting organized labor is the Davis-Bacon Act. Passed in 1931 during the Great Depression as one of those measures designed to maintain the purchasing power of the worker, this piece of legislation has effectively excluded non-union workers from federally funded construction projects. The Act stipulates that the Secretary of Labor is empowered to set wages on federally financed construction projects at prevailing wages in the region. Contractors are not permitted to pay wages less than this minimum wage if they wish to receive federal government contracts. "Prevailing wages" are usually set at the relatively high wages paid union workers, and this minimum effectively rules out competition from non-union workers willing to work for less. Contractors employing non-union personnel lose the competitive edge they would otherwise have in bidding on federal construction projects, as they are barred from paying wages lower than the prevailing union standard. With non-union workers effectively excluded from federal construction projects (some 30 percent of the nation's construction activity), they are forced to compete for jobs on those construction projects not funded by the government. This necessarily increases the competition by non-union labor for jobs on the nongovernment projects, thereby depressing wages for their services in the private construction market.

To prevent non-union workers from competing for union jobs in this case, organized labor requires the active participation of the government. In fact, it is extremely difficult for any union to prevent competition from outsiders without legal support for their monopolistic practices. The existence of union wages in excess of the competitive market standard will automatically generate non-union competition through offers to work for less. Since unions seldom have the power to prevent the hiring of non-union workers, they must secure their positions through legal restrictions.

Unions that are legally protected from competition by outsiders are often found to discriminate against racial minorities. Craft unions in the construction industry have been particularly serious offenders. A number of states require that workers serve a term as apprentices learning their trades before they are licensed to work in particular industries. At the same time these states have given organized labor control over apprenticeship programs, which allows them to control entry into the trade. One way to control entry into a trade is to discriminate against people according to race. Herbert Hill of the NAACP reported in a 1965 study of Negro labor problems that less than 1 percent of the apprentices in building and construction industries across the nation were Negro.[4] In 1961, the Commission on Civil Rights reported that only seven out of 1667 apprentices in St. Louis craft unions were black. Exclusion from apprenticeship programs naturally means exclusion from the trade itself. In 1963, Plumbers Local Number One in New York had only six blacks out of a total membership of 3000. The well-protected printers trade in New York City has also limited black participation in their union. In 1962, the NAACP found that less than 1 percent of nonjanitorial personnel working for the city's major newspapers was black.

The problem is not with the unions themselves. In fact, black membership percentages in unions as a whole exceed the percentage of blacks in the total population. Most unions do not have the power, or the inclination, to exclude racial minorities unless they are protected from competition through legal restrictions. Unions, of course, have not been passive in seeking protection through political action, for example, with minimum wage legislation. But without legal restrictions on competitive work practices, unions would be less able to limit entry through discrimination.

Where does this leave us with respect to unions as equalizers of income and economic opportunity? Unions apparently have done little, if anything, in shifting income from the capitalists to the working class. Where unions have succeeded in increasing wages, this has come at the expense of nonorganized labor. Furthermore, the strongest unions have been concentrated in the relatively skilled trades where wages were higher to begin with. The gains of organized labor must have had a disequalizing effect on the distribution of incomes. Compounding this with discriminatory practices of some unions, which adversely affect the most disadvantaged workers in society, it is difficult to see how labor unions can be pointed to as an institution that has served the goals of income equalization.

2. A Primer on Tax Evasion

With labor unions offering little in the way of income equalization, we might take a look at some government programs intended for this purpose. Certain expenditure programs of the government do help low-income families, but it is important to remember that low-income families support these programs through their taxes. If the government transfers income to the same people who paid the taxes, we are not accomplishing much in the way of income redistribution. So before turning to an analysis of expenditure programs, it will be useful to analyze the impact of the tax system on the distribution of incomes. Let's begin with a few lessons on how to beat the Internal Revenue Service.

In 1969, 301 persons earned at least $200,000 and yet paid nothing in federal income taxes. Among this group were fifty-six individuals with incomes over $1 million! How do they get away with it? Or maybe more to your interest would be the question of whether or not you can profit from their experience.

The secret is the *tax loophole*, any device which enables one to pay lower taxes than would be indicated by the straight percentages in the income tax schedules. The idea is to show a small taxable income in spite of large earnings. Your taxable income differs from gross income as the result of deductible expenses (charitable contributions, business expenses, and so on) or as the result of income received in a form that is not taxable (interest on tax-exempt bonds) or taxed at lower rates (capital gains). To illustrate, let's imagine you are one of those $200,000-and-over income earners and see how a few shrewd investments would shelter your income.

Suppose you earn $200,000 per year in a managerial position in some large corporation. You have already accumulated considerable wealth, and you are in the unfortunate position of receiving a salary, which is a bit harder to shelter than business income. But for a small fee (the price of this book) the McNown and Lee tax advisory service will show you how to avoid paying taxes on this income. You will be advised to put a large chunk of your accumulated wealth into two *tax shelters*, investments that provide access to some of the most advantageous loopholes in the tax system.

Start by investing $100,000 in a $1 million office building at 10 percent down. You will have to borrow the remaining $900,000, for which you must pay say, 8 percent interest or $72,000 per year. This interest payment and other expenses incurred in the operation of the building—taxes, maintenance, and so on—are fully deductible from whatever income you receive. Let's suppose that your rental receipts from the offices exactly offset the business expenses itemized above. If your rent is greater, you have more of that bothersome income on which you have to pay taxes; if your rental income falls short of expenses, you can deduct the differences from your salary income in computing your taxable income. What you are mainly interested in here is depreciation, an imaginary loss due to the eventual deterioration of the building. In a commercial building you may be permitted to count as much as 8 percent of the total value of the building as a depreciation loss each year. You can do this in spite of the fact that you only own 10 percent of the building and the value of the building, like most forms of real estate, is probably increasing anyway! This gives you a "loss" of $80,000, which you can deduct from your other income in computing your taxable income.

Next you put $200,000 into an oil exploration enterprise. In this business you can only expect that one out of every five wells drilled will produce oil, but your real business is tax avoidance anyway, not oil production. Suppose your share of the drilling costs on each well is $40,000, and four of the wells do not pay off for a dead loss of $160,000 (deductible of course). The fifth well produces $100,000 in oil in the first year, for which you have incurred expenses of $40,000. For a successful well about 70 percent of these expenses ($28,000) will be intangible drilling expenses, which are also deductible. In addition to this you receive a tax break in the form of the oil depletion allowance, which still exists for small operators like you. With this feature you can deduct 22 percent of the gross income from the well, or $22,000. Adding up all these deductions this operation has enabled you to write off $210,000 from your income, which now totals $300,000 ($200,000 in salary plus $100,000 in oil revenues).

Combining the results of your tax sheltering operation, your taxable income has been reduced to $10,000 (gross income of $300,000 minus $80,000 in real estate depreciation and $210,000 in losses from the oil venture). To make it into the select group which paid no taxes on their large incomes, you can arrange to donate your vice-presidential papers to the corporate library for a charitable deduction of $10,000. Without these deductions you would have ended up paying close to $95,000 in income taxes. With this scheme you pay none, and you also have a part interest in a producing oil well. You may not always be so fortunate, but such are the principles that enable people to escape a considerable fraction of their taxes.

With this scheme you have avoided paying any income taxes for one year, but it is doubtful that you will be able to get away with this over and over again. You now own two assets that are likely to start providing substantial new income or at least some capital gains. Unless you have additional wealth you can put into other tax shelters, you will not be able to find enough tax loopholes to protect your total income. You will probably still be able to lower the effective tax rate you face below the fifty percent maximum, but it is doubtful that you can get away paying no taxes year after year. Anyone you find in this position is either really losing money, cheating, or has as an only source of income the interest from tax exempt bonds.

One gimmick to lower your effective tax rate is the conversion of income to capital gains. Capital gains are the increases in value of any of your asset holdings. For example, if you buy 100 shares of General Motors at $40 per share and sell out at $60, you have realized a capital gain of $2000. This capital gain is taxable at a maximum rate of 35 percent versus a top rate of 50 percent on wages and salaries and 70 percent on "unearned" income—dividends and interest, for example.

Let's return to the business property acquired as an illustration. Suppose that in some future year you sell the property for exactly what you paid for it, and in the meantime your rental income has exactly offset interest, operating expenses, and property taxes. Apparently you have realized no profit on the venture. But this ignores what you have gained by depreciating your property. You have "lost" $80,000 per year in depreciation even though the market value of the building did not decrease during your ownership. Now you must make up for the discrepancy between your claims of depreciation and the actual market value of the property. Say you held the building for two years and were able to claim a total of $160,000 in depreciation. According to this the value of the property must have fallen to $840,000, but you were able to sell it for $1 million. The difference you may call a capital gain, which is taxed at the maximum rate of 35 percent. If you had not claimed the $160,000 in depreciation as a tax deduction in prior years, you would have paid taxes at the rate of 50 percent on this $160,000. Even though you made absolutely no direct profit from your business venture, the tax savings from this tax shelter amounted to $24,000. This investment was beneficial to you only because you wanted to protect your salary income from the steep rate of taxation on wages.

This example also illustrates why tax shelters are profitable only for the very rich. People in the top tax bracket are willing to pay a high price for investments which offer tax-shelter advantages, even if the investment itself is not likely to be directly profitable. A person with very little income to shelter does not gain much from this kind of investment and would be better off putting money in the bank. The potential gains from tax advantages keep the market value of such property high enough that the investments are not profitable for those in the lower tax brackets.

This raises some interesting points about who really benefits from tax loopholes. The demand for tax shelters by wealthy investors forces up the costs of these investments and reduces their total profitability. For example, tax-free municipal bonds pay interest rates so much lower than those paid by conventional bonds that net income after taxes from both forms of investment are fairly comparable. The fact that tax savings attract a large volume of funds into sheltered investments also implies that the supply of goods and services produced as a result of these investments will be increased. Consequently the prices of these products will be lower, so the consuming public ultimately benefits from these loopholes. Apartment rents, for example, are undoubtedly lower because of the depreciation loophole. Gasoline and other fuel prices are reduced by the existence of the oil depletion allowance.

Most loopholes were calculated to encourage people to channel money into such things as oil exploration, risky ventures, and real estate investments, but whatever the loophole's original purpose, its continuation in many cases is due to political pressure. With most of the special tax features affecting particular forms of investment—oil, real estate, and so forth—sponsors and investors in these lines of activity will find it relatively easy to organize politically for the purpose of encouraging favorable legislative action on their pet tax shelters. With the costs of a tax shelter spread over the whole populace, the costs to each little taxpayer is relatively small and not worth getting too excited about. The ordinary taxpayers will find that the individual costs of political action to close tax loopholes exceed the benefits gained. Those with tax shelters, on the other hand, have already made investment decisions based on a given tax loophole. They will find that it pays to be actively involved in political action to retain that loophole. It should come as no surprise that tax reform is indeed difficult to achieve.

3. Who Pays The Taxes?

After the previous discussion, you may have the impression that the effective tax rates for most upper income taxpayers are very low. If we consider the issue more systematically, what does our total tax system look like in terms of which income groups pay what share of the nation's taxes? In particular, is our tax structure *progressive* (meaning that the higher income groups pay a greater fraction of their incomes in taxes) *regressive* (implying just the opposite), or merely *proportional* (with every income group paying approximately the same percentage of their incomes as taxes)?

We will consider the major taxes levied at all levels of government. At the federal level this includes primarily the personal income tax, the corporate profits tax, and the payroll tax for social security levied on both employers and employees. For state and local governments, the main sources of tax revenues are the sales tax, property taxes, and personal income taxes. Determining the impact of each tax on individual income might seem to be a simple matter of adding up the taxes paid by groups of individuals and corporations, but such a procedure will be inaccurate except under some extreme assumptions. An element of uncertainty will remain in the analysis of who pays the tax, because of the possibility that the tax paid by a firm or individual is passed on to some other party.

The main controversies over the impact of taxes have to do with the corporate profits tax, the property tax, and the social security tax. With respect to the first two, one view holds that taxes on corporate profits and property are borne by their respective owners. The rate of return on capital and property is reduced by the amount of the tax, and there is nothing that capitalists can do about it. The other view suggests that corporations and property owners have some discretion over the prices they charge for their products or services and that they can, to some extent, pass the tax on to consumers in the form of higher prices. Since some element of doubt remains with respect to these two positions, we will analyze the question of tax incidence under both alternative assumptions.

The debate over the incidence of the social security tax concerns the ability of workers, through their unions, to impose some of the payroll tax on employers. The one view contends that workers are paid according to productivity considerations and that, if firms are forced to pay a tax on wages, they will simply reduce their wage payments by a corresponding amount. If a worker is worth $3.00 per hour to a firm, but the firm will have to pay five cents per hour in social security taxes, the most the firm will be willing to pay in wages is $2.95 an hour. The payroll tax is then borne by the worker in the form of lower wages. The other view holds that workers will not put up with bearing the burden of the payroll tax, but rather they force it upon the employer in their labor negotiations. Employers give in to the worker's demands but recover their costs by passing the tax onto the consumer in the form of higher prices. Why unions with this kind of market power should need the excuse of a payroll tax to impose an increased wage settlement on employers is not entirely clear. In any case, with a relatively small percentage of the labor force represented by powerful unions, this is not likely to be a phenomenon of great importance.

The ability of firms, property owners, and workers to pass some portion of their taxes on to others will certainly affect the degree of progressiveness in the tax system. Because the owners of corporate stock and property are predominantly in the upper income groups, passing the corporate profits and property taxes onto consumers makes the tax system much less progressive than if these taxes are borne entirely by the capitalists. Also because low-income groups consume very large fractions of their incomes, the taxes they pay as consumers are regressive. If workers can shift the social security tax onto the consumers, this will also tend to make the tax system less progressive.

A similar principle explains why sales taxes tend to be highly regressive. With sales taxes proportional to consumption, those groups that consume higher percentages of their incomes pay a greater fraction of their incomes to the sales tax. Since low-income groups consume higher fractions of their incomes, the sales tax is regressive. The degree of progressiveness in the entire tax system, therefore, depends on the fraction of tax revenues that come from sales taxes and other regressive taxes as opposed to the more progressive personal income tax.

Even permitting considerable uncertainty over the incidence of the corporate profits, property, and payroll taxes, we can still come to some fairly consistent conclusions about the relative impact of the tax system on income groups in society. A comprehensive study by Joseph Pechman and Benjamin Okner of the Brookings Institute based on taxes paid in 1966 by a sample of 72,000 families reveals considerable information about the *incidence* (that is, who bears the burden) of particular taxes and of the tax system as a whole.[5]

Beginning with the system of all taxes, the general picture shows that the tax structure is basically proportional or perhaps mildly progressive over most of the population. For those with incomes between $4000 and $30,000—a group composing 77 percent of the population—average tax rates fall between 24.0 percent and 26.4 percent, under the least progressive set of assumptions. Nor is the picture changed much for this group if the incidence assumptions are reversed. For the most progressive set of assumptions, the tax burden rises very gradually from 20.6 percent for those with $4000 incomes to 25.2 percent for the $30,000 income group. While this paints a picture of some progressiveness in the tax system, it is nothing to get too excited about. Based on the computed income redistributions over the entire range of incomes under the most progressive set of assumptions, the tax system reduces income inequality by only 5 percent. Incomes are approximately as unequal after taxes as they were before.

The reason for this can be seen most easily by examining the impact of particular taxes. The personal income tax, for example, is strongly progressive throughout the income range up to incomes of $500,000. The highest income tax burden falls on those with incomes between $100,000 and $500,000. That minute fraction of the population with incomes of half a million dollars or more pays taxes at a rate somewhat lower than the $100,000-to-$500,000 group, but it is still much higher than the tax rates faced by lower-and middle-income families. This evidence contradicts the impression created by the dramatic cases of income tax evasion by the super rich previously cited. Income taxes are strongly progressive in spite of loopholes in the system.

Sales taxes on the other hand, are strongly and persistently regressive. Families with incomes under $3000 pay approximately 9 percent of their incomes to the sales tax. As the level of income rises, the percentage of income spent for consumption falls and so does the average sales tax rate.

The social security tax is approximately proportional up to the cutoff level of income, beyond which the payroll tax need not be paid. All workers covered by the program must pay a flat percentage of their labor income, and this amount is matched by the employer, up to a maximum of about $14,000. Since nonlabor income is not directly taxed and tax payments cease at the cutoff income level, the payroll tax exhibits strong regressiveness at the higher income levels.

The incidence of the corporate income and property taxes remains undetermined until agreement can be reached on the ability of businesses and property owners to shift their taxes on to the consumers of their products. To the extent that they are able to shift taxes on to consumers, these taxes become less progressive. Since it is possible to discern the general outlines of relative tax burdens without disentangling the threads of this debate, we can leave the incidence of these particular taxes as an open question.

4. Political Considerations

This indeterminacy does raise interesting questions about the direction of some tax policies. Corporate profits are taxed at a maximum rate of 48 percent, a rate considerably higher than that which prevails for such a model of egalitarianism as Sweden, as well as the dynamic economies of Germany and Japan. The taxation of corporate income reduces the funds available for investment at the same time that it decreases the incentives for such investments and thus discourages the accumulation of capital. This has some real long-run costs: it retards productivity growth and consequently lowers the standard of living for future generations. There is a tendency to look at a corporation as a wealthy individual, rather than as a vehicle for organizing production, and the motivation behind the corporate income tax is apparently grounded in such a conception. If the taxation of the rich is society's goal, this can be achieved more directly and with fewer residual costs through the personal income tax. There will be less doubt about which income groups are being taxed, and less impairment of corporate investment incentives.

Unfortunately, political considerations often dominate economic ones. It is considerably easier for Congress to impose a heavy corporate profits tax, which is seemingly costless to the little man, than to tax incomes directly where the impact will be obvious. Similar considerations have led to the imposition of the payroll tax, half of which appears to be paid by the employer, and the sales and excise taxes, which nickel-dime the low-income family out of 9 percent of its income. These taxes have the appearance of being paid by "the other guy" (the corporation or businessman) or at least of being very minor in their impact. Tax policy motivated by political considerations will lead to a tax structure riddled with special exemptions and strongly characterized by short-sighted, seemingly painless forms of taxation.

5. Cash Grants vs. Consumption Subsidies

By itself, tax policy does very little to equalize incomes. But even with essentially proportional taxes, governments can achieve a redistribution of incomes by concentrating expenditures and benefits programs on particular income groups. In fact, many programs at all levels of government are intended to aid low-income groups by providing income supplements or subsidies for particular consumption activities. Each of these programs can be classified as either a cash-grant program or an income-in-kind transfer, and there is a fundamentally different philosophy behind these two approaches.

The cash-grant approach involves the direct transfer of money to those qualifying according to the rules of the program. Eligibility generally depends upon the level of family income, the number of family members, and sometimes personal attributes of the family head. The most widely known example is welfare, or Aid to Families with Dependent Children (AFDC), which provides a cash income supplement for families meeting the eligibility requirements set by individual states. The underlying philosophy of a cash-transfer program is that the recipient families can best determine their needs and will spend the money accordingly. Society is primarily interested in providing low-income families with the financial support necessary for a decent living standard. The government is not presumed to have any special knowledge about the recipient families' consumption needs, so the decision on expenditures is left entirely to the family itself.

An income-in-kind program is a subsidy for a particular consumption activity such as medical care, food, and housing. With such programs, society attempts to direct low-income families' consumption activities in particular directions, either because society as a whole is assumed to benefit, as with education, or because society deems these subsidized activities to be most beneficial to the recipient families. The presumption here is that the recipient families would not spend cash in ways that the government wants to encourage. Society's preferences differ from those of low-income families, and for their own good and the good of society, their expenditures must be restricted. The size of such in-kind transfer programs as Medicare, Food Stamps, and various housing subsidies suggests that this philosophy dominates political thinking on income redistribution.

The first and strongest argument in support of specific subsidies is that society as a whole benefits. This is undoubtedly a strong motivation behind the vast public expenditures on education. Effective government and economic growth arising out of an educated populace benefit all members of society, and without a government subsidy to education people would choose a level of education for themselves that did not account for society's gain. This argument applies to both high-income and low-income individuals, however, so educational subsidies are not directed primarily toward the poor. In fact, we have seen in the previous chapter that education can be expected to do relatively little in equalizing incomes. Furthermore, the special subsidy programs that do focus benefits on the poor—food stamps, Medicare, and public housing—provide little in the way of benefits to those not receiving the service. Hence, it is difficult to justify these subsidy programs by this generalized social-benefits argument.

The most commonly heard argument in support of in-kind transfers is that the poor are incompetent in making expenditure decisions. While this point may not be made quite so blatantly, many statements in support of in-kind programs boil down to just such a position. Housing subsidies, food stamps, old age insurance, and job training are all advocated as programs that the poor need, but might not choose if given untied cash grants. If these programs are so essential, it is surprising that the poor would not recognize these needs themselves. But this is a subtle way of saying that the poor are not competent to judge their real needs and make appropriate expenditure decisions. The assessment of competence in the management of personal affairs is extremely subjective. It is difficult to say who should pass judgment on others. Most people who are willing to make such judgments would not permit the same review of themselves.

A slight extension of this position calls for the identification of certain activities as basic "rights," which no person in our society should do without. Public support of medical care and legal aid might be supported by the argument that the right to life and equal justice are such fundamental social goals that they should be denied to no one. But this is simply the same argument just cited, with medical care and legal aid elevated to special status in our hierarchy of social preferences. If medical care and legal aid are so important to individuals, low-income families will buy them if they are given the cash. But according to some, the problem is that people may not recognize the importance of these services—that is, they are incompetent—and might squander their money on useless consumption items.

Some services are subsidized for the poor because society would like them to adopt a particular set of attitudes. This is one reason behind the movement to provide public support for child care. Those wishing to free women of the traditional housewife's syndrome see free child-care centers as a vehicle for getting women out of the house and into the working world where they will acquire new attitudes and values. Many who would not use money at their disposal for child care would still accept child care as a second-best solution to their low-income problems. They then might adopt new ways of thinking about the role of women in society. Here we have another form of the government-knows-best argument—this time in a judgment over what values people should have. We all tend to think our values are superior to those of others, and by subsidizing particular activities we can convert other members of society.

These are all nice intellectual arguments, but when it comes down to implementation, political considerations will shape the ultimate direction of income equalization policy. Here the arguments for grants-in-kind dominate. For every special subsidy program there will be a special group, other than the poor, which stands to gain or lose by the program. These groups are actively involved in the design of the program to see that their interests are looked after as well as those of the poor. The medical profession looks after Medicare, agricultural interests are behind food stamp programs, and the construction industry benefits by public housing. Unfortunately, this political interaction does not guarantee that the resulting programs provide much in the way of benefits for the poor. Where nonpoor special interest groups dominate the political process, we can anticipate that a substantial share of the benefits will end up in the pockets of the middle-and upper-class members of society. When we recognize that low-income groups pay a proportionate share of their incomes as taxes, it is apparent that many in-kind expenditure programs do not achieve an equalization of incomes.

One in-kind subsidy that illustrates most of these principles is the food stamp program. Beginning with the initiating legislation in 1964, liberal concern for the nutritional needs of the poor combined with agricultural interests in an effective political coalition enabling the enactment, and later expansion, of the food stamp program. By 1974 federal government bonuses to 13½ million food stamp recipients totaled $3 billion. Since eligibility requirements for the program are primarily based on income deficiency and family size, food stamp benefits appear to accrue mainly to the neediest families. In this sense the program does achieve significant advantages for the poor. The question remains, however, whether or not the poor would benefit more from a direct income supplement.

One consideration relevant to this question is the cost of administering the food stamp program. Nine percent of total government expenditures on the program go to administrative costs, which provide no direct benefit to food stamp recipients.[6] In addition there is a substantial element of "waste" resulting from the fact that food stamp recipients consume more food products than they would if they were simply given an equivalent value of income supplement. To illustrate this, consider a family of four with a monthly income of $300. This family can purchase $150 worth of food stamps for $83, which increases the family's real income to $367 ($300 + $150 − $83). Forty-one percent of this income ($150 ÷ $367) is spent on food, and this is a much higher percentage of income going to food consumption than this family would probably choose if it had simply been given a $67 monthly income supplement. The difference between what the family spends on food under this program and what it would choose to spend on food if it were given an extra $67 is a measure of "waste" in the food stamp program.

However, food stamp advocates argue that the administrative costs and "waste" from extra food consumption are justified. These additional food expenditures constitute a desirable redirection of spending toward those goods the low-income families need most. Society as a whole may benefit psychologically from the higher nutritional levels thus realized. Unfortunately it does not quite work out this way. A study of recipients' food-expenditure patterns in 1969–70 revealed that no significant improvement in nutritional levels resulted from the program.[7] Total food expenditures by the poor did rise, but much of this increase was directed towards luxury foods (packaged prepared foods) and items of low nutritional value (soda pop and junk foods). There is no evidence that the food stamp program has achieved anything which could not be more economically realized through a program of income supplements.

A number of other in-kind expenditure programs have been subjected to similar scrutiny elsewhere.[8] To avoid repetition at this point, the rest of our discussion will focus on the most prominent income supplement programs—Social Security and the welfare program.

6. Social Insecurity

By far the largest income transfer program in the United States is the Social Security program. Designed initially as low-budget insurance to provide income support to those who lived beyond their years of useful employment, Social Security has expanded to a $45 billion per year program. Although it has the image of a mandatory insurance scheme, there is very little connection between insurance as most people understand it and the operations of Social Security. It comes much closer to being an income transfer program, although the nature of the transfer is widely misunderstood as well. By close examination, we will see that the Social Security system is an income transfer program financed by a highly regressive tax and distributed in a fashion that is at best capricious.

Present law requires tax payments at the rate of 5.85 percent on all wages under $14,100 per year to be paid by workers with a matching contribution by employers. Wages over $14,100 are not taxed. If everyone earned only wage and salary income and no one earned more than $14,000 per year, the tax would be simply proportional. Because wage income over $14,100 and nonlabor income are not subject to the tax, the burden of the payroll tax falls most heavily on low-income groups. A worker earning $10,000 per year, for example, pays Social Security taxes at the rate of 5.85 percent, while an individual with earnings of $32,000 pays taxes amounting to only 2.5 percent of total income. Additionally, there are no personal exemptions enabling low-income workers to escape or reduce their taxes; the 5.85 percent is certain and unavoidable.

Nor should we be fooled by the employers 5.85 percent contribution. Most likely this is borne by the workers also, as firms lower the level of wages offered to compensate for the tax payments they must make. Even if workers are able, through union pressure, to prevent a compensating wage reduction, the tax will simply show up as higher prices for goods and services. In this case the tax is borne, like a sales tax, in proportion to families' consumption levels. No matter which way you look at it, the tax falls most heavily on the low-income groups.

Unfortunately, the relative size of this tax has increased substantially since its inception. In 1974, Social Security taxes collected were equal to more than half of the revenues received from the personal income tax. As the share of total tax revenues accounted for by the Social Security tax increases, the entire tax structure becomes increasingly regressive.

Nor is there much solace for low-income groups on the benefits side. Lower-income workers tend to retire later and die earlier than high-income people, so the expected number of years for which benefits will be received is considerably less for the poor than for the rich. Since the poor usually start work earlier and therefore make contributions for a larger number of years (with no corresponding change in benefits received), this is really adding insult to injury.

But this is only part of the problem on the benefits side. People living on Social Security are permitted to earn from their labor services an annual income up to $2400 without any effect on their benefits. For incomes above this figure, they start losing fifty cents in benefits for every dollar of income earned. This does not apply, however, to those receiving a nonlabor income. Nelson Rockefeller may retire with an income from dividends and interest in the millions and still be eligible for the full Social Security benefit. But whoever chooses to work industriously enough to receive an income in excess of $2400 will be penalized by a reduction in benefits, and it is not too difficult to see that this provision is likely to have the greatest effect on low-income workers.

But the absurdity does not stop here. Not only does the aged worker lose benefits at the rate of 50 percent of income over $2400, on top of this he or she must pay the Social Security tax. The effective rate of taxation due to the Social Security program alone is 61.7 percent for aged workers earning over $2400 per year![*]

In spite of these inequities and inefficiencies Social Security benefits do provide substantial income support. Given the rates of taxation that prevailed in the past and the current level of benefits, a worker who is now retired can anticipate quite a windfall. His net gains are the result of recent increases in benefit and tax payment levels. But if benefits were to continue to increase at present rates up to the year 2000, total Social Security payments would then exceed the gross national product projected for that year. This is, of course, impossible, and in fact it is quite likely that recent trends will have to be

---

[*]This assumes that the worker bears the burden of the employer's contribution. The rate of taxation is then 50 percent (the rate at which benefits are taxed away) plus 5.85 percent (own contribution) plus 5.85 percent (employer's contribution actually borne by the worker).

reversed with payment levels reduced sometime in the future. Because ratio of retired people to the total working population is presently quite small, present payments into the program by workers and employers are sufficient to make the legally mandated payments to the retired. However, with the onset of zero population growth, the age distribution of the population twenty or thirty years from now will be such that a relatively small working population must support the Social Security payments of a large number of retired people. This phenomenon is aggravated by the growing tendency towards early retirement. Faced with the burden of huge Social Security payments for the retired, it is not too clear how the future working generation will react.

This may be hard to grasp if one continues to think of the Social Security program as insurance. Under private insurance plans, your contributions are invested in safe securities, easily convertible to cash upon death or retirement of the policy holder. Private insurance companies are actually required to hold assets equal to all claims outstanding against them. There is no possibility that your benefits will fall short of your payments, because the money you put into premium payments is actually held by the insurance company until your death or retirement. But Social Security does not operate this way. By the standards of private insurance practice, the Social Security program is actuarily unsound. Under existing legislation, claims against the program amount to $500 billion, while the present holdings of the Social Security Fund amount to $1/10$ that amount—enough to cover one year's payments.[9] The *Wall Street Journal* has valued the discrepancy between payments and receipts over the next seventy-five years under reasonable assumption about population and economic growth to be $1.3 trillion. Existing levels of benefits cannot be maintained without substantially increasing the revenues of the program.

The obvious answer seems to be the elimination of the ceiling on incomes beyond which the payroll tax need not be paid. This would eliminate most of the *regressivity* in the system at the same time that the level of revenues would rise. But the program has tied itself into a kind of Gordian Knot: every escalation of the maximum level of payments legally obligates the Social Security Administration to increase the level of benefits for those making the maximum contribution.

As a final illustration of the financial problems of the system, there is the increased burden imposed by the cost-of-living escalators, which have recently provided automatic increases in benefits commensurate with increases in the price level. In principle, indexing of this kind does provide a reasonable means for protecting the elderly from an erosion of their living standards due to inflation. However, in the design of this piece of legislation, increases in benefits were instituted without due regard to where the money would come from. Payments into the Fund were legislated to increase at a rate equal to the inflation rate, but the level of benefits to which current contributors will be entitled will grow more rapidly than prices. At some sufficiently high inflation rate a retired worker can receive more from Social Security than he did on the job!

When so many incongruous sounds are emitted from such a machine, it is time for an overhaul. Reform of the Social Security program will come about only if we stop pretending that it is an insurance program, and take it for what it is: a means for transferring income from the working generation to the retired. Without the social insurance mythology, it is not a difficult matter to design a system of income transfers that avoids many of the problems which have plagued the Social Security program.

7. Encouraging Dependency

One program which does effectively transfer income to the poor is the welfare program, or Aid to Families with Dependent Children (AFDC). This is one of the few programs that is truly a cash-grant program with no elements of an in-kind transfer. Eligibility is determined primarily by income deficiency, and there are no restrictions on how the money is to be spent.

However, serious problems in the design of the system have fostered the growth of dependency. In most states eligibility is limited to families without a male head of household. In many situations, a father is unable to earn a salary that is as great as the payments his family could receive from welfare if he were to desert them. With this kind or incentive system, the number of absent-father families quadrupled between 1961 and 1972, and this fact alone can explain a significant amount of the increase in welfare dependency over this period. A second problem is that because each state sets its own eligibility rules and benefits levels great disparities exist between the programs of various states. In Mississippi, for example, the average monthly payments for a family of four are under $50 while these payments for a comparable family in New Jersey average $265. In general, benefits levels are relatively high in the Northern industrial states, and this encourages migration of welfare families out of the South and rural regions into the already congested Northern cities.

There have been numerous proposals for reforming the welfare system ranging from tracking down deserting fathers to a liberalization of benefits and eligibility requirements. One proposal worthy of our attention is the negative income tax or guaranteed minimum income plan, a proposal which has been advanced in one form or another by politicians of widely divergent ideologies, including Richard Nixon and George McGovern.

A guaranteed minimum income (GMI) plan sets a floor below which incomes will not be permitted to fall. Families earning no income receive cash payments equal to the income guarantee. For families with positive earnings, the cash payments are reduced by some percentage of the amount earned. A hypothetical GMI scheme is illustrated in table one.

This plan calls for an income guarantee of $3000 and a 50 percent rate of taxation or benefit reduction. Every family is guaranteed an income of at least

TABLE I   Hypothetical GMI Plan: $3000 Guarantee and 50% Tax Rate

Earnings	Deduction From Supplement (50% of Earnings)	Income Supplement ($3000 − Deduction)	Total Income (Earnings + Supplement)
$ 0	$ 0	$ 3000	$ 3000
1000	500	2500	3500
2000	1000	2000	4000
4000	2000	1000	5000
6000	3000	0	6000

$3000, even if earnings are zero. For every dollar of income earned government payments are reduced by fifty cents; at an income level of $6000 (the cutoff income level) and higher, no government transfer is paid.

The GMI scheme is an attempt to satisfy three essentially contradictory objectives. First of all, it tries to maintain the greatest possible work incentive by insuring that the total level of income (earnings plus the supplement) rises as earnings increase. From column four in table one, it can be seen that this program does accomplish this goal. In fact, any such scheme with a tax rate of less than 100 percent will insure that incomes rise as earnings rise. This feature preserves the incentive for family heads to seek work and strive for increased earnings.

Prior to some reforms enacted in the AFDC program in the late sixties, every dollar of earnings was offset by a dollar's reduction in government payments—a 100 percent rate of taxation. Obviously the incentive to work was severely impaired under such a system. Presently the rate of taxation under the AFDC program is 67 percent, a rate which provides less of a work incentive than our hypothetical example, but certainly better than what existed prior to the reforms.

The second objective is the elimination or reduction of the extent of poverty. This could easily be accomplished by increasing the income guarantee to the poverty line (approximately $5000 today for a family of four). The program outlined in table one will reduce, but not eliminate, poverty because there will still exist families with earnings under $4000, leaving their total income below the poverty line. Because a large fraction of the poor come from families whose head does work full-time for some part of the year, poverty reduction for this group would, however, be considerable.

Finally, the design of the program has to consider cost. The program must be funded by taxes, which have a multitude of other uses and cannot be raised indefinitely without impairing the work incentives of the taxpayers.

Taken together, these three objectives outline an irresolvable conflict. Poverty elimination can be accomplished by raising the minimum guarantee, but this would substantially increase the cost. It would not only increase the level of benefits to present recipients, but it would also open eligibility to the large number of families in the lower-middle-income range. A reconstruction of table one with a $5000 minimum and the same 50 percent rate of taxation, for example, extends the cutoff income level to $10,000, which is just slightly below the median income level in the country. The higher guarantee could also adversely affect work incentives.

We could get around the problem of extended coverage by increasing the rate of taxation. A program with a $5000 guarantee and a 75 percent rate of taxation, for example, has a cutoff level of income at $6666—only slightly higher than under our original plan. However, such a high rate of taxation coupled with the high guarantee is going to tempt people to stay away from the work force in droves.

Finally, we could maximize the work incentive by reducing the rate of taxation, but this increases coverage to large numbers of new people and magnifies the total cost of the program.

There is no perfect GMI plan that meets all three objectives. The scheme different individuals will find most appealing depends upon the relative value they place on poverty reduction, the maintenance of work incentives, and total taxpayers' cost. This kind of proposal does, however, represent a significant advance over the existing system by eliminating the incentives for family dissolution and providing potentially stronger work incentives.

There is a temptation to try to achieve these goals by a redesign of the existing system. With uniform payments and eligibility standards for all states and coverage extended to all low-income families regardless of sex and employment status of the family's head, the AFDC program would become a GMI program in all essential respects. The rate at which earnings are taxed could be changed from the present 67 percent level if that were found to be injurious to work incentives. The problem with integrating a GMI scheme into the existing network of programs is that there are a number of other benefits programs that have payment schedules and eligibility requirements geared to earnings levels as well. A family earning no wages may be eligible for food stamps, medical care, and public housing benefits, as well as the income transfer. As earnings rise, food stamp benefits are reduced and eligibility for medical aid and public housing subsidies disappears. This together with, say, a 50 percent rate of taxation from the GMI program can lead to a situation where total income including benefits will actually decline as earnings rise. Even if this can be avoided, effective rates of taxation are bound to be extremely high. For the GMI plan introduced under the Nixon Administration, which proposed a 50 percent rate of taxation on the income supplement, the effective rate of taxation taking into account reductions in all benefits payments, was estimated to be 80 percent.[10] Few would argue that this provides much in the way of a work incentive for the poor.

The implementation of a program that holds to the objectives of the GMI scheme would require the elimination of the existing network of benefits programs. The savings provided by their elimination would permit the funding of a large-scale GMI program. Unfortunately, there is little prospect for the implementation of such a plan in the near future. The vested interests which have grown up around the existing benefits programs—agricultural interests, the medical profession, the construction industry—are not eager to have these programs reduced in scope.

Proposals which pay heed to the interests of the beneficiaries of existing programs will necessarily fail to achieve meaningful reform, while radical reforms are scuttled by opponents of change who benefit from the present welfare system. Caught in this political roadblock, we are left with a system which perpetuates poverty, aggravates welfare dependency, encourages family dissolution, and adds to the burdens and frustrations of the taxpayers.

DISCUSSION QUESTIONS

1. From time to time politicians have proposed the adoption of a value added tax (VAT) as a means of increasing government revenues. A VAT imposes a constant percentage tax on the value added to a product at each stage of production. The tax is either absorbed by the producer at each stage of production or passed on to the consumer disguised in the form of a higher price. Which of these is most likely to occur? Why? What effect would such a tax have on the progressivity of our tax system? Why? What are the political advantages of such a tax?

2. How would you design an equitable tax structure? Which taxes would you increase and which would you reduce? Would you add any new ones? Does your tax system retain work incentives?

3. Explain why families in low tax brackets would actually lose money by investing in a tax shelter that benefits the rich.

4. What is the effect of a large Social Security program on the volume of private savings? Why? What effect does this have on investment and hence the rate of economic growth? How could Social Security be redesigned to avoid these effects while maintaining adequate provision for income of the aged?

5. When confronted with the argument that the union sector gains at the expense of the non-union sector, defenders of labor unions respond by advocating total unionization for the whole economy. Would this substantially alter the fact that some labor groups gain at the expense of others? Why? Which groups would gain most by total unionization? Which ones least?

6. What are the features of a sales tax and a payroll tax which make them politically attractive?

chapter **II**

Exploiting National Differences Through Trade

In this chapter we turn our attention to the issue of international trade. We will look into why countries find it advantageous to trade with each other, what impact foreign trade will have on the economy of trading countries, what lies behind many of the arguments for restricting this trade, and what are the effects of these restrictions. In the next chapter we will discuss international finance and such issues as the balance of payments problem and the exchange rates between different countries.

Trade with other countries is an important economic activity for almost all economies. Some countries are almost totally dependent on foreign trade. A country like Kuwait effectively has a one-product economy. That one product is oil, which is very valuable. However, Kuwaitis, just like everyone else, like a little more variety in their consumption bundles than petroleum products can provide, so they trade most of their oil to other countries in return for most of their investment and consumption goods. An economy as large and diverse as that of the United States is much less dependent on international trade. But even the United States finds substantial advantages in trading with other countries. In 1974 the United States imported slightly over $100 billion worth of goods and services from other countries while exporting close to $97 billion worth of commodities. This means that for the year 1974 a little over 7 percent of our total output was traded to foreign countries in order that we could consume many of the products produced in these countries.

There are obviously benefits from international trade, as shown by how extensively it is practiced. Yet almost everyone can give several reasons why they think trade with foreign countries should be restricted, if not in some cases eliminated.

140

1. Arguments for Import Controls

Most people would probably acknowledge that free international trade sounds good as a general principle, but they will then cite reasons why it wouldn't be good for practical policy. Some of these reasons are not based entirely on economic considerations and as such can't be adequately considered with strict economic reasoning. Other criticisms of free trade sink or swim almost entirely on the basis of their economic validity. Unfortunately, some of the most popular economic arguments for restricting trade are almost totally void of substance. Although we will not critically analyze the reasons given in this section for obstructing the free flow of trade until later in the chapter, they should be read with a critical eye.

Perhaps economic considerations alone would dictate that we produce much less of a commodity than we desire and import the remainder. But if reliable supplies of the commodity are critical to the nation's welfare, for example, because of national defense considerations, it may be advisable not to become overly dependent on foreign sources. In situations of this type it is often argued that barriers should be erected against the importation of the good in question in order to encourage domestic production. An example of this is our foreign trade policy regarding petroleum. Obviously petroleum is crucial to the running of our modern industrial economy. A substantial percentage of our petroleum comes from the Middle East, a politically volatile area that hasn't always been reliable. In response to arguments that national security would be weakened if we became too dependent on such foreign sources for crude oil, the United States established an oil import control program in 1959. Until the spring of 1973, when the import controls were significantly relaxed, the program protected our domestic oil industry from foreign competition and undoubtedly resulted in a larger domestic industry than we would have had with free trade.

National security considerations are not the only reason some may find it desirable to restrict trade in order to maintain a large domestic industry of a given type. A country may feel, for example, that it is culturally desirable to maintain a large agricultural population even though much of its food could be imported more cheaply than it can be produced domestically. Obviously arguments of this type can't be evaluated strictly in terms of economic considerations. However, economic analysis is not without its uses in providing information necessary for assessing particular types of trade restrictions.

A strictly economic and widely accepted argument for restricting foreign trade centers around the fear of cheap foreign labor. The United States has the highest paid workers in the world. Obviously the wages workers receive are important consideration in the prices of the commodities they produce. The concern is that foreign firms, with access to low paid labor will be able to produce products much more cheaply than can domestic firms. If this is the case, free trade would allow the foreign firms to compete business away from domestic firms which would result in higher unemployment and lower wages for our labor force. Those who hold this view feel that the only way to keep lower-paid foreign workers from depressing the wages of domestic workers is for our government to restrict imports. These restrictions could take the form of tariffs, which would increase the price we have to pay for foreign goods, or import quotas, which would make it illegal for us to purchase as much of the foreign produced goods as we would like.

When consumers in the United States purchase commodities produced abroad money flows out of the economy. When foreign consumers purchase goods produced in this country, money will flow into the economy. The mechanics of how these imports and exports are actually financed is the topic of the next chapter. But regardless of mechanics, a common feeling is that it is undesirable for money to flow out of the economy and desirable for money to flow in. This attitude is reflected in a statement supposedly made by Abraham Lincoln, "I don't know much about the tariff. But I do know that when I buy a coat from England, I have the coat and England has the money. But when I buy a coat in America, I have the coat and America has the money."

Those who hold this view are likely to find tariffs, or other import restrictions, desirable because they will entice more people to purchase domestically produced goods and therefore keep the money at home. On the other hand encouraging exports is seen as desirable, again because it results in money flowing into the economy rather than out of it. In fact, the federal government currently has a policy of subsidizing companies to export commodities. This policy allows some commodities to be sold to foreign consumers at lower prices than we can purchase them in this country.

Yet another argument in favor of restricting imports has to do with protecting infant industries. It may be the case that a new industry is not efficient enough initially to face the competition of well-established foreign competitors. But given the chance to get started, such an industry may soon become very efficient and be able to offer domestic consumers lower prices than they could get by importing. Obviously this situation would provide a strong case for providing an industry temporary protection against foreign imports.

The infant-industry argument for tariff protection has been an important one in the history of the United States. It was first recommended in 1791 by Alexander Hamilton in his well known "Reports on Manufacturing." Certainly in the early years of our country this was an often used argument for tariff protection.

2. Export Controls

Exports are normally seen as desirable because they cause money to flow into the country, and stimulate domestic employment and business. But some advocates of restricting trade have not ignored what they see as advantages of restraining exports. Foreign demand for domestically produced goods can have the effect of driving up their prices and making them less available to domestic consumers. For example, one of the factors behind the sharp increase in the price of United States beef in 1973 was the increased foreign demand for it. In the summer of 1973 President Nixon, in response to this price increase, imposed a price freeze on beef. This put us in a situation where foreign consumers were willing to pay more for our beef than we could legally pay for it. Without further controls this would have left us with little beef because suppliers found it more profitable to sell abroad. So along with the price freeze on beef, Nixon also applied export controls that restricted foreign sales of this product.

In the last few years there has also been sympathy for restricting the export of other products. For example, in 1973 the price of lumber was increasing rapidly at a time when Japan was buying large quantities of our timber. There was strong support for restricting lumber exports so domestic users would have larger supplies and lower prices. In the same year we imposed temporary restrictions on our exports of soybeans to Japan. In the summer of 1973 soybeans were almost four times as expensive as they had been a year earlier, and again export controls were seen as the best way of protecting United States consumers against the competition of foreign consumers. Wheat sales to the Soviet Union have recently been attacked because they drive up the price of wheat to the U.S. consumer.

We haven't presented an exhaustive list of the arguments that have been advanced for restricting trade with foreign countries. Some of the more common complaints against free trade have been mentioned, however, and these are typical of other arguments against unrestricted trade. Before taking a critical look at these arguments, let us discuss the economic rationale for trade.

3. Mutually Advantageous Trade and Absolute Advantage

Why is trading such a pervasive fact of economic life? Before answering the question we can quickly dismiss a couple of commonly heard explanations for trade. It is often implied that trade occurs when each party to the trade has more of some commodity than they want. The statement, "Trade between the Mediterranean and the Baltic developed when each area produced a surplus of some good," which comes from a popular history text is illustrative. It is undoubtedly true that, in many exchanges, someone unloads an item that he or she is glad to get rid of. Some of the best examples of this are probably found at garage sales. But this isn't typical of most trades, particularly international trade. The commodities we export are things we would prefer to have more of, not less.

Another common misconception about trade is that it normally is motivated by an opportunity for one party to get the best of the other, or profit at the expense of the other. Fortunately this is not generally true. Many people have entered into exchanges that they subsequently regret, but with few exceptions both parties to an exchange see it as an opportunity to improve their well-being. Only the most accomplished incompetent will consistently enter into bad trades.

Why is it that trade results in both parties being better off, in spite of the fact that both give up something they value? The most obvious explanation is that each trades away goods that are of less value to him than those he receives in return. If, for example, U.S. trade with France finds computer equipment going to France in return for fine wines, there is every reason to believe that we placed a higher value on the imported wines than the exported computer equipment, and vice versa for France. Any time two countries (or individuals) place different relative values on commodities, the situation allows both countries to benefit from trade.

Obviously the fact that different countries have different customs and preferences is an important explanation for international trade. But even without this difference we would still find advantages from trade. This arises from the fact that each country is more efficient at producing some commodities than are other countries. For example, Americans love coffee, yet almost no effort is made to grow coffee in the United States.° On the other hand Colombians like to drive automobiles, but they devote few of their resources to auto manufacturing. It's not that we can't grow enough coffee to satisfy our current demands (coffee will grow nicely in Maine if enough resources are devoted to green houses and other artificial environments), or that cars can't be produced in Colombia. But it takes much less effort to grow a ton of high quality coffee beans in Colombia than in the United States, and with the industrial base of the United States it takes less effort to produce automobiles here than in Colombia. Therefore more coffee and automobiles will be produced if we specialize in auto production and Colombia specializes in the production of coffee. Specialization and trade allow each country to have a more desirable combination of cars and coffee than it could have otherwise.

We have just discussed an example where each country has an *absolute advantage* over its trading partner in the production of a commodity. When a country has an absolute advantage in the production of a commodity, it'can produce a given output of that commodity with fewer resources than other countries can. When two countries each have an absolute advantage over the other, the desirability of trade is really quite obvious. But different absolute advantages are not necessary for trade to be desirable. Two countries will normally find it mutually advantageous to trade even if one of them has an absolute advantage over the other in the production of everything.

4. Comparative Advantage and Trade

Let's go back to our example of trade between the United States and Colombia, but with a hypothetical modification. Pretend that the discovery of a new wonder bean has made it possible to grow coffee with less land, labor, and machinery in the United States than it takes in Colombia. Among agricultural

---

°Actually there is some coffee grown in the United States. From two to three thousand acres of coffee is harvested annually in Hawaii.

experts this becomes known as the bean revolution. The United States has an absolute advantage over Colombia in the production of both coffee and automobiles. Now the question is whether or not there is any economic basis for trade between the two countries.

Why import coffee from Colombia when we can produce it more cheaply here? But let's not be hasty. Is coffee production really cheaper in the United States than in Colombia simply because it takes fewer resources to produce a ton of coffee in the United States? Not necessarily. If we are to avoid making errors in our economic reasoning the concept of opportunity cost must be kept in mind. The cost of producing any commodity is measured in terms of the most valuable forgone alternative. Since we are considering only two goods, automobiles and coffee, the cost of producing a ton of coffee is given by the number of automobiles that could have been produced instead. The productive resources that are directed into coffee production could have been used to produce automobiles.* For purposes of our example, let's assume that in the United States the resources necessary to produce a ton of coffee could also be used to manufacture half an automobile. In other words, the cost of producing a ton of coffee in the United States is half the value of an automobile.

We now consider the cost of producing coffee in Colombia. Let's assume that if the resources necessary to produce a ton of coffee in Colombia were used to produce automobiles in Colombia only one-fourth of an auto could be completed. In other words the cost of producing a ton of coffee in Colombia is one-fourth the value of an automobile.

In our example, it is twice as expensive to produce coffee in the United States as it is in Colombia. The United States must give up half an automobile to produce a ton of coffee, whereas one ton of coffee costs Colombia only one-fourth of an auto. This means that although the United States has the absolute advantage in producing coffee, Colombia has the *comparative advantage*. When comparing the productivity of coffee production to automobile production, we find that Colombia is more efficient in coffee production than is the United States. This means that more of both commodities can be produced if each country pursues its comparative advantage, the United States specializing in auto production and Colombia in coffee production. For every car that the United States produces for Colombia's consumption, two tons of coffee will be sacrificed. However with Colombia not having to produce that auto (importing it instead), four tons of coffee can be grown. With no sacrifice in autos we have an extra two tons of coffee. With specialization resulting in more goods, each country will be able to obtain more coffee and autos through specialization and trade than if trade were not allowed. Without the possibility of

---

*This isn't to say that a coffee picking machine could be used to produce automobiles. But the resources that were used to manufacture the coffee picking machine could have been directed into the production of a machine to stamp out fenders or to cast engine blocks.

trade, the country that wanted to consume both coffee and autos would be forced to give up some of the benefits of pursuing its comparative advantage and use productive resources in the production of both commodities.

The benefits from pursuing comparative advantages aren't confined to countries and international trade. We individually make very important decisions based on our personal comparative advantages. Most people seek employment in productive activities where they expect the largest reward, considering such things as income, life style, and training costs. These productive activities are normally very narrow in that each will produce only a few of the many goods and services that individuals like to consume. Individuals do not expect to achieve a desirable bundle of goods and services directly from these productive endeavors. They produce those things in which they feel they have a comparative advantage and trade these things for those commodities they want to consume. The fact that there are intermediate steps involved, with money being received for productive effort and then used to purchase goods, does not change the fact that workers are specializing in the production of a few goods and trading them for other goods.

By specializing in an area where we have a comparative advantage, we are more productive (produce more value for a given expenditure of scarce resources), and can earn a higher income. There is no law against being a jack-of-all-trades and personally producing everything you consume. But few people go that route because they would be very poor indeed.

As a general rule, few people attempt to be a jack-of-all-trades because most of us are very poorly equipped to perform certain tasks. We have absolute disadvantages in many areas. But, just as in the case of trade between countries, even if an individual had an absolute advantage in many activities, it would still pay for that individual to specialize. As an example consider the case of Jack Nicklaus. Most people are aware that Nicklaus is one of the best golfers in the world. But what few have considered is the fact that he could also be one of the world's greatest caddies. If Nicklaus decided to turn caddie, there can be little doubt that he would be the best. Can you think of another caddie who would be better at giving advice on which club to use, how to correct flaws in a swing, and which way a putt will break? Yet, even though Jack Nicklaus has an absolute advantage in golfing and caddying, we don't find him playing in one tournament and caddying in the next. Nicklaus specializes in that activity where his comparative advantage lies, golf.

5. Arguments for Restricting Trade: A Second Look

Now that we have taken a detailed look at the economic advantages of international trade we are in a better position to analyze the arguments put forth for restricting it.

Self-Sufficiency An argument that is ideally suited for many industries which want import restrictions is that national security would be compromised if we became too dependent on foreign supplies. This argument undoubtedly contains some truth and can't be analyzed in traditional economic terms. How self-sufficient we want to be in our consumption of particular commodities is not strictly an economic question. But economic considerations are certainly important, since the cost of reducing our dependence on foreign sources will be weighed against the benefits in any attempt to decide how self-sufficient we should be. Also economic considerations will be important if we are to achieve a given level of self-sufficiency at the least cost. Using these economic considerations it is possible to question some of the specific proposals that are commonly put forth as the means to reduce dependency on foreign countries for important commodities.

Reducing our reliance on foreign governments for petroleum supplies is an important case in point. The Middle-East oil embargo of 1973–74 underscored the desirability of being able to satisfy our demands for petroleum internally. Long before the embargo the oil industry was stressing the importance of minimizing our dependence on oil imports. They emphasized the national security aspects of relying on imports and their arguments were instrumental in convincing the government to establish oil import quotas in the 1950s. These quotas were in effect until May 1973. But were those quotas (a policy designed by the oil industry) the cheapest way of achieving our national security objectives? There are strong reasons for believing they were not.

The import quotas cost the United States consumer dearly. It was estimated that in the late 1960s and early 1970s United States consumers were paying $5 to 7 billion annually more for energy than they would have without import quotas. It's just possible that this was as important to the oil industry as national security. Stockpiling oil or developing productive oil fields and leaving them unexploited, while continuing to import oil from cheaper foreign sources, would have been a more economical means of insuring adequate supplies of oil in our emergency situation. Also, such a strategy would not have encouraged the extensive depletion of domestic oil reserves which was encouraged by the imposition of oil import quotas.

It's worth pointing out in this connection that cutting ourselves off completely from foreign energy sources, as some advocates of "project independence" suggest, would certainly not be the cheapest way to maintain adequate self-reliance in energy. In a study done for the Brookings Institute, economist William Nordhaus estimated that it would cost an extra $8 billion per year to rely completely on domestic energy production as opposed to maintaining an open import policy and storing a full four-year supply of oil.

National security arguments may justify developing a large measure of self-reliance in certain commodities. But many times there are ways of accomplishing this without establishing severe restrictions on imports. National security doesn't have to be pursued with policies that protect domestic industries from foreign competition.

Cheap Foreign Labor   One of the most widely accepted arguments for import restrictions is that without them foreign firms, which have access to cheap labor, would be able to compete unfairly with domestic firms. Fortunately, it simply isn't true that cheap foreign labor puts United States firms at a competitive disadvantage. First there is a reason United States workers are so much better paid than most of their foreign counterparts. That reason is productivity. Because of the capital and highly developed transportation and communication networks they work with, plus their relatively high level of training, United States workers are much more productive than those workers in foreign countries whose wages are very low by United States standards. While we are worried about our ability to compete against cheap foreign labor, a common concern in foreign countries is their ability to compete against highly productive United States workers. When wages are figured on the basis of labor cost per unit of output, it isn't at all clear who has the cheap labor.

Also, the concept of comparative advantage is important in pointing out the fallacy of the cheap foreign labor argument. This argument implies that because of the low wages paid abroad, foreign industries can produce almost all goods more cheaply than the United States. But this ignores the principle of comparative advantage. When any commodity is produced, resources are used that could have gone into the production of other commodities. The cost of producing a commodity has to be measured in terms of the value of this forgone production. Because of this, no country can be the cheapest producer of everything. As in our example of the United States and Colombia, each country will have a comparative advantage in the production of some commodities, which means a comparative disadvantage in the production of others. This is true even if one country requires fewer resources in all productive activities, has lower paid workers, subsidizes exports or what have you. Each country will be better off to specialize in those areas in which it has a comparative advantage and import those commodities in which it has a comparative disadvantage. The fact that money wage rates differ from country to country doesn't affect the benefits of specialization and trade in the slightest.

This is not to say that some of the fears of those who have used the cheap foreign labor argument to support import restrictions are without foundation. Labor groups have traditionally resisted the elimination of trade barriers because of the fear that many jobs would be lost as foreign imports replaced domestic production. In one important respect this is true. Trade restrictions inevitably result in a country devoting resources into productive activities where it doesn't have a comparative advantage. For example, if trade restrictions severely limited the amount of Colombian coffee we could buy (quotas) or significantly increased its domestic price (tariffs), we would probably find it desirable to devote some resources to domestic coffee production. In this situation the advantage of domestic coffee production would be an artificial one. If trade restrictions were then eliminated, consumers would then find it easier to purchase Colombian coffee and those who were employed in the domestic coffee industry would lose their jobs. So to the extent that trade restrictions have encouraged employment in those activities in which we have a comparative disadvantage, the removal of these restrictions will cause people to lose their jobs.

But opening up trade, by allowing us to concentrate more resources in the activities where we have a comparative advantage, will also create new job opportunities. What is commonly seen as the negative consequence of trade, the elimination of some jobs, is really a benefit, the release of labor and resources from inefficient uses so they can be employed more productively.

Obviously shifting productive resources from one activity to another is not without its costs. Many workers will be unemployed, at least temporarily, as they seek other opportunities and develop the skills necessary to pursue them. Some people will find that the jobs they have trained for are no longer in demand. Others will have to move from communities and friends they have known for years. Some will have invested in businesses which suddenly become unprofitable.

These are significant costs and they shouldn't be ignored. However, they are not as great as the costs of devoting scarce resources into productive efforts in which we have a comparative disadvantage. With trade restrictions these costs will continue indefinitely, while the adjustment costs which would accompany the elimination of these restrictions would be temporary. Any time opportunities are taken to use scarce resources more productively, whether through specialization and trade or technological advances, adjustment costs will be incurred. But it's because we have seized these opportunities in the past that our material standard of living has improved, and at the same time the work week and human effort required to produce this wealth has declined. Removing import restrictions would result in some temporary unemployment and hardships, but in the long run it would contribute to a higher standard of living for people in this country and elsewhere.

Keeping Our Money at Home   The argument for restricting imports so we can have the advantage of keeping our money at home requires studied illiteracy in the simplest notions of economics. If we restrict imports it's true that domestic consumers will spend more money in this country. But they will spend it on commodities which, without import barriers, could have been purchased cheaper from foreign countries. Also, just because we are able to get domestic consumers to spend more money in this country doesn't mean that we are getting more money spent at home.

When we import commodities from foreign countries, we pay for these commodities with dollars. The dollars shipped out of the country, however, are not the cost of our imports. The cost of these imports is equal to the value of our domestic products that foreign consumers buy with our dollars. The dollars that flow out will eventually flow back in again. They will flow back as a claim on the goods and services produced in the United States. We would be fortunate indeed if we could pay for the importation of valuable commodities with dollars that would not come back to divert our production away from domestic consumption and into foreign consumption. If we could we would be able to benefit from the productive efforts of others at a cost no greater than that of printing money. As we will see in the next chapter, the United States has enjoyed such a fortunate situation to some extent for a number of years.

Those who worry about keeping our money at home are often concerned about adequate aggregate demand to guarantee a fully employed domestic economy. But any conceivable contractive influence our foreign trade would have could easily be offset with appropriate monetary and fiscal policy without having to deny ourselves the advantages of free trade.

Import barriers don't result in more money being spent in this country. They simply hamper the international trade that would allow us to get more for the money that is spent here.

Protecting Our Aging Infants   It may be true that there are industries in which we would have a comparative advantage once they were established, but they couldn't compete successfully with foreign imports when first getting started. Import restrictions have been seen as a means of protecting such industries in their infancy, allowing them to grow up into strong and viable adults ready to make it on their own in world competition.

Whether this argument provides a strong justification for protection is debatable. Most enterprises will find that the initial period of getting established is relatively rough. It's not unusual for losses to prevail for the first few years in productive ventures that go on to be very successful. We find such ventures being undertaken without governmental help because many investors are concerned with long-term returns on their investments. As a result they are willing to take short-term losses if the long-term prospects appear strong. So it's not necessarily true that an industry in which we have a long-run comparative advantage will require government protection from imports to get started.

But even if you feel that there will be situations where temporary tariff protection is desirable, it's worthwhile to recognize a couple of problems. One problem involves identifying those beginning industries for which temporary protection would provide legitimate social benefits. For sure, all beginning industries that must compete with imported commodities will want protection. To accommodate all, however would involve protecting industries that would be viable without special advantages as well as those that would never be able to compete against imports without protection.

Once import protection has been provided to an infant industry, there is the problem of deciding when the infant has grown up enough to be weaned. We can't expect objective information from the protected industries in making the decision. Import restrictions will invariably result in higher prices for the protected products, and even the most efficient industry can be expected to resist removal of restrictions. What we tend to find is that protection is not eliminated as our infants become of age. In fact, as an industry becomes established it is quite likely to be able to obtain even more favorable protective arrangements. This is largely explained by the responsiveness of the political process to well-organized interest groups.

Export Controls   So far we have discussed only trade restrictions that apply to imports. But what about export barriers that prevent foreign demand from driving up the prices of domestically produced commodities? Aren't these trade restrictions desirable since they help maintain lower prices for domestic consumers?

It's true that by restricting exports we can keep prices lower on some domestically produced goods. But it's also true that such a policy will limit some very desirable options and will result in higher prices for other goods.

The big advantage seen for export controls is that they would allow us to purchase some domestically produced goods at prices lower than what foreign consumers would be willing to pay. Without these controls, producers would increase their shipments to foreign countries in order to take advantage of the higher prices. This would leave a smaller supply and higher prices for domestic consumers. But we must always remember that trade is a two-way process. Selling domestically produced commodities to foreign consumers provides us with foreign currency with which to purchase foreign-produced goods. The more foreign consumers are willing to pay for our goods, the more foreign commodities we can get for our productive efforts. For example, without an export embargo on soybeans in 1973, we could have bought approximately twice as many Sony TV's, Hondas, French perfumes, Peugeot racing bikes, and so on, with a given quantity of soybeans than we could have a year earlier. This is because of the higher prices the Japanese and others were willing to pay. So while the soybean export embargo did help maintain lower prices on soybeans, it prevented us from taking advantage of some attractive bargains on foreign goods.

Also export controls tend to divert resources away from activities in which we have a comparative advantage. With export controls preventing us from taking advantage of some attractive exchanges on foreign goods, we will end up devoting more resources to the domestic production of commodities that could have been obtained cheaper through trade. By motivating an inefficient allocation of our scarce resources, export controls are just as wasteful and pernicious as import controls.

6. David Beats Goliath in the Political Arena

Countries will be better off if they devote their efforts and resources to those activities in which they have a comparative advantage and trade for the bundle of goods they want to consume. Trade restrictions, by making it more difficult to get desirable goods from foreign sources, cause countries to devote resources to the production of commodities they would like to consume but in which they have a comparative disadvantage. As a result, trade restrictions make a country worse off. Then why has there always been a great deal of political pressure for trade restrictions?

To answer this question we have to recognize that the advantages of free international trade are not uniformly distributed throughout the population. As consumers we all benefit from free trade by being able to purchase goods from the most efficient producers. The competition fostered by free trade not only forces producers to specialize in those areas where they have a comparative advantage, but it also makes sure that the resulting efficiencies are passed on to consumers in lower prices and higher quality. But what's good for all of us as consumers isn't always welcomed with open arms by particular producer groups. For example, try to convince someone working in our textile industry of all the advantages of having the price of textiles drop as a result of opening their industry up to foreign competition. We're all in favor of lower prices for the things we buy, but lower prices for what we sell is an entirely different matter. Representatives of domestic industries that face foreign competition consistently urge legislation that will increase tariff duties on competitive imports. Of course, consumers will have a vested interest in urging the political process to resist such increases.

How does the political process respond to these conflicting interests, one favoring import restrictions on particular products and the other favoring free trade? If we think of political decision being made in response to the majority, it is clear that the free trade sympathizers would carry the day on each tariff proposed. Those who consume the product of a particular industry will far outnumber those who work for it. We might expect that consumer interests would outweigh producer interests, and legislation to restrict imports would be defeated. Unfortunately, this conjecture doesn't fit the facts. By far the majority of the goods imported into this country are subject to tariffs or other trade restrictions. While tariff duties have fallen in recent years (from an average of approximately 60 percent of value in 1930 to approximately 12 percent today), the number of nontariff restrictions have increased. In the area of import restrictions the political process has been more responsive to the minority interests of producers than to the majority interests of consumers.

This shouldn't be surprising if we recall our discussion in chapter six. In that chapter we saw that the political process is often much more responsive to small interest groups than to large ones. The reason for this phenomenon, concentrated benefits versus dispersed costs, is particularly applicable here. Those who work for a given industry have a major interest in its ability to attract customers and charge high prices. Restrictions on trade that reduce competition from foreign sources will mean more employment, better wages, and higher profits for the protected industry. Therefore we can be sure that members of a particular industry will be aware of any legislative proposal to protect their industry from imports and will work for its enactment. Such a well-defined group with a strong common interest is relatively easy to organize for exerting political pressure. Elected representatives will be made aware of the fact that their position on protective legislation will be watched with great interest by the industry group. Politicians will know that a vote in favor of protection will be remembered and appreciated by those who benefit.

But what about all those consumers who will end up paying higher prices if the trade restriction is passed? To what extent can we expect them to lobby against protection? Probably very little. Each consumer's income is spread over thousands of different commodities. An import restriction on one of them, while increasing its price, will normally not have much impact on the individual consumer. As a result few consumers will feel their welfare threatened by a specific piece of trade-restricting legislation. Few will even be aware of such legislation or how their political representatives voted on it; even if they were, they would be unlikely to take any action.

Assume, for example, that a consumer was informed that the United States tulip industry was about to push through an exorbitant tariff that would double the price of tulips. Do you think he or she would start an anti-tulip-tariff campaign? Even if this consumer has a fetish for tulips (a tulip freak), the cost of starting such a campaign would surely outweigh the probable benefits. For most people the perceived benefits of resisting such a tariff, even if they thought this resistance would be effective, wouldn't justify the cost of a stamp and the time to write their representatives in Congress.

An example of the success of a relatively small special-interest group to restrict domestic use of foreign services is given by our maritime unions. Over the years they have been able to get political support for legislation protecting the United States maritime fleet against foreign competition. For example, in 1920 the Jones Act was passed, which made it illegal for any ship other than ones built in the United States and owned by a citizen of the United States to carry cargo between any two points in the United States. This law is still on the books and currently means that United States shipping costs along these United States routes are approximately twice as high as those charged by foreign flag ships. Considering just the cost of transporting oil from Texas and Louisana to the east-coast states, the Jones Act costs United States consumers at least $100 million every year.[1]

Because the benefits of such protective legislation are concentrated on a relatively few well-organized groups (members of maritime unions, ship owners, and ship builders), these groups have been very active and effective at influencing political decision makers. In December of 1974 Congress responded to their influence and passed the Oil Cargo Hauling bill, which requires that at least 20 percent of all oil imports be carried on United States tankers, with the percentage going to 30 percent by 1977. Despite the fact that the United States Department of Commerce estimated that this bill would cost United States consumers an additional $315 million a year, it got the vote of many legislators who claim to be for consumer protection.

Of course legislators can pass themselves off as advocates of consumer interest while voting for legislation like the Oil Cargo Hauling bill or the Jones Act simply because the cost of any one of these acts is small to the individual consumer. Few individuals are even aware of the Jones Act, for example, and those that are aware of it cannot see any personal benefit from lobbying against it.

This reasoning does not explain the enactment of all trade barriers. In particular, it is hard to argue that export restrictions will be fought for by the industry primarily affected, the one doing the exporting. An industry will welcome the opportunity to enlarge its market by selling abroad and can be expected to resist efforts to restrict exports. So export restrictions, which have been justified as a means of preventing foreign demand from increasing prices for domestic consumers, cannot be explained by our argument that small industry groups exert more political influence than consumers. But our argument is consistent with the fact that export controls have been infrequent and insignificant relative to the incidences of import restrictions, and often not long-lived. Export controls on beef and soybeans, for example, did not last long. Our argument is also consistent with the fact that the export subsidies are more prevalent than are export restrictions. In the United States some corporations can defer federal taxes on half the income they earn from exports. In 1974 this subsidy program cost the United States Treasury approximately $1 billion in revenue.[2] Obviously a governmental policy of export subsidies will be more to the liking of exporting industries than will restrictions. And in the political arena the small-interest group has the advantage over the Goliath of consumer interest.

7. On to International Finance

In order to consider the basics of the economics of international trade, we have been talking as if goods were being exchanged for goods. Considering only ultimate effects there is little harm in this. However, it ignores some important and interesting issues concerning the financing of international trade.

We all know that few exchanges actually involve trading one commodity directly for another. Normally there is an intermediate step that involves trading a commodity (it may be human labor) for money and then exchanging the money for another commodity. This intermediate step can be an important influence on the process of exchange. This is especially true in the case of international exchange. When United States consumers buy a commodity made in Germany, they want to pay for it with dollars, but the sellers want to be paid in marks. Obviously some mechanism has to exist for determining the value of dollars in terms of marks and for allowing dollars to be exchanged for marks. The issues involved in financing international exchanges come under the heading of international finance and is the topic of the next chapter.

DISCUSSION QUESTIONS

1. Our discussion seemed to indicate that a country either had a comparative advantage in the production of a good (in which case the good would be domestically produced and not imported) or a comparative disadvantage (in which case the good would be imported and not be produced domestically). In the real world we observe that a country will both produce and import the same type of good. Explain how this fact is consistent with the principle of comparative advantage. Could trade restrictions explain this observation in cases where it couldn't be justified by comparative advantage?

2. It seems widely accepted that selling wheat to the Russians is inflationary since it increases the price of wheat. Formulate a rebuttal to this point of view, arguing that selling wheat to Russia actually has the effect of reducing inflation.

3. Occasionally an ad will appear in the local newspaper attempting to convince the area residents to support their local merchants by making their purchases close to home. Do you think such ads have much impact on consumers? Do you feel there would be a net advantage to the community if everyone made a real effort to spend their money locally?

4. A French economist once wrote a satire about candlemakers who petitioned the legislature to impose a tariff on the use of sunlight since the abundance of sunlight kept employment down in the candle industry. In principle, is this any different from imposing a tariff on French wines or Japanese cameras? Explain how either tariff would have the effect of making our economy less productive.

5. Some have argued that we need trade restrictions to protect our country against "dumping." By dumping we mean that other countries are selling their goods in this country below their cost of production. Can you think of any reason why, rather than being fearful of this practice, we should applaud and encourage it? Do you think there is really much danger of a widespread movement among foreign countries to dump on us?

chapter 12

Deep Float:
The Economics of
International Finance

Have you wondered why foreign cars have become so expensive in recent years? If you have traveled abroad in the last several years, did you notice how expensive tourism has become for Americans? Did you ever wonder why so many Japanese suddenly have the financial means to travel in the United States? All of these events are the direct result of a fundamental change in our system of international finance that has taken place since August of 1971. An understanding of this change is often obscured by the language of international finance—an elegant tongue that includes such nice sounding terms as devaluation, Eurodollars, capital flows, and floating currencies. You will meet some of these creatures in this excursion through the world of international finance, and by the end of this chapter you should have a pretty good idea of what this all means and how it may be important to you individually.

International trade requires particular financial institutions. In particular, trade between countries requires a mechanism for expressing the value of one currency in terms of another. If you want to purchase an Italian Fiat with dollars, the manufacturer will want to know what those dollars are worth in lira. The manufacturer must convert your dollars into the kind of money needed to pay Italian workers, suppliers of raw materials, and so forth. If it is known that one dollar will exchange for 600 lira and the total cost of production (including a nice return to the entrepreneur) is 1.8 million lira, then the cost to you will be $3000. For $3000 you get the car, the dollars are exchanged for lira, the Italian workers get their wages and the manufacturer takes home a profit.

If the business of international finance were simply a matter of reading *exchange rates* between currencies from some table, we could wrap up this discussion right here. But how is this exchange rate established, and what, if anything, could cause it to change? This sort of question is connected with the particular institutions and regulations that govern international finance. The issue is made even more complex by the fact that every country is pursuing different economic policies and experiencing different sorts of structural economic changes. As the western world has come to realize in the last several years, the factors underlying international trade are not static. They change dramatically over time. These changes are reflected in the institutions of international finance, such as exchange rates between currencies, and most importantly they have repercussions on our own daily economic lives.

Our first consideration is to measure how we stand with respect to the rest of the world in terms of money flowing in and out of the country. This is usually referred to as the *balance of payments*. Thankfully we do not need to get involved in the details of balance of payments accounting; we will merely outline the most important items that involve money flows in or out of a country. Following this will be a discussion of the systems which have been employed throughout history to settle international transactions and some of the special institutions that characterize the world of international finance today.

1. Balance and Imbalance

Up to now our discussion of international economics has focused primarily on the trading of goods and services between countries. In the sense that merchandise trade is the largest single item among international transactions, this is appropriate, and most considerations of international finance are concerned with facilitating this activity. But not all transactions between countries necessarily involve the flow of goods and services; a substantial fraction of financial activity across international boundaries takes the form of investment. By 1973, for example, more than $100 billion worth of capital in other countries had been accumulated by United States citizens and corporations. At the same time foreigners have made considerable investments in the United States, particularly in the form of loans to the United States government. Such investments necessarily involve some means of financing, just as is the case for exports and imports of goods.

In order to facilitate trade and investment, a system of international finance must establish an acceptable medium of exchange or "money" for financing international transactions. Gold, for example, has served as a means for settling international transactions for much of the world's commercial history. At times the currencies of particular countries have also been employed as international exchange media. We will refer to those foreign currencies that are acceptable in financing international transactions as *foreign exchange*. A country's holdings of gold and foreign exchange are referred to as *foreign reserves*.

Foreign reserves must be sacrificed by a country whenever one of its citizens or its government spends money abroad. When the United States imports goods from other countries or when Americans travel abroad, these activities must be paid for with gold or foreign exchange. Likewise the purchase of stock in a foreign corporation by a United States firm must be financed by giving up foreign reserves. A grant by the United States government or private citizens to foreigners will also involve the flow of "money" out of this country. Any such transaction is referred to as a *debit item* in our balance of payments accounts.

For the most part these are offset by *credit items*, which are transactions financed by the flow of foreign reserves into the United States. Our exports to other countries, income U.S. corporations receive on their foreign investments,° and investments foreigners make in the United States are the major credit items in our accounts. Any such transaction obligates a foreign citizen or country to part with some amount of international exchange media, and this involves the flow of foreign reserves into this country.

We are accustomed to hearing or reading about a deficit or surplus in our balance of payments. Simply put, a *deficit* in the balance of payments arises if we are spending more abroad than foreigners are spending in the United States. This deficit must be financed by borrowing from foreigners or by selling whatever holdings of gold or foreign currencies are held in the United States. If West Germany, for example, lends the United States one billion German marks, we will be able to make expenditures abroad in excess of what foreigners are making in the United States by an amount of one billion marks. If we are unable to arrange such a deal, but we have holdings of one billion marks accumulated from past years, we may use these holdings to spend in excess of what foreigners want to spend here. Finally, if this is not possible, we may sell gold abroad in exchange for foreign currencies, which we may then use to make foreign expenditures.

In the opposite case, when foreigners desire to spend and invest more in the United States than we want to spend and invest abroad, we say our balance of payments is running a *surplus*. With a surplus on our account, we will accumulate foreign reserves or make loans to other governments. If the balance of payments account is in either a surplus or a deficit, it is said to be in *disequilibrium*. If there is neither a surplus or a deficit, we have a balance of payments *equilibrium*.

The alarming thing about a deficit is that we cannot always expect the arrangements used to finance it to last indefinitely. Certainly we, and other

---

°Investment activity complicates things a bit. When a United States corporation uses some of its domestically earned profits to make a foreign acquisition, this act involves the flow of money out of the United States and hence is a debit item. If the investment funds are obtained in the financial markets of the country in which the investment is made, no country's balance of payments is affected. After the investment has been made, profits sent back to the United States become a credit item. If they are reinvested in the foreign enterprise, again there is no capital flow across national boundaries and hence no effect on the balance of payments.

countries for that matter, have only limited holdings of gold and foreign currencies. In addition we cannot count on foreigners to lend us their currencies without end. For the most part countries can expect to finance only temporary deficits through foreign borrowing or gold and currency sales. Other corrective measures must be adopted in the longer run.

Notice, however, that if we were able to continue a deficit in our balance of payments, we could increase our economic welfare at the expense of other countries. A deficit means that we are spending and investing more abroad than foreigners want to spend and invest in the United States. We, as consumers, benefit from imports, while exports are the unfortunate, but usually necessary, cost of securing imports. Exports are the flow of goods out of the country, and hence they detract from the stock of goods available to satisfy our consumption desires. Imports, on the other hand, increase the volume of goods available for our own consumption and hence raise our standard of living. Consequently a deficit can be looked upon as desirable because it enables us to attain a higher standard of living. If foreign governments could be convinced to lend to us indefinitely, we could continue to make expenditures and investments abroad without incurring the costs of giving up U.S. goods to foreigners. As we will see shortly, the United States had managed to achieve just such a position for a number of years, primarily because of the institutional arrangements that existed for settling international transactions.

2. The Golden Calf

For most of recorded hisory gold has been the universal medium of exchange. This history, more than any intrinsic properties of the metal itself, accounts for the lasting sacredness of gold in our various systems of finance.

Prior to the establishment of the Federal Reserve system, the United States and most of our trading partners were on a system of international finance most closely akin to the *gold standard*. For the hundred years following 1834, except for a period extending from the Civil War to 1879, the United States Treasury maintained a commitment to buy and sell one ounce of gold at the fixed price of $20.67. In addition to this, gold was an important component of the monetary base prior to 1914. The Treasury issued notes that were fractionally backed by and redeemable for gold, and these Treasury notes as well as gold in private circulation could be used as reserves by private commercial banks in the creation of bank notes and deposits. Gold was the foundation of the whole monetary system. In order to maintain convertibility between Treasury notes and gold, the Treasury had to restrict its issue of notes according to its holdings of gold; banks in turn were limited in their deposit and bank note creation activities according to their holdings of gold and Treasury notes. The total supply of money—gold, Treasury notes, bank notes, and deposits—was thus controlled by the domestic supply of gold.

Two conditions establish a gold standard for a country, and prior to 1914 the

United States met them both: the value of the dollar was legally defined in terms of a fixed quantity of gold, and the domestic money supply was controlled by the quantity of gold in the country. Because the currencies of our trading partners were also valued in terms of gold, exchange rates were fixed. There was a great deal of certainty about the terms at which international trade could take place.

The second condition—letting a country's money supply be determined by the quantity of gold held in that country—established an automatic mechanism for achieving an equilibrium in the balance of payments. Suppose, for example, that the United States was running a persistent deficit in its balance of payments arising from a surge in demand for French wines, German Porsches, and Scotch whiskey. This deficit would have to be financed by the sale of gold to foreigners in order to obtain the foreign currencies necessary to purchase these products. Gold would be drained from the coffers of the Treasury and from the vaults of commercial banks causing the money supply in the United States to shrink. A shrinkage in the money supply would ultimately lead to a reduction in the general level of prices in the United States. At the same time our exports of gold to our trading partners would add to their gold holdings and hence to their own money supplies, and this would cause their price levels to increase. United States goods would become relatively inexpensive because of both of these changes, and consumers, both American and foreign, would be encouraged to purchase United States products rather than foreign products. As long as gold continues to leave the United States for foreign countries, this process would continue, lessening the magnitude of our balance of payments deficit until equilibrium were restored.

This process as just described has a mechanical beauty like that of the movements of the celestial spheres. Unfortunately in practice the gold standard never worked so smoothly. You might recall that a number of business depressions in the pre-Federal Reserve period originated with the movement of gold out of the country in anticipation of some political or economic crises. In any case the immediate effect of such gold outflows was not a smooth downward adjustment in the price level, but rather an unpleasant and sometimes abrupt contraction of business activity and employment. Those nasty lags in adjustment, which have plagued our attempts to deal costlessly with inflation in modern times, also spoiled the smooth adjustment process of the gold standard. A reduction in the money supply, caused in this case by a shrinking gold stock, led first to a reduction in output and employment and only later to a reduction in prices. The reliance on a system that required frequent and possibly severe disruptions of normal business conditions was too costly a means for achieving a balance of payments equilibrium.

Even when these adjustments could be made smoothly, there were significant social costs arising out of the persistent changes in the price level forced on the economy by the rules of the gold standard. For the twenty-year period following our resumption of the gold standard in 1874, there were few discoveries or little mining activity to increase the world's supply of gold. At the same time there was a fairly strong growth in the level of real output, at least in the United States. With a relatively fixed supply of money, this greater volume of business activity could only be financed at lower average prices. The gold standard forced the United States to adhere to a restrictive monetary policy at a time when expanding business activity called for an expansionary policy. The result was a severe and persistent deflation, or reduction in the general price level, which imposed significant hardship on the debtor classes in society.

By the beginning of the twentieth century, the desirability of a domestic monetary policy independent of external or foreign trade considerations had become obvious. Most countries, including the United States, began to abandon the strict gold standard, and there was an evolution toward an alternative system. In the United States the establishment of the Federal Reserve system in 1914 loosened the link between the money supply and our gold holdings. The Fed was permitted, and during the twenties demonstrated its willingness, to compensate for gold flows by offsetting open market operations. When gold was flowing into the United States and tending to cause an undesired monetary expansion, the Fed simply sold some of their holdings of government securities, thereby withdrawing some money from private circulation. The opposite kind of action could be taken at a time of gold exports, and in this way the domestic money supply could be determined entirely independent of international financial considerations.

The establishment of the Federal Reserve began the evolution of a new system of international finance. World War I was followed by several years during which countries did not adhere to fixed relationships between their currency values and gold. Exchange rates between currencies were therefore flexible. This brief period of flexible exchange rates was brought to an end by agreements reached at Genoa, Italy, establishing fixed values of every currency in terms of gold. However, the widespread economic crises of the thirties led many countries to abandon these fixed currency-price agreements, and the instabilities accompanying World War II prevented the establishment of a new international financial system until 1944. The agreements reached at Bretton Woods, New Hampshire, in 1944 reestablished the *gold exchange standard* of the Genoa agreements. This system called for fixed exchange rates between currencies, but each country was permitted, within bounds, to pursue an independent monetary policy. The gold exchange standard, together with the particular institutions set up at the Bretton Woods Conference, provided the framework for financing the tremendous expansion in trade that took place after World War II.

Under a gold exchange standard the price of every currency was set in terms of a certain quantity of gold as was the case with the strict gold standard. In actuality the Bretton Woods agreement assigned to the dollar a primary role in the new system. The dollar's value was set in terms of gold (at $35 per ounce), and the value of every other currency was specified in terms of dollars (for example, one German mark = $.25). This amounted to having every currency defined in terms of gold, but emphasizing the key role of the dollar in the system. Under the gold exchange system countries were not required to permit their money supplies to contract and expand with gold movements, but they were obligated to undertake whatever policies were needed to maintain the fixed exchange rates between currencies.

3. Wheelings and Dealings in the Gold Exchange System

While the general characteristics of a gold exchange system have already been defined, it is useful to direct our analysis towards the particular institutions that arose during the 1944–71 period to make the system work. With domestic money supplies determined independently of gold flows, there was no longer a mechanism to automatically maintain an equilibrium in a country's balance of payments. With its money supply determined independently of gold flows, a country could run a deficit in its balance of payments year after year without being forced to take the traditional medicine of the gold standard, namely, a monetary contraction. Theoretically this country could continue to run a deficit until its holdings of gold and foreign currencies were depleted, at which point it would no longer be able to meet its obligations to foreign creditors—the country would be in a state of bankruptcy. Naturally institutions and procedures were set up to prevent such a possibility. This was an attempt to achieve the benefits of the gold standard system without its costs.

The guiding principle of the 1944–71 financial system was that countries facing a disequilibrium in their balance of payments should take corrective action in the form of an expansion or contraction of their domestic economies. Deficit countries were obligated to undertake contractive fiscal and monetary policies which would reduce prices in those countries relative to prices in other countries. This would increase the demand for the deficit countries' products and reduce the tendency for deficit countries to import from other countries. The opposite changes would take place in surplus countries. Thus the traditional medicine of the gold standard was prescribed, but in a form that was intended to be less painful and a dosage that was more controllable than before. Countries were to be permitted time in initiating corrective policies, and responses needed to be made only if a country faced what appeared to be a long-term fundamental disequilibrium. Temporary deficits arising from, say, speculative flights of money out of a country would not be permitted to influence a country's money supply, and a degree of domestic monetary tranquility above that permitted under the gold standard was possible.

The institution that was to have made all this possible was the International Monetary Fund (IMF), an organization of the major trading nations of the world. Each country participating in the system was assigned a quota stipulating a quantity of that country's currency that would be pledged to the Fund. The IMF thus possessed a substantial holding of the currencies of every major trading country participating in the system—dollars, marks, pounds, francs, and so on—which could be lent to countries facing a deficit in their balance of payments. A deficit country wishing to postpone or ease into a domestic economic contraction thus had several means at its disposal for financing its deficit: it could use whatever holdings of foreign currencies and gold it might possess; it could attempt to borrow foreign currencies from other governments; or it could borrow foreign currencies from the IMF. The extent to which a country could pursue a domestic policy independent of international financial considerations was determined by its ability to secure funds for financing a deficit from any of these sources. The main accomplishment of the IMF was to permit countries with small foreign currency holdings and few credit facilities to finance a temporary deficit by borrowing from the Fund. Loans from the IMF were tendered with the reminder that the country was obligated to adopt domestic policies which would correct the deficit.

The system had several advantages over the pure gold standard. A country's domestic money supply did not have to respond to temporary financial changes arising from political or economic uncertainties. The potential effects of such temporary deficits could be neutralized by appropriate monetary policies. Persistent or fundamental deficits did require corrective action, but countries were permitted sufficient time to enact contractive policies so as to minimize the costs of adjustment. The monetary contraction did not have to be so severe as to induce a business depression as was sometimes the case under the gold standard; all that was required was fiscal and monetary restraint, which would hold the rate of price increase in the deficit country below that of its trading partners. Finally, the world's total supply of money was not dictated by the quantity of gold held by various monetary institutions. Each country was free to increase or decrease its own money supply, within the constraints imposed by the balance of payments. Monetary expansions required to finance an increased volume of business did not need to await new gold discoveries; deflation and inflation became the result of conscious policy actions rather than the product of luck and innovation.

The achievements of the gold exchange system, as supervised by the IMF, were measurable and dramatic. This system, augmented by the Marshall Plan assistance extended by the United States to European countries, nurtured the recovery of economies that had been devastated by World War II. Economic recovery required the importation of goods in a volume that exceeded the capacity of these devastated economies to produce goods for export. The persistent deficits of these countries had to be financed by loans from the United States and the IMF until recovery became sufficiently advanced. So successful was the recovery that these countries, once dependent upon the United States for financial aid, became serious competitors for our markets.

The other major accomplishment of the system was the tremendous growth in world trade, which it fostered. During the fifties and sixties the volume of international trade expanded at the rate of 7 percent per year, reaching a level of $300 billion by the end of the sixties. For over two decades the international financial system was able to accommodate and stimulate this phenomenal growth in world trade.

4. The IMF Boondoggle

The record shows that the United States during this period was possibly the main beneficiary of the IMF system. Our exports and imports quadrupled during the fifties and sixties, as we participated evenly in the growth in world trade. But more importantly, because of the position of the United States dollar in the IMF system, our net gain was considerably higher than what might be indicated by our growth in foreign trade. The United States began the postwar era in a financial position that was clearly much stronger than that of our major trading partners. Prior to and during World War II, large holdings of gold were transferred from Europe to the United States because of the greater uncertainties facing European countries. The threat of war and political turmoil induced many people to transfer their wealth to the safer environment across the Atlantic. In order to make investments in the United States, European currencies had to be exchanged for gold, which was then shipped to the United States to finance the acquisition of American assets. By the end of the war, United States gold holdings were valued at $20 billion, and they amounted to somewhat more than half of the total gold holdings of monetary authorities throughout the world. Our vast holdings of this key international money were obviously important in the world's assessment that the dollar was as good as gold. Also the United States exited from the war with its productive capacity virtually unscathed, while the economies of most of our major trading partners had been ravished. The demand for American products was strong, while the ability of Europe and Japan to produce for export to the United States was extremely weak. Consequently the United States was running whopping surpluses on our balance of payments during the late forties, which incidentally translated into increased United States holdings of gold.

Due to these factors the United States dollar held the position of a *key currency* in the system. The dollar was in strong demand because of the goods it could purchase. It was as good as gold because of our huge gold holdings, and it served as an alternative to gold in financing international transactions. Furthermore, with the total world holdings of gold in the hands of foreign governments in relatively short supply, the United States dollar was the only means available to finance the increasing volume of trade. To accommodate the growth in trade, the United States supplied increasing quantities of dollars to foreign countries, at first in the form of grants and loans under the Marshall Plan, later in the form of United States balance of payments deficits.

A number of factors contributed to the conversion of this country from a surplus into a deficit position. Undoubtedly the most important factor was the

recovery of the economies of European countries and Japan from the devastation of the war and their consequent increase in productivity. By the late fifties
these countries were cutting seriously into many of our important export
markets while increasing their volume of sales to the United States. Add to this
the burgeoning expenditures by this government on foreign alliances and
military escapades such as the war in Vietnam, as well as nonmilitary grants-
in-aid to other countries. Finally consider the boom in foreign investment made
by United States corporations in foreign countries in search of higher profits
abroad. In ever-increasing amounts United States citizens, corporations, and
the federal government were spending more abroad than foreigners were
spending in the United States. Because exchange rates were fixed by the 1944
agreement and fundamental structural changes had occurred in various economies since the end of World War II, there was a persistent disequilibrium in
the United States balance of payments with respect to the rest of the world.
Because it was possible to purchase foreign currencies with dollars at the
relatively cheap terms established in 1944, foreign products themselves were
relatively inexpensive and the volume of United States expenditures abroad
grew tremendously in response.

These deficits were financed in part by sales of some of our gold holdings, but
primarily by the willingness of foreign citizens and governments to hold dollars.
Because the dollar continued to be a key currency in the world financial system,
foreigners still desired to acquire dollars to finance the ever-growing volume of
international trade. Our excessive level of public and private expenditures and
investment abroad was financed simply by foreign acquisitions of U.S. dollars.
Goods and services we purchased from foreigners were paid for with dollars,
and the dollars remained in the hands of foreign corporations and governments,
who used them for international trade. In effect we were able to finance our
higher level of expenditures and investments through the creation of dollars or
new dollar deposits—obviously a fairly costless activity! As long as foreigners
wanted to hold dollars or dollar deposits for foreign trade purposes, we could
get away with running deficits in our balance of payments. This was the best
something-for-nothing scheme since water was turned into wine.

Our trading partners, however, soon caught on to this boondoggle, and they
began to pressure the United States into curbing its extravagant ways. By the
sixties our balance of payments deficits were so large that foreign holdings of
dollars and dollar deposits were increasing to levels beyond what was desired
for international trade purposes. The dollar glutted the foreign exchange
markets.

At this point the member countries of the IMF were in a peculiar bind. They
recognized that the United States was able to increase the level of expenditures
and investment through the costless creation of new dollar deposits. We were
thus able to improve our standard of living by increasing our imports, while
holding down the level of exports at their expense. At the same time some
increase in foreign holdings of dollars was desired to satisfy the financial needs

for the growing volume of international trade. In addition, from the point of view of the export industries in the other countries, measures taken by the United States to curb imports would not be desirable. These industries gained by our profligate ways and hence were reluctant to encourage any change that would cut into their sales to the United States. Finally it was recognized that because of the dollar's role in the system as a key currency, a change in the relation between the dollar and the other currencies in the system would undermine the gold exchange system as it had existed since 1944. The ultimate solution—a change in the exchange rate between the dollar and other currencies to make the dollar cheaper—was shunned as long as possible. Not only would such action destroy the system that had prevailed so successfully since 1944, but also it would leave most countries holding a large bag of dollars worth considerably less than what they had paid for them. It is not hard to see why the final solution was put off until the last possible minute.

5. Crises and Speculation

The obvious solution in this case, and in any other case of fundamental disequilibrium, was to change exchange rates to make it cheaper for foreigners to purchase United States products and make investments in this country, while at the same time increasing the costs of such activities by Americans in other countries. In 1965, for example, it was possible to buy four German marks with one United States dollar. With this exchange rate you could buy a bratwurst and a beer for thirty-five cents, (1.40 marks), a dinner at the student cafeteria for fifty cents (2.00 marks), a dormitory room with board for a month for $60.00 (240.00 marks), and a VW beetle for $1200 (4800 marks—purchase price in Germany). Change the exchange rate to three marks to the dollar, and the prices become forty cents for the beer and wurst, sixty-seven cents for the student meal, $80 for room and board, and $1600 for the VW. Consumption of these products by American citizens is going to be significantly reduced by this change in exchange rates. At the same time, of course, there is a corresponding reduction in the price of the dollar in terms of marks and hence in the price of United States products faced by Germans. Consumption of United States products by Germans rises as the United States consumption of German products declines, restoring an equilibrium in the balance of payments. This action is referred to as a *depreciation* of the dollar with respect to the mark (or an *appreciation* of the mark with respect to the dollar).

Fixed exchange rates had been quite successful in creating the financial climate that stimulated the tremendous growth in trade during the 1944–71 period. There was naturally a great reluctance to give up a winning system. Barring the possibility of currency depreciations or appreciations, other methods were available to deficit countries to restore a balance of payments equilibrium. There was always the classic remedy of the gold standard: initiate contractive fiscal and monetary policies thereby stagnating business activity until prices in the deficit country fall relative to those in other countries. The economic costs and the political limitations of such a policy should be fairly obvious. Deficit countries thus sought other relatively "painless" ways of discouraging expenditures abroad and encouraging foreign expenditures in the deficit country. The balance of payments battles fought in the United States and Great Britain are rich with examples of these "painless" policies: limitations on tourist travel and the amount of money travelers can take out of the country; constraints on the foreign investment activities of business firms; tying foreign aid grants to purchases in the deficit country; increasing tariffs and other trade barriers; providing export subsidies; requiring the use of domestically owned merchant ships for particular activities; and "Buy American" or "Buy British" campaigns. The main characteristic of any such "painless" solution is that it curbs the kinds of activities that we wanted our system of international finance to encourage in the first place.

Another feature of such controls is that they are seldom effective. In both Great Britain and the United States, trade and investment controls did little to stem the tide of balance of payments disequilibrium. Piecemeal controls can do little to offset the effects of long-term structural changes in different economies. Also, humans have a limitless ability to circumvent controls and negate their intended effects. In 1964 the British pound, once proud ruler of the seas, was depreciated; in August 1971 so was the dollar.

In addition to control programs, postponing the currency depreciations disrupted international trade and investment in other ways. A nation fighting off the pressures of depreciation falls prey to those bad guys of international finance, the speculators. When it becomes obvious that a country is under pressure to depreciate its currency, speculators step in to help it along. Speculators in the markets for foreign currencies are people, firms, and financial institutions who buy and sell various currencies in the hope of making a profit and/or avoiding losses. Some speculate by choice, others because it is a natural sideline to some other international business operation, such as international banking. Successful speculation requires reliable forecasts of future currency price changes, so that the speculator can purchase and hold onto those currencies which will appreciate and get rid of those what will decline in value. While this is a tricky business in most circumstances, there is one situation in which currency depreciation is not hard to predict. Consider a country which had run a deficit consistently for the past eleven years; a country which had experienced a decline in its merchandise trade balance (exports minus imports) from over $5 billion to near zero over the past decade; a country which had almost $70 billion in highly liquid claims against it held by foreigners and only $12 billion in gold holdings and other reserve assets to meet these claims; a country that had taken numerous measures to restrict imports and foreign investments. For such a country currency depreciation is only a question of when, not if, and speculators are certainly astute enough to realize this. Any manager of the foreign currency office of a bank or corporation who wants to hold onto his job had better reduce the company's holdings of such a country's currency to a bare minimum. This was exactly the situation in which the United States found itself in 1971.

Years of fighting the depreciation of the dollar were finally coming to a climax. Speculators abandoned the dollar in that year at a rate that could not be sustained for long. During that year the United States government incurred $27 billion in new liabilities to other governments, which were helping absorb the surplus dollars speculators were unloading. Speculators had been "waging an all-out war on the American dollar," President Nixon informed the nation, August 15, 1971, and we were forced to protect what was left of our precious gold hoard by refusing to honor our commitment to convert dollars into gold. *Convertibility* between the dollar and gold was suspended, and the system of international finance that had prevailed since 1944 came to an end.

This sort of change does not come about easily, and it is a credit to the system which followed that these events caused little disruption in international trade. Under the system of fixed exchange rates, currencies were depreciated and appreciated, but only after long periods of accumulated pressure against existing exchange rates and the development of a crisis atmosphere accompanied by massive speculation. When exchange rates did change, these changes were generally large enough to impose substantial costs on parties engaged in trade who had not protected themselves against such a possibility. The abruptness and magnitude of exchange rate changes together with the fact that they were accompanied by a speculative crisis made official depreciations and appreciations potentially disruptive tools. Unfortunately, however, no other viable means for correcting a fundamental disequilibrium in a country's balance of payments was available under the IMF system. Minor or temporary disturbances in a country's balance of payments could be accommodated by the system, but fundamental departures from equilibrium resulting from long-run structural changes could not be handled smoothly under the gold exchange standard.

6. The Accident of Flexible Exchange Rates

In August 1971 President Nixon terminated convertibility between gold and the dollar. The equivalences between the dollar and other currencies, which had been determined by the 1944 agreements, were undone. The relations between currencies became subject to the influences of private supply and demand in the various markets for foreign exchange. Because dollars were in surplus at the old exchange rates, there was downward pressure on the price of the dollar in terms of the other currencies. There were more dollars around than people or businesses wanted to hold for international trade purposes. Dollars became acceptable in exchange for other currencies only at terms more favorable to the recipient of dollars. Exchange rates were permitted to float up or down to new levels free of the artificial influences of the old fixed exchange rates. At the end of 1971 new agreements were reached on a new set of exchange rates, and it seemed as if the old system of fixed exchange rates would be resurrected. Under the new agreements the dollar was depreciated with respect to most of our trading partners, for example, by 17 percent with respect to the Japanese yen and 13.6 percent with respect to the German mark. At the same time the dollar was devalued in terms of gold with the price of gold increased from $35 to $38 per ounce. The devaluation of the dollar with respect to gold was a purely artificial operation. Its sole purpose was a minor embarrassment for the United States. Devaluation of the dollar entailed a certain loss at prestige for the United States—an admission that we were not the world power in international trade that we once had been. Actually we had not bought or sold gold on the open market for a number of years, so changing the price of gold had little real impact.

During 1972 the depreciation of the dollar seemed to have little effect on our balance of payments position. Our trade balance continued to worsen, running into the red for the first time since the end of World War II. While the exchange rate changes did lower the prices of American goods to foreigners and raise the prices of foreign goods faced by Americans, people were slow to adjust their consumption behavior to these new relative prices. It takes time—sometimes considerable time—to accumulate information and make the adjustments in life-style necessary to respond fully to new relative prices. However, while these effects might reasonably have been anticipated, the continued deterioration of the United States balance of payments during 1972 certainly did nothing to reassure speculators that the new exchange rates could be maintained. Having once devalued, there would certainly be less reluctance for the United States to do so again. Speculative pressure against the dollar rose again, and in February 1973 a second devaluation and depreciation of the dollar was announced. This act was the final blow to the fixed exchange rate system. There was no longer any confidence that exchange rates could or would be maintained, and most countries abandoned their attempts to support currency prices. Official exchange rates became meaningless, and currency prices began to move up and down according to the influences of supply and demand. This system, or nonsystem, of floating exchange rates has persisted to the present time.

7. The Float

With governments no longer guaranteeing the price of one currency in terms of the others, exchange rates ceased to be fixed. Exchange rates were permitted to vary in response to changing conditions in the markets for currencies (foreign exchange). Basically exchange rates are determined through the interaction of supply and demand for various currencies.

Take a simple example of two countries—the United States and Switzerland. United States citizens and corporation will have a demand for Swiss francs that depends upon their desire to purchase Swiss products, partake of the beauty of the Swiss Alps, or make investments in Switzerland. Changes in technology or preferences that increase Americans' desires to engage in these activities will correspondingly increase their demand for Swiss francs. The quantity of Swiss francs demanded by Americans is also likely to be strongly influenced by the price. A 20 percent increase in the amount of dollars needed to buy 100 francs implies a 20 percent rise in the cost of purchasing Swiss products, and Americans will be discouraged from engaging in such activities. Similarly if the dollar price of the Swiss franc falls, Americans will be encouraged to increase their level of expenditures and investments in Switzerland, and the quantity of Swiss francs demanded will rise.

At the same time a quantity of Swiss francs is made available to Americans by firms and citizens of Switzerland wishing to make expenditures and investments in the United States. In order to purchase American soybeans or invest in United States corporations, the Swiss must acquire United States dollars by offering Swiss francs in exchange. The quantity of francs supplied to Americans depends upon the desire of the Swiss to engage in these activities. Obviously one important determinant of their willingness to spend in the United States is the price at which they can acquire dollars. An increase in the number of dollars offered for 100 francs increases the attractiveness of spending and investing in the United States, and hence increases their willingness to supply francs to acquire dollars.

Putting these two sides of the market together, it is apparent that there is only one price of francs at which the quantity of francs demanded by Americans is exactly equal to the quantity of francs supplied by the Swiss. Suppose this price is equal to forty cents for one franc. At any higher price Americans will be discouraged from buying Swiss watches or acquiring Swiss bank deposits. The quantity of francs demanded will fall off. The Swiss on the other hand can acquire a greater quantity of dollars in this case, and they will increase the quantity of francs offered in exchange for dollars. More francs are supplied on the market for foreign exchange than are demanded, and currency traders will discover that they cannot get rid of the surplus francs at such a high price. They will have to reduce the price of francs back down to forty cents in order to get rid of the surplus. This is an *equilibrium price* in the sense that departures from that will automatically generate shortages or surpluses which push the price back to forty cents.

Naturally over time this equilibrium price will change as the result of changing tastes and technologies in the two countries. A surge in white-collar crime in the United States will lead to an increase in the demand for Swiss bank accounts and hence an increased demand for Swiss francs. This would tend to increase the equilibrium price for francs in order to bring the quantity of francs demanded and supplied into balance again. Similarly cost reducing innovations in the United States computer industry would lead to an increase in Swiss demand for United States goods and hence an increased willingness to supply francs in exchange for dollars. The extra francs offered on the foreign exchange market would depress the equilibrium price of the franc.

Notice that in this process two things are automatically accomplished through the interaction of supply and demand. First of all the exchange rate between the two currencies is automatically determined by market forces. There is no need for governmental action to determine exchange rates, though governments may choose to participate in some foreign exchange dealings. Secondly, fluctuations in the exchange rates automatically equalize the quantity of each currency demanded with the quantity supplied. A persistent disequilibrium in the foreign exchange market and hence in the balance of payments is impossible. Only when exchange rates are artificially supported at an arbitrary level can a disequilibrium persist. The whole balance of payments problem has become a red herring under the system of flexible exchange rates.

8. Pros and Cons

There are significant advantages to this system over the previous one. First, the nation is freed from balance of payments considerations in its decisions about domestic policy. A program of economic expansion need not be constrained by fears of an increasing balance of payments deficit. If a domestic expansion leads to increased demand for foreign products, exchange rate adjustments will automatically take place to restore equilibrium in the balance of payments. It seems appropriate that adjustments to a disequilibrium in international trade take place in the market for foreign exchange rather than permitting this disequilibrium to affect in a costly way the domestic economy. The second major advantage is that adjustments in exchange rates take place gradually in an orderly fashion, thus avoiding the atmosphere of crisis, which accompanied depreciations under the previous system. The adjustments are automatic and do not require eleventh-hour meetings between finance ministers in the midst of a speculative crises.

But if this system is so good why was it so long in coming? A substantial number of economists had been advocating the adoption of such a system during the waning years of the fixed exchange rate system, and yet flexible or floating exchange rates were adopted only as the result of a failure to secure agreement on an alternative. The opposition to flexible exchange rates is grounded in both political and economic considerations.

9. Speculation

The primary economic concern of opponents of the flexible exchange rate system has been that speculation in foreign exchange markets would tend to cause radical fluctuations in currency prices and that this would have a harmful effect on world trade. Since February 1973 there have, in fact, been substantial fluctuations in exchange rates. The German mark appreciated relative to the dollar by 30 percent between February and July of 1973. The mark then depreciated by 22 percent over the next six months, only to regain its July 1973 value within another five months. However, it is not at all clear that these fluctuations were due to speculation. Major changes in international product markets, such as the quintupling of petroleum prices and a sharp restriction in supplies of agricultural products, provide reasonable explanations for radical fluctuations in exchange rates. The floating of exchange rates eased the transition of the world economy through these troubling conditions.

Furthermore the adjustment from the old system was a significant accomplishment in itself. After years of mounting United States balance of payments deficits, a huge volume of surplus dollars was held by foreign citizens and governments. The dollar was over-priced, and new exchange rates had to be determined with very little information on the effects of exchange rate changes.

It should be pointed out that speculators share a common interest with and provide valuable services for those who would like to conduct business with a minimum of exchange rate uncertainty. Successful (profitable) speculation necessarily moderates the magnitude of exchange rate changes. Speculation tends to be destabilizing only if speculators as a whole are losing money. Recall the famous dictum for profitable speculation: buy low, sell high. Successful speculators will purchase currencies when their prices are abnormally low, thereby adding to the existing demand for such currencies and providing some support for those prices. They will also sell currencies that are unusually expensive, thus augmenting the supply of these relatively scarce currencies and moderating the extent of their price rises. We need only fear destabilizing speculation if we believe that speculators as a whole are dumb enough to consistently buy high and sell low.

Aside from the potentially stabilizing nature of profitable speculation, active speculative markets in foreign exchange provide a means by which businesses can protect themselves from unanticipated changes in exchange rates. Suppose, for example, that you are an American distributor of electrical appliances and that you wish to place an order to receive delivery of 1000 Sony television sets six months from today. Sony agrees to sell the TV's at a price of 100,000 yen apiece, payment to be made at the time of delivery. Checking your copy of *The Wall Street Journal*, you see that 100,000 yen is equivalent to $340, which is sufficiently below your selling cost to allow a nice margin of profit. But what if between now and six months from today the yen becomes significantly more expensive, so that you end up paying $380 for 100,000 yen. This knocks $40 off the profit. You could of course purchase today all of the yen you will need at the time of settlement, but that would involve an outlay of $340,000 now—money you might not have sitting around In any case it's a sum you do not want inactive for a period of six months. Enter your friendly neighborhood speculator, probably in the guise of a foreign exchange officer in a large commercial bank. You can sign an agreement with him today to purchase 100,000 yen six months from now at a price which is stipulated in the contract. You may have to pay a slight premium for this contract, but at least you will be guaranteed the right to purchase your yen at terms known to you today. Even if the market price of yen rises between now and the time of delivery, you don't have to pay a nickel more than the price specified in your agreement. Such an agreement is referred to as a *forward contract*; it permits the conservative businessman to insure himself against business losses due to unanticipated changes in exchange rates. The speculator assumes the risk of currency price changes in exchange for some commission.

10. Dirty Float

The second potential problem with flexible exchange rates is part economic and part political. It involves the possibility that governments may intervene in foreign exchange markets to influence the movements of currency prices away from the free market equilibrium. The motivation here comes primarily from a country's exporting industries, which fear that an appreciation of their own currency would cut off a large amount of their sales abroad. Such an attitude was in fact exhibited for the first several months after the United States decision to suspend convertibility (August 1971). The large surplus of dollars held by foreigners was causing dollars to become cheaper and other currencies, particularly the mark and yen, to become more expensive. The increase in the price Americans would have to pay for German and Japanese currencies would discourage some demand for the products of these countries. Wishing to maintain their export markets, these countries were forced to intervene in foreign exchange markets and buy up the surplus dollars in an attempt to maintain the exchange rates. This sort of intervention in foreign exchange markets can take place at any time under the nonsystem that exists today. The result is that those exchange rate changes necessary to restore equilibrium in countries' balance of payments cannot take place, and some countries face a persistent deficit with sagging levels of exports, while others run a healthy surplus.

But why should that be a matter of concern? If Germany wants to keep the mark cheap by purchasing surplus dollars, then that's all the better for us. Cheap marks mean cheap German products and low-cost visits to the beer halls of Bavaria. If Germany is content to let us pay for these goodies with costlessly produced dollars, then we are able to reap the increase in living standards that comes with a large volume of imports and low exports. Why should we complain?

The complaining, of course, is done not by United States consumers, but by United States industries and their workers who are displaced by the large volume of German goods that we import. Theoretically these workers can be re-located in other productive pursuits, but the practical problems of such a policy are similar to those discussed in the previous chapter. The political aspects are likely to become overwhelming. In any case the possibility of exchange rate wars, with various countries attempting to secure an export advantage through a depreciation of their own currency, is something that cannot be ruled out under the present system. One of the major tasks confronting financial representatives of the world's trading nations is agreement on rules governing the official intervention into foreign exchange markets. So far the system has functioned successfully without such rules, and perhaps fears of an exchange rate war are unfounded and rules are unnecessary.

11. Eurocurrencies

No discussion of the current situation in international finance is complete without mention of the Eurodollar or Eurocurrency markets. A *Eurodollar* is simply a deposit in a foreign bank, usually European, with a value stated in United States dollars. If a company holds a deposit in a German bank with the amount of that deposit stated in dollars rather than marks, it is referred to as a Eurodollar deposit. A combination of factors makes the holding of Eurodollars preferable to other kinds of bank deposits. First of all, the dollar is still, despite its recent battering, the major means for financing international transactions. The dollar continues to be extremely useful for financing trade and investment activities between nations. However, people and firms do not want to hold dollars in the form of cash, for cash yields no interest income. In addition the rates of interest paid by United States banks on deposits in this country range from zero to minimal. For the investor who wants to hold some wealth in the form of a dollar deposit but also wants a decent return on his money, the Eurodollar market provides the answer. The Eurodollar deposit is in dollars, but it pays the high rates of interest offered by European banks.

Such arrangements have led to a tremendous expansion of these deposits in recent years. With the growing importance of other currencies in international finance, other forms of *Eurocurrency* have become prominent. Euromarks (deposits denominated in marks held outside West Germany), Eurofrancs (deposits denominated in Swiss francs held outside Switzerland), and others provide the capability of holding wealth in a number of different ways. The Eurocurrency market has expanded from $44 billion at the end of 1969 to $132 billion by the end of 1973. This latter figure amounts to approximately 15 percent of the total world money supply, a fact which poses particular problems for monetary authorities.

The Eurocurrency expansion has taken place largely outside the control of the monetary authorities of various countries. The surplus holdings of dollars by foreigners generated by our massive balance of payments deficits in the years prior to depreciation have found their way into the European banking system as Eurodollars. There they are subject to multiple expansion-and-deposit creation similar to the process described in chapter five. The growth in this market has provided an ample source of funds for investment and business activities independent of any domestic monetary restraint that foreign governments may try to impose. No doubt the recent worldwide inflation of 1973 and 1974 can be at least partially attributed to the expansion in funds available through the Eurocurrency markets.

12. International Economics: Who Cares

It is often not particularly obvious how all of this has anything to do with our own day-to-day lives. Why should anyone other than speculators in foreign exchange be interested in whether the franc is going up or down? Why should we pay much attention to international economic events when such a small fraction of our consumption consists of foreign products and such a small fraction of our production is sent abroad? The impact of foreign markets on our own economic lives is considerably greater than you might expect, and changes in exchange rates can have a significant impact on your economic affairs even if you never try to purchase a franc yourself.

Through specialized production and exchange, international trade enables nations to reach a higher level of economic welfare than would be possible for a country that remained cut off from world trade. Thus in very general terms international trade affects our lives. It was also seen in the preceding chapter how changing conditions leading to larger imports in particular markets will cause the decline of certain industries in the United States and the displacement of workers. These changes reflect in some sense the "real" side of international economics—effects that are independent of financial institutions and depend only on real differences in productivity.

In addition to these real factors the particular financial arrangements for settling international transactions can affect our personal economic lives. The fact that the dollar was the key currency under the old IMF system meant that we could purchase foreign goods by costlessly creating new dollars. This enabled us to maintain a level of imports much higher than would have been possible if foreigners had not been willing to hold dollars for international trade purposes. The depreciation of the dollar in 1971 and since that time has made it increasingly expensive to purchase foreign-made products and travel in other countries. Consider how much more an imported car costs now as compared with 1971, even relative to the general rise in automobile prices that has occurred since that time. Or if you have ever traveled abroad you will be painfully aware of how much more your basic food and living expenses have become. A depreciation of the dollar means that it takes more dollars to buy other currencies, and hence it is more expensive to buy foreign products of any kind.

Now you may imagine that such effects are likely to be minor for people in the United States, which is considerably more independent in terms of our volume of trade relative to GNP than, say, most European countries. In 1974 our exports and imports each amounted to about 7 percent of our gross national product. It might appear from that figure that changes in international markets will have only a minor effect on our own economy. In fact if this is analyzed in a Keynesian aggregate demand framework, the important magnitude is net exports (exports minus imports). The net addition to aggregate demand by the foreign sector is given by the amount of United States products demanded by foreigners (exports) less the amount by which our own consumption or investment demands are satisfied by the purchase of foreign products (imports). In the post World War II period net exports have never amounted to as much as 1 percent of aggregate demand from domestic sources so the macroeconomic impact of foreign trade might as well be ignored.

But things are not quite so simple. The influence of international markets in our own economy is seriously understated by the Keynesian line of reasoning. Our dependence on the rest of the world is more accurately represented by the total volume of goods that are *potentially tradable*, not the quantity that actually flows across international boundaries. Take a timely example—oil. The United States was importing about 36 percent of the oil used in domestic consumption prior to the embargo in 1973. But when the price of oil was increased by the OPEC countries, this didn't just affect the price on the imported oil. Nobody was going to buy imported oil at $12 per barrel if they could get domestic oil for $3. The price of domestic oil was quickly bid up to equal the foreign price of $12 per barrel.* Only if the United States production of the good were so large as to swamp the effect of the foreign price increase would our markets be unaffected by price changes in international markets.

Extend this illustration to the market for any tradable good and an important lesson emerges. Prices of products in the United States will be influenced by price changes in international markets as long as the product is potentially tradable. This conclusion holds regardless of the quantity of the product that actually crosses international boundaries. The potentiality for trade is sufficient to transmit price changes from international to domestic markets.

From this it can be seen that the total volume of exports or imports relative to GNP gives a misleading picture of the effect of foreign markets on our economy, particularly in connection with prices. The relevant measure of our interdependence with the rest of the world is the percentage of GNP that consists of potentially tradable goods. Some reflection would lead one to exclude most services, government activities, buildings, and heavily tariffed goods from this category of tradables, but not much else. Apparently a very large fraction of GNP is potentially tradable and thus subject to the influences of foreign markets.

---

*In the United States oil market this is not strictly true. The federal government has controlled the price of oil produced from old (precontrol period) wells, while the price of oil from new wells has been permitted to rise to the predicted levels. The implications of this dual pricing scheme are interesting, but they would take us far afield. See Lee and McNown, *Economics in our Time: Concepts and Issues*, chapter nine, for a discussion of some issues related to government intervention into the markets for natural resources.

It is therefore not surprising that considerable interdependence has been observed in recent years between the price movements in *the major industrial countries of the world*. The inflation we experienced in 1973 and 1974 was also felt in Western Europe and Japan. Inflation rates in the industrialized world averaged 12 percent in both of these two years. The ensuing recession was also world wide. The strength of the apparent interdependence exceeds anything explainable by the simple effect of net exports on a country's aggregate demand. International markets have a great importance even for a country as seemingly self-contained as the United States.

DISCUSSION QUESTIONS

1. In one of Ian Fleming's James Bond thrillers, the villain Goldfinger attempted to contaminate the U.S. gold hoard at Fort Knox, Kentucky, with radioactivity from an atomic bomb. Ignoring the fact that most our gold is stored in New York, rather than Fort Knox, what would be the effects of a successful Goldfinger operation on international financial markets (a) under a gold standard and (b) under the present system?

2. Most of the U.S. gold hoard was accumulated at a price of $35 per ounce. The going price on the private gold market is currently (October 1975) $135 per ounce. The U.S. government could sell all of our gold at this higher price and reap a huge profit. What would be the effect of such action on (a) the price of gold and (b) the ability of this country to finance foreign trade?

3. Is it advantageous for a country to accumulate vast holdings of foreign reserves by repeatedly running a balance of payments surplus? Why?

4. Classify each of the following operations as either debit or credit transactions on our balance of payments accounts: a U.S. corporation borrows from a foreign bank; German tourists increase their travel in the U.S.; American citizens give money to Israel; foreign earnings of a U.S. corporation are distributed to the stockholders. Under a system of flexible exchange rates, in what direction would the price of the dollar (in terms of foreign currencies) move in response to each of these occurrences?

5. Some economists have argued for a return to fixed exchange rates on the grounds that that system provided a control on the free-spending and easy-money policies of central governments. In what way do fixed exchange rates constrain expansionary tendencies of national governments? How would you support or criticize this position?

chapter **13**

Outgrowing the No-Growth Imperative

Implicit in most of our previous discussions has been the idea that economic growth is a good thing: the larger the output of goods and services generated by our economy, the better. Periods of employment are considered a problem in part because they prevent the economy from growing as rapidly as otherwise possible. Inflation is often seen as undesirable because it can disrupt the productive process and impair the economy's ability to churn out goods and services. The interest that has been given to monetary and fiscal policy reflects the hope that these tools can be used to prevent fluctuations in economic activity, which reduce the long-run rate of economic growth. The advantage we saw with free international trade was that our resources would be allocated toward their most productive uses, so as to maximize output.

1. Some Pros and Cons

Citing the advantages of a growing economy is not a difficult task. Although the United States has an abundance of goods and services at the disposal of its consumers, few would argue that more wouldn't be desirable. A growing economy has meant in the past, and will mean in the future, more medical research and medical care, better housing, more education and cultural opportunities, safer and more reliable transportation, as well as innumerable other items, conveniences, and opportunities that make life more pleasant and exciting. There is no evidence that we have come close to satisfying consumer desire for more, and as long as this remains true, there will be some strong justifications for a growing economy.

Throughout this chapter our use of the term *economic growth* will mean growth in the per capita production of goods and services. Obviously, this requires a comparison between the growth in the production of goods and services and the growth in population. When we think of economic growth as being desirable, we are surely considering a situation in which output grows more rapidly than population. Only in an economy experiencing growth in the per capita sense will individuals be able to effectively express their desire for more goods and services.

Of course, we can always find those who, while not necessarily against economic growth, are against the type of goods and services that our economy produces. Some will say we are producing too many cars; some complain about the proliferation of electric utensils, with the electric can opener and tooth brush singled out for ridicule; others are fond of citing hula hoops and silly putty as evidence of our perverted priorities. Largely unbeknownst to these critics, their complaints indicate a healthy economy. We have millions of consumers in our economy, all with different tastes and preferences. Any economy whose productive sector is designed to respond to individual desires, as ours in large measure does, is going to produce a diverse bundle of goods. This is desirable in that it provides consumption possibilities for everyone's tastes, no matter how idiosyncratic they may be. Those who feel that they know best what others should consume will always have something to complain about as long as the economy allows each individual a large measure of control over his or her consumption decisions.

Of course there is the problem that some in the economy will have little income with which to express their preferences in the market place. It is with regard to this problem that continual growth has much to recommend it. A growing economy has traditionally offered new opportunities for the economically motivated and, as a result, has fostered much upward mobility. The figures cited in chapter nine are evidence of this. But even if an individual's economic situation doesn't improve relative to others, he or she can still expect an improved standard of living in a growing economy. In a no-growth economy, the only way the poor in society could hope to gain more affluence would be to do so at the expense of the not-so-poor. This certainly isn't a situation conducive to social harmony. Even in a growing economy, where people who amass wealth usually do so by producing goods and services that benefit society at large, the poor are likely to resent the wealth of the more affluent. In a no-growth economy this is sure to be the case since it will only be by reducing the benefits accruing to the wealthy that the poor could escape their poverty. Likewise, we would expect the wealthy to be much less sympathetic to the plight of the poor in a no-growth economy than in a growing one where helping the poor wouldn't require lowering their own standard of living. Economic growth provides opportunities for mitigating social conflict.

The advantages of economic growth are so obvious and visible that for years economists felt no need to justify growth as a social goal. But this has changed. The desirability of continued economic growth has come under recent attack by some economists and other social thinkers who feel the cost of this growth is greater than the benefits. As a result, the goal of economic growth is no longer immune to critical evaluation. It is now acknowledged that there are costs associated with economic growth, even by those who remain strongly in favor of it.

The critics of economic growth have primarily been concerned with two problems. First, they are concerned with the environmental disruption that has been associated with the growth of our producing and consuming activities. It is felt by some that continued economic growth will soon place on our ecological system stresses that will be both unfortunate and unalterable. Second, there is the concern that continued economic growth will soon exhaust our natural resource base, leaving a ravished planet denuded of fertility, minerals, metal ores, and fossil fuels as our legacy to future generations.

Many aspects of the current controversy over economic growth are best viewed after looking at some of the economic prerequisites to this growth. The problems that had to be overcome in the past to permit economic growth are related to those that will require resolution in the future if this growth is to continue.

2. The Requirements of Growth: The Present vs. The Future

Rapid economic growth of the type we have experienced in the last century is a relatively recent phenomenon in the human experience. For most of human history economic growth was nonexistent or, at best, extremely slow. The economic well-being of one generation was largely indistinguishable from that of the next. With few exceptions the work and lifestyle of the parents became that of the children and upward economic mobility was practically unheard of.

The reason for the lack of economic growth was quite simple. There was little innovation and change in the techniques of production. A given amount of human effort and natural resources devoted to production produced about the same quantity of output from generation to generation. Economic growth as we know it today requires the constant development and dissemination of new techniques for getting more output with the same quantity of human effort. This is technical progress and means finding more efficient ways of transporting and organizing existing productive resources, as well as discovering useful properties in previously unusable resources (for example, before the techniques were developed for refining kerosene from crude oil, petroleum was of little use). Of course, technical progress has been going on ever since human beings conceived of throwing a rock to accomplish a desirable end. Discovering the wheel and uses for fire are important examples of early technical progress. But it wasn't until the last 200 years or so that knowledge and the application of it progressed at a pace rapid enough to appreciably affect the economic well-being of the masses. Of course, all countries have not shared equally in this economic growth. Some have experienced rapid economic growth only in the post World War II period. Unfortunately, others have never had any significant economic growth. But where economic growth did occur, an indispensible prerequisite for that growth was technical progress.

As important as technical progress is, however, it cannot, by itself, insure economic growth. Simply because new techniques of production exist doesn't mean they will be implemented. First of all, new types of physical capital, such as automated machinery, improved roads, transportation networks, and communication systems, have to be put in place. Secondly, people have to receive the training necessary for developing the new skills demanded by new technologies. The development of this human capital is just as crucial, probably more so, than the development of physical capital. Countries whose physical capital has been devastated by war, such as Germany and Japan, have managed spectacular economic recoveries because of the knowledge and skill possessed by their citizens. Their human capital had been left intact. On the other hand, many underdeveloped countries whose people are largely illiterate and unskilled have been unable to achieve significant economic growth despite the availability of modern physical capital.

Although there are obvious differences between physical and human capital, they have much in common. The development of either physical or human capital requires a reduction in current consumption. To increase our stock of either type of capital requires that productive inputs be diverted away from the production of food, clothing, shelter, and leisure activities, as well as other items that can be consumed directly and immediately. While this may be more apparent for the production of physical capital, it is no less true of human capital. People who are being educated and trained in various skills obviously have less time to devote to the production of consumable goods.

The value of this forgone current consumption is the cost of increasing the stock of capital, whether physical or human. This cost has to be paid immediately, while the benefits of increased output permitted by the added capital come in the future and are spread out over the lifetime of the capital.

This characteristic of capital investment goes a long way in explaining the difficulty many of the less developed countries of the world have getting their economies started along a rapid-growth path. The necessary sacrifice in current consumption is very costly to a country whose per capita consumption is hovering around the minimum level for subsistence. When a little extra current consumption is the difference between going hungry or not, the thought of current sacrifices in the hope of a more productive future isn't likely to sound very appealing. For the individual who is hungry, the future is now.

For reasons that are now obvious, economic growth has traditionally been thought of as future oriented. It has been through the mechanism of economic growth that the fruits born of the creativeness, effort, and sacrifice of one generation have been passed on for the benefit of succeeding generations.

3. Accentuating the Negative

Unfortunately, economic growth isn't an unmitigated blessing. There are costs to this growth, and some feel that the most important of these costs have been ignored as a result of our emphasis on more and more material goods. The costs that are of primary concern to those who are skeptical of continued growth are related to the availability of productive inputs and the effect of our economic outputs. Although these concerns are related, we will discuss them separately, beginning with the question of long-run resource adequacy.

The physical supply of all our natural resources is strictly limited. Many of these resources are crucial to our current productive processes, and it's difficult to imagine how our standard of living could be maintained, much less increased, without ample supplies. Yet our empahsis on economic growth seems to have blinded us to the eventual prospect of exhausting our resource base as we consume ever-increasing quantities of these resources year after year.

Some see this as establishing an imperative for bringing economic growth to a halt. It is felt that the earth will not be able to support much longer the type of exponential economic growth that many countries have been experiencing.° Also, continued population growth is viewed as a major threat to our long-term prospects. Even without increased economic growth (recall that this refers to per capita economic growth), at current rates of world population growth, enormous and eventually unsupportable demands will be put on our resource supplies.

So it's not only a halt in economic growth, but zero population growth as well, that is seen by some as an essential policy for the future. It is felt that unless restraints sufficient to halt growth are self-imposed, they will be brutally imposed by circumstances. This is a view that dates back to Thomas Malthus, who did his writing during the early years of the nineteenth century. His main thrust was that unless policy restraints are imposed, human populations will increase until further increases can no longer be supported by the natural environment. To Malthus and many of his followers, past and present, this means that the standard of living has a natural tendency to decline until people have only enough to maintain life. This is obviously not a very cheerful view of the world and was not without influence in getting economics tagged as the dismal science.

Of course, the predictions of Malthus haven't been universally realized. Living standards have increased worldwide since Malthus' day, in some parts of

---

°Exponential growth refers to increases each year by a constant percentage rate. Such growth becomes larger and larger in absolute terms even though its percentage growth remains constant, since the percentage is applied to an increasing base. Over time the effects of this growth can be quite dramatic. For example, at a 7 percent annual growth rate economic output would, in comparison to its initial size, double in 10 years, quadruple in 20, be 8 times larger in 30, and in 100 years it would have grown by a factor of 1,024.

the world dramatically so. Malthus failed to foresee the tremendous advances in technology that were just getting under way during his lifetime and have permitted growth in goods and services to outpace population growth ever since. While most have seen this as a desirable turn of events, those who recommend no-growth policies see things in a different light. To them, the predictions of Malthus haven't been invalidated, just postponed. In this view, technology, while giving us a temporary reprieve from the plight of subsistence living, can't continue to rescue us from a diminishing resource base. In fact, technology has been seen as more a curse than a blessing, since it has permitted a huge growth in population with the eventual Malthusian condition simply applying to a much larger number of people. The Malthusian result that only starvation and misery will check population growth has been referred to by economist Kenneth Boulding as the "dismal theorem." The corollary to this is that any improvement in production technology will ultimately mean more people living in misery, and Boulding refers to this as the "utterly dismal theorem."

The only possible way no-growth advocates see to avoid the worse consequences of the Malthusian specter is to move toward a zero-growth society, with respect to both production and population. If nothing else, this would postpone the day of reckoning and, more optimistically, give us more time to come up with solutions to what now seem like intractable problems. What's interesting to note here is that the proponents of no growth see themselves as the ones effectively concerned about the future, not those pushing for economic growth. As far as they are concerned, persistent attempts at passing on ever more sophisticated technology, increasing stocks of capital, and growing flows of consumable goods will only result in the devastation of the earth's natural amenities and natural resources.

4. Accentuating the Positive

These arguments for zero economic and population growth are not to be dismissed lightly. Continued exponential growth would eventually result in consumption and population figures of overwhelming magnitude. For example, if current world population growth rates continue, within a few centuries the mass of human bodies would exceed the mass of the earth. You think you have trouble finding a parking space now. Yet the response of most economists to the preceding arguments is much more optimistic than may seem warranted at first glance. The previously cited economist, Kenneth Boulding, once said that anyone who believes exponential growth can go on forever in a finite world is either a madman or an economist. While this comment was intended more for its humorous impact than its reflection of reality, it's not completely wide of the mark. Obviously, economists don't believe exponential growth can continue indefinitely. But neither do most economists take very seriously the dire warnings of those who base their gloomy predictions on the comparison of continual exponential growth to finite quantities. This is explained by the fact that economics is fundamentally a study of how society responds to the problem of resource scarcities. Because of this, economists are aware of the fact that response mechanisms exist in the economy that provide economic decision makers with the information and motivation necessary to respond in desirable ways to increasing resource scarcities. As a result, economists tend to be unsympathetic to predictions based on the notion that current trends will continue relentlessly with starvation being the most creative response the human race can muster.

Obviously, world population growth rates, which are currently doubling the world's population approximately every thirty-five years, will not continue indefinitely. Although no one can absolutely deny that starvation will be the primary check on this growth rate, there are other possibilities. Social mores do change in response to changing social conditions, albeit sometimes slowly. The large families that served useful purposes in less crowded agrarian settings cease to be beneficial in more crowded circumstances, and over time this can be expected to retard population growth. Government policies can supplement this process by providing economic incentives for smaller families through any number of possible tax adjustments.°

Although much is unknown about the effects of social and economic conditions on fertility rates, there is evidence that affluence serves as a rather attractive check on population growth. Countries that have experienced rapid economic growth and achieved high levels of per capita incomes have moved toward population growth rates that, if maintained, will eventually stabilize their populations. As countries become more industrialized children cease to be economic assets as they are in lesser developed countries. Rather, children are more likely to be considered as consumption items, and expensive ones, competing with such things as larger homes and frequent trips abroad. Whether or not this explains the lower birth rates that have been observed in the more affluent countries or if these lower birth rates will continue in the future are open questions. But there are reasons for being hopeful that affluence, rather than starvation, can serve to moderate future population growth.

While controlling population growth through increasing affluence is a pleasant thought, it doesn't get us out of the woods as far as resource adequacy is concerned. Fortunately, there are reasons to be optimistic in this regard, at least for the foreseeable future. This optimism is based on several considera-

---

°Government policies in the area of population control have been justified on the likelihood that "free riders" will frustrate noncoercive efforts at controlling population. Even though it is widely acknowledged that society at large would benefit from population controls, individuals may still perceive personal advantages from large families. In this situation, each couple realizes that they can benefit from having their own large family without offsetting any overall reduction in growth rates resulting from the moderation of others. Obviously, when most are hoping to benefit from the birth control practices of others, effective birth control is likely to be frustrated.

tions. As a resource becomes more scarce, its price will increase relative to the prices of other productive resources. This motivates users of the resource to economize on it by using it more carefully and efficiently and by switching to substitute resources that aren't as scarce. The higher price will also make it worthwhile to incur more expense in obtaining the resource, so motivation will exist to augment its supply as well as the supply of substitute resources. Added to this will be incentives to develop new technologies for using the scarce resource more efficiently, for discovering and recovering it more efficiently, and for making use of other resources that were of little or no previous value. In effect, it is possible for the relevant resource base, the quantity of resources that are recoverable and usable at existing prices and with available technology, to expand.

Adjustments to increasing resource scarcities are much more than theoretical possibilities. Economic history is full of examples of these types of responses to changing resource conditions.

In the ninth and the tenth centuries, Europe's agriculture was expanding and had encroached on much of the available timberland. Evidence indicates that the price of wood relative to other commodities increased by approximately 1000 percent during this period. As a result of the higher price for wood, consumers found ways of using it more sparingly. But the thing that ended this wood crisis was the motivation the high price of wood provided for developing substitutes for wood. This motivation resulted in the development and spread of tunnel and pillar mining techniques which greatly increased the supply of coal. The result was that coal became a much cheaper source of fuel than wood, and the demand for wood dropped, as did its price; the wood crisis was over.

During the nineteenth century another major fuel crisis developed. This time it was whale oil and sperm oil (an oil taken from the head of the sperm whale). Whale and sperm oil were the major sources of artificial light in the early years of the nineteenth century, and whaling was the second most important industry in the United States, second only to agriculture. It was about 1820 that the effects of a depleting whale population began to appear, and as a result the price of whale and sperm oil started to rise. The price of sperm oil increased from forty-three cents per gallon in 1823 to $2.55 a gallon in 1866, almost a 600 percent increase. Whale oil was twenty-three cents a gallon in 1832 and $1.45 a gallon in 1865, an increase of over 600 percent in price.[1]

There were several responses to these price increases. First, more effort was made to search out whales. Between 1820 and 1847 whaling vessel tonnage increased over 600 percent. Also, improved methods for extracting the oil from whales were developed. But the most significant response was the strong motivation for creative and industrious people to develop a low-cost substitute. It was this motivation which hastened us into the petroleum era.

People had known about crude petroleum for centuries. In some areas it formed in small pools above ground and the Indians recommended it to the Pilgrims for its supposed healing powers. While crude petroleum was known to burn, it gave off a nauseous, dirty smoke and was considered largely worthless. But because of high whale and sperm oil prices, people began looking at crude petroleum more carefully as an alternative fuel source. In an effort to obtain quantities of oil large enough to experiment with, Colonel E. L. Drake began drilling for oil near Titusville, Pennsylvania, in 1858. In 1859, a well came in and efforts began in earnest to refine crude petroleum into a usable product. By 1863, approximately 300 refineries were working on this problem, and in 1867 kerosene was developed. With the availability of kerosene, a cheap and effective substitute for whale and sperm oil, the price of whale and sperm oil plummeted. In 1896, sperm oil was selling for forty cents a gallon, cheaper than had ever been previously recorded. The increasing price of whale and sperm oil had stimulated the search for alternative fuels and as a result, an entirely new resource was developed.

These examples of how resource scarcities have been successfully overcome in the past are not devoid of current significance. For one thing they show that the relevant resource base is dependent on much more than the physical attributes of natural resources. Just as important are the relative prices of different resources and man's ingenuity. For example, if the price of crude petroleum increases much more, it will be economically feasible to begin extracting oil from tar sands and oil shale. These are resources which have been of no value at historical prices of oil, but which have the potential of yielding quantities of oil many times greater than we can realize from sources of conventional fossil fuels. Price increases can also be expected to stimulate improvements in technology, which will also have the effect of expanding our usable resource base. Technological advances in the extraction of oil from the sands and oil shale, for example, could turn these into viable energy sources even without a price increase.

There are many examples of past technological advances that have enlarged the resource base. In 1880, the lowest grade of copper ore that could be used had to contain at least 3 percent copper. Today, 0.4 percent copper ore can be successfully refined. Similarly, technological advances have created useful resources of iron, bauxite, and many other mineral deposits that used to be considered waste. Technological advances in nuclear power generation have turned Vermont granite into a potential energy source, since the uranium in each pound of Vermont granite has the energy potential of 100 pounds of coal. Future technological breakthroughs in nuclear fusion could turn the practically unlimited quantities of deuterium found in sea water into an enormous source of energy. Each pound of deuterium in a fusion reactor provides the combustion energy of over 1.1 million gallons of gasoline.

The importance of technology in expanding our resource base cannot be overemphasized. Despite the fact that we have been using our resources at ever-increasing rates over the past 150 years or more, we now have a larger usable resource base than ever before in history. The resources that were absolutely useless to our forebears of a few centuries past are utilized by our current generation to provide us with services and conveniences that could only have been explained as magic in the past. We shouldn't be surprised if continued technological advances turn things that we see as useless today into resources of enormous utility in the future. Our resource base will undoubtedly continue to grow.

Let's look at our prospects with regard to some of our conventional resources of today. Are we about to run out of some of our more important resources? Before looking at some numbers, it will be useful to reconsider for a moment our examples of the wood and whale oil crisis. In both of these cases there was a gradual but persistent increase in the price of the depleting resource relative to the price of other goods over a prolonged period of time. Long before the resource was actually in danger of being physically exhausted, prices were informing consumers and producers that some adjustments would have to be made and motivating these economic decision makers to make these adjustments. Assuming that markets are reasonably free to operate, this will always be the case. Long before we were about to run out of any important resource, its enhanced future value will be anticipated, and owners of the resource will begin reducing its current supply in order to realize the higher future prices.°

Now let's look at what has happened to the price of some of our most important resources relative to the price of labor. The price of coal relative to the price of labor was 4.59 times greater in 1900 than it was in 1970. This means that the real price of coal as measured against the value of labor has decreased substantially since the turn of the century. The price of copper relative to the price of labor was 7.85 times higher in 1900 than 1970. The price ratio of iron to labor has also declined significantly, 6.20 times greater in 1900 than in 1970. An even more dramatic decline has been experienced in the real price of crude petroleum. Relative to the price of labor the price of crude petroleum was 10.34 times greater in 1900 than in 1970. But there are even larger declines. The price of aluminum relative to labor was 31.50 times greater in 1900 than in 1970.[2] Similar declines in real price have also been experienced for phosphorus, molybdenum, lead, zinc, sulfur, and gold. In fact, in an extensive study of long-term resource price movements covering the period from 1870 to 1957, the only natural resource whose real price exhibited any upward tendency was wood.[3]

Price patterns of this type certainly aren't consistent with the view that we are about to run out of important resources. Rather, they indicate that our technical ability to discover and recover natural resources has outpaced the effects of their physical depletion, actually increasing the availability of natural

---

°This argument is dependent on the resource being privately owned. When a resource is commonly owned (everyone having free access to it), each individual realizes that what they conserve today will probably be grabbed by someone else. As a result, no one perceives any personal benefit in reducing current consumption. Common property resources tend to be overexploited. A notable example is the blue whale.

resources. To be more specific we cite some recent estimates, prepared for the U.S. Geological Survey, of how long the natural resources in the United States will last at current consumption rates. These estimates are based on how much of the resource is thought to be ultimately recoverable, given current prices and technology. In this sense it is a conservative estimate since either an increase in relative price or an improvement in technology will increase the amount of a resource that is recoverable. According to these estimates we have enough copper for another 340 years, iron for 2,657 more years, phosphorus for 1,601 more years, lead for 162 more years, zinc for 618 more years, sulfur for 6897 more years, uranium for 8,455 more years, and aluminum for 68,066 more years.[4] As far as energy is concerned it has been estimated that relying only on fossil fuels we could sustain current consumption rates another 520 years, and if we throw in currently available nuclear technology another 8,400 years.[5]

These figures may appear surprisingly large to the reader who has heard much more pessimistic pronouncements to the effect that at current consumption rates we only have a few more years of vital resources left. Fortunately, these pessimistic estimates are based on what are known as proven reserves, the amount of a resource already located and shown to be recoverable at current prices and with current technology. These proven reserves will always be low simply because it costs a lot to explore for resource deposits and develop them into profitable sites. Therefore, companies aren't going to spend large amounts now to discover deposits that won't be needed until far in the future. Using figures on proven reserves will always show that we have only a few years of petroleum left. In 1950, people were saying that Middle East oil would be depleted by 1970, but in 1970 proven reserves were four times what they were in 1950. According to figures on proven reserves we only have about twenty-three years supply of aluminum left, even though we have seen that according to estimates on recoverable quantities there is enough aluminum to last over 68,000 years at current consumption rates. Figures on proven reserves aren't very meaningful for measuring resource availability.

It appears that calls for curtailing economic growth because we are about to exhaust our natural resource base are premature. There is little reason for believing that resource availability will act as a significant brake on economic growth in the foreseeable future.

5. Focusing Our Concern

But simply because our technology allows continued economic growth by expanding our base of usable resources doesn't establish the feasibility or desirability of continuing this growth. Converting raw resources into desirable goods and services inevitably results in the production of by-products. Many of these are of no value to those generating them and are disposed of as waste. Unfortunately, much of this waste is harmful when discharged directly into the environment. Up to a point the discharge of most waste products is of little concern since they are assimilated by the natural processes of the environment.

However, rapid economic growth has been accompanied by a rapid increase in the quantity of waste generated and discharged. We have already reached the point in many areas where the assimilative capacity of the environment has been overloaded and severe environmental disruption has resulted. Air pollution from automobiles and electrical generating plants and water pollution from industrial and municipal wastes are all too familiar examples of this phenomenon. The question is, can our environment survive a continuation of economic growth and the accompanying increase in the generation of waste products? If not, choking in our affluence may spell the end to economic growth long before resource scarcity becomes an important factor.

In order to gain a useful perspective on the question of whether or not controlling economic growth is the desirable response to our pollution problem, we need to consider the economic cause of pollution. First, we have to consider the fact that the use of the environment as a waste-sink is a valuable service, one that is just as essential to life as the air, water, food, and minerals provided us by our environment. It is an essential input into any productive process, whether we are producing electricity, transportation, musical instruments, textbooks, or any other item you can imagine. As opposed to most productive inputs, however, no mechanism currently exists for charging environmental polluters for the cost their use of the environment imposes on society. If, for example, a firm hires a skilled worker it will have to pay that worker an amount which approximates his or her productive value elsewhere in the economy. This alternative value has to be paid if the firm hopes to retain the services of the worker and represents opportunity cost. But when a firm discharges wastes into the atmosphere or a body of water, no payment has to be made even though the cost to society is a real one.

This goes a long way in explaining why we are experiencing problems with pollution. Since there is no private cost associated with using the environment for waste disposal, economic decision makers have no motivation to economize on its use. The result is too much pollution. Most of the technological advances that have been developed have the effect of economizing on the use of productive inputs that carry a price tag. This is no accident. The development of this type of technology has the potential of paying large returns to those who direct their money and effort into this development. On the other hand, it has only been recently and under the threat of government penalties that any significant effort has been made to develop technologies that economize on the use of the environment as a waste-sink. There is no doubt that such technologies would have been developed long ago if individuals had seen any private benefit from doing so.

One of the implications of this discussion is that setting up a mechanism for charging economic decision makers for discharging waste into the environment would be a major step in addressing our pollution problems. Pursuing this idea, however, would distract us from our primary concern, the relationship between economic growth and pollution.

It should be clear from the above discussion that halting economic growth is not the only way to contain the growth in pollution. By attacking the problem of pollution directly, pollution levels can not only be maintained, but actually reduced, without bringing economic growth to a halt. At best, controlling aggregate economic growth is a crude means of combating pollution, particularly when compared with what can be accomplished by focusing our efforts directly on the problem.

A recent study was done by the research organization Resources For The Future to investigate the relationships between population and economic growth, resource availability and environmental quality. The principal finding on cleaning up the environment was that the important factor is environmental policy rather than economic growth, population growth, or even technology. According to the study, pollution levels could be dramatically reduced from current levels if we devoted from 2 to 2½ percent of our gross national product to an active pollution control policy, and this could be accomplished while experiencing rapid economic growth. For example, such an active policy would, by the year 2000, reduce the emissions of hydrocarbon to less than 50 percent of their 1970 emission rate, and this with rapid population and economic growth. The situation for many other pollutants is similar.[6]

So there is little support for the view that the best way to clean up the environment is stopping economic growth. In fact, once it has been decided that environmental quality is a goal worth pursuing, we will probably find it is more easily achieved in a growing economy. In a growing economy we are most likely to have the technological growth that can be directed toward environmental problems. Also, in a growing economy improvements in environmental quality can be made without reducing our consumption of more traditional goods, so we can hope for wide support for environmental protection. In a no-growth economy, where devoting more resources to the solution of environmental problems means a reduction in the output of other desirable goods, there is likely to be little sympathy with environmentalists. This is especially true of the relatively disadvantaged in society who are quite intent, and justifiably so, on improving their material well-being.

If we want to clean up the environment we should get on with the task directly. At best, a policy of stopping economic growth is a roundabout approach to improving our environment, and more realistically it is a policy that would impede serious efforts at protecting and improving environmental quality.

6. Implementing a No-Growth Policy

So far, the thrust of our argument has been that a policy of halting economic growth isn't the answer to important social problems, as claimed by no-growth advocates. We now turn our attention to some of the problems that would be encountered in actually implementing and running a no-growth economy. For the most part, these problems have been brushed aside by those pushing for a halt to economic growth. According to E. J. Mishan, one of the most articulate advocates of zero economic growth (in his words a steady-state economy):

> The actual means whereby a steady-state economy is to be brought into being—the rationing of raw materials, the controls on technology, etc.—and the level of affluence to be sought are important subjects of discussion. But in the existing state of social awareness, they are perhaps premature . . . . The aim of the ecologist and environmentalist is not a no-growth economy per se. It is to win *acceptance* by the public at large of a no-growth society.[7]

One may also say it is premature to feel an urgency to convince the public of the desirability of a proposal until it has been fully thought through. Certainly a consideration of the implementation and functioning of a zero-growth economy is crucial in assessing the overall desirability of such an economy.

There is the obvious question of how growth in the economy is to be halted. The motivating force behind our economic growth has always been the desire of individuals to improve their economic well-being and that of their children. Government policy can help by creating a stable political environment, protecting property rights, and not destabilizing the economy with inappropriate monetary and fiscal policy. But without individuals seeking to improve their lot by working, innovating, saving, and investing, economic growth would not take place. This means, of course, that achieving a no-growth society would require denying people many of the opportunities and freedoms they now have to improve their situation. The question of how this is to be accomplished poses problems that go beyond the merits and liabilities of a no-growth economy.

Certain attributes are desirable in any economy, whether growing or not. One of the most important of these is that our resources be used as efficiently as possible to produce those goods and services most valued by consumers. Certainly this has to be considered an important attribute to those who feel that a dwindling resource base makes holding down economic growth an imperative. Stopping economic growth clearly shouldn't mean halting technological improvements that allow a given set of consumer desires to be satisfied with reduced demands on our resources. If a no-growth policy stifled this technological growth, it would frustrate the mechanism that has provided us with a growing relevant resource base in the past and can continue to do so in the future. But as we are about to see, the implementation of a no-growth policy is very likely to hamper technological advances. In so doing such a policy would probably hasten the very problems its advocates claim it will postpone.

In a market economy the efficient use of resources is accomplished primarily by private producers responding to prices of productive inputs and outputs. Output prices provide information on consumer preferences, with the relative price of a good increasing in response to an increase in consumer demand, which in turn motivates producers to increase their production of the good. Prices of productive inputs reflect their value in their most productive employments in the economy. Therefore, with producers responding to these input prices in their attempt to produce as cheaply as possible, the cost of producing commodities is kept to a minimum, with substantial rewards going to those who can innovate more efficient ways of producing.

Without a large amount of freedom afforded to the individual to spend money as he or she desires and to allocate productive resources and talents as he or she sees fit, much of the advantage of the market mechanism is negated. This brings us face to face with the problem of how zero economic growth can be achieved without obstructing the desirable allocation of our resources among competing uses.

It may seem quite simple to design an effective policy imposing zero economic growth. The government could pass and enforce a law requiring the value of production to remain constant from year to year. However, some problems come immediately to mind. First of all, what mechanism can the government use to insure that output doesn't increase? One possibility would be to place quotas on the quantity of each good to be produced. If this is done a major problem is that of determining which goods should be produced and in what combination. As previously discussed, a crucial goal of any economy is that these decisions be made to conform to consumer preferences. These preferences vary widely from individual to individual and change unpredictably through time. It takes an extraordinary amount of information to keep the productive process responsive to these consumer preferences. It is optimistic indeed to hope that any government agency would be able to keep abreast of this information and maintain a desirable production quota system. Optimism would require not only tremendous confidence in the government's ability to keep current or changing preferences, but also great faith in its ability to make decisions independent of political pressures.

Assume, for example, that consumers began to sour on the automobile as the almost exclusive form of personal transportation and that millions of individuals decided that bicycles offered a more desirable alternative. With production decisions being made in response to market forces, we would find a reduction in auto production as auto manufacturers found fewer people willing to buy their product at prices that covered their cost. On the other hand, with increasing numbers of people willing to spend money on bicycles, producers of bicycles would expand output in response to higher profits. It's hard to imagine this adjustment occurring so smoothly if the decision of auto versus bicycle production was under the control of a government agency. Under these circumstances automobile manufacturers would find it to their advantage to invest heavily to lobby against any reduction in their production quotas. They could come up with any number of "justifications" for maintaining high production levels for autos. Of course, bicycle manufacturers could, and probably would, lobby for an increase in their production quotas, but being much smaller and less influential politically, they would have an uphill task getting their quota enlarged at the expense of the automobile quota. The bicycle manufacturers certainly wouldn't get any help from the oil industry or the highway lobby. Meanwhile, the consumer, who should be the important decision maker, will hardly be heard from in the decision making process.

Extend our example of autos and bicycles to include razor blades, running shorts, motor boats, tennis balls, insect repellant, shoe repair services, dental repair, textbooks, soy beans, etc., and it is clear that vesting in government the authority to determine the allowable production of each conceivable good and service would be a frightfully clumsy and wasteful way to halt economic growth. But there are further difficulties involved in direct government control. Once the quota for a good has been established, decisions as to which producing units are to fill that quota would have to be made. Suppose, for example, that Jonathan Jones developed a new technique for making sleeping bags, and as a result thought he could give consumers a better bag than was currently available at a lower price. Operating under the market mechanism. Jones could invest his money in manufacturing and promoting his sleeping bag. If his assessment of his bag wasn't consistent with that of the consumer, he would soon find it advantageous to direct his talents and money elsewhere. On the other hand, if consumers did find his sleeping bag preferable to existing bags, his production and revenue would expand while the production and revenue of his competitors would fall. Of course, eventually our innovator's techniques would be imitated and all producers would be producing better bags for less, much to the consumer's benefit.

If a government agency was responsible for deciding for each product which firms could expand output and correspondingly which firms had to reduce output, it's doubtful if the interests of the consumer would be promoted. For practical purposes it would be impossible for a government agency to have the information on changing productive techniques necessary to know, for each product, which firms should be expanding and which should be contracting. Not having this information the agency would soon find itself relying on the expertise of the existing firms in each industry in order to make its decision. Each firm in an industry would soon learn that in order to protect or enlarge its market share, it has to appeal to the judgment of the regulatory agency rather than that of the consumer. Technological improvements and product innovations would be found less useful to the aggressive firms than its lobbying activities and influence with the right regulators. Unfortunately, this wouldn't create the type of environment that a new firm with an improved product or lower price will find very hospitable. Well-established firms in the industry could be expected to use their influence to prevent such intruders from ever getting their product to market.

This is more than conjecture. We have had plenty of experience with government agencies regulating market share and entry in many of our industries. For example, since the Civil Aeronautic Board was established in 1938 to regulate our airline industry not one new airline has been permitted to enter into long haul competition with the existing airlines. Another example comes from the Interstate Commerce Commission (ICC), an agency of the federal government charged with regulating interstate ground transportation. In 1961, Southern Railroad had developed a grain-carrying car that allowed them to cut their freight rates on grain by 60 percent and requested the ICC to permit this reduction. It was estimated that this innovation would save consumers millions of dollars annually. Yet the ICC in sympathy with barge lines, trucking firms, and other railroads, all of which competed with Southern Railroad, refused to allow the rate reduction Southern requested. It wasn't until 1965, after the case was nine times before lower federal courts and twice before the U.S. Supreme Court, that the ICC quit fighting the rate reduction and allowed it to go into effect.[8] Many other examples could be given indicating the tendency of agencies charged with regulating industries to completely lose sight of the consumer interest.[9] But by now our point should be clear. Attempting to halt economic growth by controlling the permitted output for each good and service would be inconsistent with the goal of using our resources as efficiently as possible to produce a combination of goods and services compatible with the preferences of consumers. The cost of halting economic growth in this way would be so high that only the most enthusiastic no-growth advocate would find it acceptable.

Having a government agency decide on the combination of goods and services to be produced, isn't the only way zero economic growth could be imposed. Another possibility is to let consumers spend their incomes as they see fit, but limit the total income that can be earned in the economy. This would seem to have the advantage of allowing consumers to decide what should be produced and encouraging producers to be innovative and efficient with their use of resources. But, of course, we now have the problem of controlling incomes. And, unfortunately for this approach, there is a strong relationship between how consumers exercise their preferences for goods and services and how individuals earn their incomes. People earn their incomes by responding to the desires of consumers, producing and perfecting those things on which consumers are most anxious to spend their money. As we have already pointed out this provides the incentive for producers to use resources efficiently and creatively in order to provide consumers with better products at lower prices. But people get rich doing this, and in so doing they invariably enrich countless others by creating highly productive jobs and permitting consumers to have more for less effort. So any attempt at controlling the incomes consumers have to spend will require strict controls or strong disincentives against creative responses to the wishes of consumers. This doesn't necessarily mean that the government would have to apply direct restrictions on innovative behavior. A high enough tax on profits or investment returns could sufficiently discourage investment in capital and technological improvements to be consistent with a no-growth economy. But whatever the means, only by discouraging producers from responding to the consumers' desire for better products at less cost will it be possible to prevent incomes from increasing. It's hard to see, therefore, where this approach to controlling economic growth has eliminated the disadvantages of direct controls on output. Both approaches will have the effect of insulating the actions of producers from the desires of consumers.

Attempting to control incomes and dampen investment presents another, but related, problem. The necessity of controlling innovative responses to consumer preferences means controlling one of the most important sources of income mobility in the economy. We saw in chapter nine that there is a substantial amount of income mobility in the United States from one generation to the next. There are plenty of opportunities for the ambitious and capable individual to become wealthy even though born into poverty. Likewise, being born into wealth is no guarantee that an individual can remain both indolent and affluent for long. The primary source of this mobility is that those who are productive (producing those things consumers value) are rewarded while those who are unproductive aren't. Attempts to control income would surely reduce income mobility in our society by hampering the mechanism that produces it. Restricting people's ability to develop more productive techniques or train for more productive employment would restrict the means by which individuals have been able to improve their economic situation. It also restricts the competition that forces those who have made it economically to either remain responsive to consumer desires or move down the economic ladder.

Designing and enforcing a policy to halt economic growth would be a difficult task. If such a policy were actually imposed some of the consequences would be unfortunate. It would reduce the influence that consumers have on the choice of what is to be produced. Coupled with that is the stifling influence implementing such a policy would have on motivations to produce efficiently and creatively. We would also find a more regimented society with far less chance for the relatively disadvantaged in society to improve their situation with ingenuity and hard work. The likely consequence of this calcification of society would be disruptive social unrest or the emergence of a caste system in which people knew their place and accepted it. One of the nicest things one could say about such an economic order is that it would be dull.

Fortunately, there is little urgency for establishing a no-growth economy. The problems that such an economy is supposed to solve either constitute no threat in the foreseeable future (natural resource depletion) or can better be solved with direct action employed in a growing economy (environmental pollution). Solving the fundamental economic problem of using our resources efficiently to provide for the well-being of our population is difficult enough in a growing economy.

DISCUSSION QUESTIONS

1. Some people seem to think that we will eventually have to cease using petroleum because its supply will be diminished to the point where it will be impossible to discover and extract any more. Why is it more likely that petroleum will cease to be used even though it could still be recovered in large quantities?

2. What do you think would have been the result of a government program to solve the ninth-century wood crisis by putting price controls on wood?

3. How do you think an economy's growth rate is related to people's willingness to save (postpone current consumption for additional future consumption)? Do you think economic growth would increase or decrease if (a) it was discovered that the sun was going to burn out in five years, (b) a wonder drug was discovered that increased life expectancy to 1000 years, (c) people really believed the statement of Thoreau's, "man is rich in proportion to those things he can do without."

4. If you were convinced that the world was rushing blindly towards the near term extinction of important natural resources, how could you make yourself a lot of money and at the same time perform an extremely useful function for society?

chapter 14

An Overview

It should be apparent by this point that our economy suffers from a number of serious problems. Periods of inflation are followed by episodes of widespread unemployment. Significant disparities in income exist in our population. The interdependence of the world economy adds to our problems of economic stabilization. Finally there are the costs of continued economic growth, in terms of resource depletion and environmental degradation. Some of these problems are the natural by-product of economic advancement; others are problems specific to the decentralized market system that our economy approximates; and some are brought about, or aggravated, by misguided attempts by the government to lessen the problems of the private macroeconomy.

In formulating macroeconomic policy, economic analysis combines with political decision making to produce a program that retains both political and economic features. The errors of macroeconomic policy have resulted from faulty economic analysis as often as they have been the result of short-sighted, narrowly motivated political decisions. Throughout this book we have attempted to point out the problems inherent in implementing macroeconomic policy, whether these problems were of a political nature or due to inadequacies in economic understanding.

The first problem of macroeconomics was unemployment. It was the depression of the thirties, with unemployment rates approaching one-fourth of the labor force, that gave birth to the field of macroeconomics in the writings of John Maynard Keynes. Keynes first hinted that the problem of unemployment is grounded in a deficiency of aggregate demand. Although workers could theoretically offset a reduction in demand by offering to work for lower wages and thus avoid unemployment, imperfect information about labor market conditions as well as institutional rigidities prevent wages from responding to the demand deficiency. Presumably a sufficiently long period of unemployment would reduce wages enough to restore full employment, but society appears unwilling to suffer the costs incurred by a policy of benign neglect. This naturally brings up consideration of the policy tools available to the federal government, as the largest economic decision maker in the country, to bring about a more rapid restoration of full employment.

The success of government policies to manage aggregate demand depends on the behavior of private decision makers—producers and consumers—in response to these policies. The theories of consumer and producer behavior outlined in chapter three and the interaction of these sectors as summarized by the multiplier indicate how aggregate demand is likely to change as a result of alternative policy actions. This was made more concrete in chapters four and five, in which the relative effects of fiscal and monetary policies were discussed. Here the lessons of the past are particularly enlightening, pointing out the disastrous outcomes of policies based on incorrect economic knowledge. Hopefully our understanding of macroeconomics is now sufficiently advanced to enable us to avoid the errors committed during the Great Depression, but it is not at all clear that we have the detailed understanding of the economy or the political will to engage successfully in a policy of carefully managed aggregate demand.

The dangers of on-again off-again policies designed to fine-tune the economy become particularly acute when we consider the nature of macroeconomic decision making. The political context in which these decisions are made makes it likely that many macroeconomic policy decisions will be short-sighted responses to immediate problems with little heed to longer-range implications. With reelection foremost in most politicians' minds, an existing recession is going to be much more heavily weighed than the more remote dangers of a future inflation. Unfortunately the timing in the responses of inflation and unemployment to policy actions tends to aggravate this problem. An expansionary policy will have its first effects in raising the level of employment. Only later, as productive capacity is strained, do prices begin to rise.

The tendency towards fiscal expansion is aggravated by the relatively strong influence special interest groups are likely to exert on political decision makers. The benefits of many expenditure programs are concentrated on a relatively small number of citizens, while the costs are spread more or less evenly throughout society. Therefore, lobbying in support of expenditures is likely to exceed general taxpayer resistance.

This tendency towards expansion in expenditure programs combined with the politician's natural desire to minimize explicit taxes on constituents has led to the use of "painless" methods of financing expenditures—the expansion of the government debt and the creation of new money. Expenditures not financed directly through taxes are likely to be financed by the hidden tax of inflation.

With the momentum towards fiscal expansion difficult to break, the government has turned to other "solutions" to the problem of inflation. As demonstrated in chapter eight, price controls do little to curb inflationary pressures in the long run, but they do impose significant costs in distorting the important signals transmitted by the price system. The alternative of indexing is worth further investigation.

The problems of political decision making also take their toll in attempts to implement effective programs of income redistribution. Chapter ten suggests that the major institutions of income redistribution, including labor unions and the tax system, have done little to alter the distribution of incomes as determined in the marketplace.

Policy towards international trade is also influenced by similar considerations. Politically powerful industries, represented by both management and labor, have been effective in protecting themselves from foreign competition. The tremendous potential expansion in economic welfare attainable through free trade has not been fully realized because of trade barriers and international financial policies geared towards producer interests.

The entire discussion has implicitly assumed that economic expansion is a worthwhile objective. Full utilization of our resources, capitalizing on potential gains from international trade, designing income redistribution policies which retain work incentives, and other such concerns are worthy of attention only if human welfare really is increased by an expansion of economic activity. The pros and cons of economic growth are addressed in chapter thirteen, where many of the anti-growth arguments are seen to have little substance.

Economics is an evolving field of study. Many of the issues do not have satisfying solutions, and much remains unknown about the behavior of the macroeconomy. We should not, however, despair about the usefulness of economics in helping us to deal with our economic problems. The problems of inflation, unemployment, income distribution, international trade, and economic growth are important ones with substantial impact on our own lives. The failures of policies of the past, often designed in ignorance of economic principles, should establish the importance of careful economic analysis in designing policy recommendations for the future.

Chapter Notes

Chapter 2

1. Figures from *Wall Street Journal*, Dec. 23, 1974, p. 1.
2. These figures were taken from Martin Feldstein, "The Economics of the New Unemployment," *The Public Interest*, Fall 1973.

Chapter 3

1. Council of Economic Advisors, *Annual Report*, 1963.

Chapter 4

1. Franklin D. Roosevelt, *The Public Papers and Addresses of Franklin D. Roosevelt*; quoted in Stein, *The Fiscal Revolution in America*, Chicago: University of Chicago, 1969, pp. 44–45.
2. Richard M. Nixon, *Six Crises*, Garden City, New York: Doubleday, 1962, pp. 309–11.
3. John Maynard Keynes, *The General Theory of Employment, Interest and Money*, New York: Harcourt, Brace and Co. 1936, pp. 119–20.

Chapter 5

1. Friedman and Schwartz, "Money and Business Cycles," *Review of Economics and Statistics*, vol. 45, no. 1, part 2: supplement (Feb. 1963).

Chapter 6

1. See Lee and McNown, *Economics in Our Time: Concepts and Issues* Palo Alto, Calif.: Science Research Associates, 1975.
2. Reported in M. E. Jewell and S. C. Patterson, *The Legislative Process in the United States*, New York: Random House, 1973.

Chapter 7

1. *Historical Statistics of the United States, Colonial Times to 1957*, Washington, D. C.: U.S. Bureau of the Census, 1960.

Chapter 8

1. This information and much more on the economic effects of inflation is contained in the second chapter of a very interesting book by G. L. Bach, *The New Inflation: Causes, Effect, Cures*, Englewood Cliffs, N.J.: Prentice-Hall, 1973.
2. For some data on this and a good discussion of it, see the previously cited book by Bach, pp. 27–31.
3. This information was obtained from "Have Monetary Policies Failed?" by Milton Friedman, *The American Economic Review*, May 1971, p. 15.
4. For a more thorough discussion of what may be referred to as the illusion of cost-push inflation, see Lee and McNown, *Economics in Our Time: Concepts and Issues*, pp. 46–50.

Chapter 9

1. U.S. Internal Revenue Service, *Statistics of Income, 1966: Individual Income Tax Returns*. Washington, D.C.: U.S. Government Printing Office, 1968.
2. Robert Lampman, *The Share of Top Wealth-Holders in National Wealth*, Princeton: Princeton University Press, 1962, p. 24.
3. Irving Kristol, "Taxes, Poverty, and Equality," *The Public Interest*, no. 37, Fall 1974, p. 11.
4. *The Denver Post*, May 27, 1975.
5. R. M. Solow, "Technical Change and the Aggregate Production Function," *Review of Economics and Statistics*, vol. 39, August 1957, pp. 312–20.
6. Christopher Jencks et al., *Inequality: A Reassessment of the Effect of Family and Schooling in America*. New York: Basic Books, 1972, p. 224.
7. The previous data is taken from I. B. Kravis, *The Structure of Income*, Philadelphia: University of Pennsylvania Press, 1962, p. 124.
8. Sources: Column 2: B. F. Haley, "Changes in the Distribution of Income in the United States," in J. Marchal and B. Ducros (eds.), *The Distribution of National Income*, New York: St. Martins Press, 1968. Columns 3 and 4: U.S. Census Bureau, *Current Population Reports*, Series P-60, no. 75, table 11, p. 26.
9. United Nations Economic Commission For Europe, *Incomes in Postwar Europe: A Study of Policies, Growth and Distribution*, Geneva: United Nations, 1967.
10. Lampman, *The Share of Top Wealth-Holders*.
11. Peter M. Blau and O. D. Duncan, *The American Occupational Structure*, New York: Wiley, 1967, table 3.5, p. 102.

12. Blau and Duncan, *Occupational Structure*, table 12.1, p. 434.

13. Jencks, *Inequality*, p. 215.

14. Jencks, *Inequality*, table 7–1, p. 210.

15. Jencks, *Inequality*, p. 219.

16. James N. Morgan et al., *Income and Welfare in the United States*, New York: McGraw-Hill, 1962, p. 89.

17. Jencks, *Inequality*, p. 220.

18. Jencks, *Inequality*, p. 263.

19. *The Wall Street Journal*, January 24, 1975, p. 8.

Chapter 10

1. Albert Rees, *The Economics of Trade Unions*, Chicago: University of Chicago, 1962.

2. Data from *Handbook of Labor Statistics*, tables 153 and 175; and Kravis, *The Structure of Income*.

3. Lee and McNown, *Economics in Our Time: Concepts and Issues*, chapter 3.

4. Herbert Hill, "Racial Inequality in Employment: The Patterns of Discrimination," *Annals of the American Academy of Political and Social Science*, 357; January 1965, pp. 30–47.

5. J. Pechman and B. Okner, *Who Bears the Tax Burden?*, Washington, D.C.: Brookings, 1974.

6. K. W. Clarkson, *Food Stamps and Nutrition*, Washington, D.C.: American Enterprise Institute, 1975.

7. Ibid., p. 50.

8. Lee and McNown, *Economics in Our Time: Concepts and Issues*, chapter 13.

9. R. L. Miller, "Social Security, The Cruelest Tax," *Harpers*, vol. 248, no. 1489 (June 1974) pp. 22–27.

10. M. Friedman, *An Economist's Protest*, Chicago: Thomas Horton and Company, 1972, pp. 138–39.

Chapter 11

1. See Richard B. Mancke, *The Failure of United States Energy Policy*, New York: Columbia University Press, 1974, pp. 122–123.

2. *The Wall Street Journal*, May 9, 1975, p. 10.

Chapter 13

1. These figures, as well as those on the whale crisis, are taken from W. Philip Gramm, "The Energy Crisis in Perspective," *The Wall Street Journal*, November 30, 1973.

2. These figures are contained in William D. Nordhaus, "Resources as a Constraint on Growth," *American Economic Review*, May 1974, p. 24.

3. See Barnett and Morse, *Scarcity and Growth: The Economics of Natural Resource Availability*, Baltimore: Johns Hopkins Press, 1963.

4. See Nordhaus, "Resources as a Constraint on Growth," p. 23. These figures are based on the assumption made by the U.S. Geological Survey that approximately .01 percent of the quantity of resources that exist to a one kilometer depth are recoverable.

5. Ibid., p. 24.

6. This study is cited and summarized in Fisher and Ridker, "Population Growth, Resource Availability and Environmental Quality, "The American Economic Review, May 1973.

7. E. J. Mishan, "Ills, Bads, and Disamenities: The Wages of Growth," in *The No-Growth Society*, eds. M. Olson and H. H. Landsberg, New York: Norton, 1973, pp. 81–82.

8. For a more complete discussion of this case, see Louis M. Kohlmeier, Jr., *The Regulators: Watchdog Agencies & The Public Interest*, New York: Harper & Row, 1969, pp. 121–128.

9. See ibid., and Lee and McNown, *Economics In Our Time: Concepts and Issues*, chapter 6.

Index

Economics in Our Time: Macro Issues is set in 10 point
Laurel.
Typesetting was done by Dharma Press, Emeryville,
California.

Sponsoring Editor: Bruce Caldwell
Project Editor: Carol Harris
Cover Design: Michael Rogondino